Thinker Tailor Soldier Spy

One Man's Journey

Harry Beckhough

First Published 2007
by DSM
The Studio
Denton
Peterborough
Cambs PE7 3SD

British Library Cataloguing in Publication Data
A catalogue record of this book is available from the British Library

ISBN 0 9547229 3 0

Historical advisor: Dr Penny Starns

Produced by
DSM
The Studio
Denton
Peterborough
Cambs PE7 3SD

Foreword by Rt. Hon. Michael Ancram QC MP

When I first encountered Harry Beckhough in the Devizes Conservative Association office in Marlborough, I met what appeared to me a dapper, serious and somewhat conventional figure, of the sort that my political life seemed to throw up at every turn. I am embarrassed to think that my initial reaction may well have reflected this. If it did, I couldn't have got it more wrong!

It only took a week or so to realise that beyond this conventional exterior, there lay in wait a most exceptional man. Behind the serious demeanour the eyes twinkled and the neat frame shook with gentle and genuine laughter. Behind the initial monochrome perception, lay a kaleidoscopic treasure trove of colour. Behind what at first sight might have appeared a pretty ordinary life, emerged a saga of adventure and initiative which, as this book so ably demonstrates, puts the rest of us to shame.

I first met Harry Beckhough when he moved from Yorkshire to Wiltshire, to be close to his family. I was the local MP, and here was this octogenarian knocking on my door - not to ask me to help him, but as to how he could help me. At a time of life when slippers and the comfortable cardigan might have been regarded by many men of his age, as among the priorities and certainly the prerogatives of life, here was Harry seeking action, knocking on doors, delivering leaflets, arguing politics, taking a determinedly pro-active part in my constituency association, and eventually becoming a key driving force within it.

Harry has strong political opinions which he is not shy in advancing. But he is no armchair politician. He likes to get down to where the action is, to take his politics into the streets and onto the doorsteps. In his politics, as in everything else he has turned his hand to in his long and distinguished life, he has shown himself to be every inch a 'doer'.

The variety of his life well illustrates and explains this better than any foreword by me. Student, soldier, code-breaker, intelligence officer, educationalist, teacher, textile manufacturer and political activist; all that was and still is Harry. Father, grandfather, writer, thinker; it is all there in this remarkable book. Remarkable not only for Harry Beckhough's quite amazing power of recall, often of the most intricate detail, but above all for its sense of humanity.

In this book we meet many Harrys:

The mischievous, inquisitive son of Bristol already aware of the value of learning. His account of his family life and his school days, gives an early indication of that spirit of independence that even today motivates him.

The student Harry, part serious on his way eventually to securing his doctorate, part adventurous as he began to explore the politics, the passions and the tensions of a turbulent pre-war world. Harry quite evidently was no mere observer; he was a participator. His sojourn in Germany in 1933, clearly opened his eyes to the unfolding horrors of Hitler's National Socialism.

Then the young man about town Harry, with his early loves, his purchases on the street from the young Charles (later Lord) Forte, his enterprising move north to shirt-making in Wakefield, leading (not causually I hasten to add!), to the onset of the Second World War.

And then another Harry appears, determined to fight for King and Country, enlisting and finding a particular outlet for his skills in code-breaking and intelligence both at home and overseas. He has of course written about this fascinating period of his life elsewhere, but his aptitude in these disciplines is another vital key to unravelling the real Harry. I have an inkling that this was the most challenging and, therefore, rewarding part of Harry's life. He was doing absolutely crucial work which, in no small way, contributed to the war effort and to ultimate victory.

And then in the aftermath of war, his unsung achievements in rebuilding German university education, and his encounters with great post-war German statesmen such as Konrad Adenauer.

And so back to England, to Yorkshire, to Harrogate, to marriage and family, and on into a successful textile business of Atkinson Rhodes, which set-up he ran for twenty-five years. During this time he also founded and set up the Cundall Manor preparatory school, which still thrives today. Either of these challenges at any one time would have been enough for most men. Harry undertook them at the same time.

And then to Wiltshire and the Devizes Conservative Association. Harry Beckhough is not a man who does things by halves. Having committed himself to the Association, he became almost certainly its most active member, prepared to do any job as long as there was a potentially positive, political outcome at the other end of it. He entered wholeheartedly and with great wisdom into the strategic planning of election campaigns, both national and local, all of which he has recorded in this book. Having been a Conservative member for more than seventy years, his is a record which I doubt will ever be anywhere near matched. He was rightly given a standing ovation for his political service at a national Conservative Conference.

No foreword can ever do justice to the glorious variety of skills and experiences which is Harry Beckhough. You need to read this book to begin to comprehend the breadth and the scale of them. And then you have to bring them together to understand and appreciate this very remarkable man.

Putting all the Harrys together, you end up with a very special person and a very special life of achievement. And when you wonder how any one human being can fit so much into a single life, then you have to see Harry Beckhough in his tenth decade, still motivated, still arguing and debating, still planning, still researching - and above all still laughing.

As this book shows so clearly, Harry's motivation stems from a sense of duty and of loyalty. To his family, to his country, to his party and to his friends. Through this book he will continue to be an example and an inspiration to the rest of us.

I am indeed lucky to be able to count him as my friend.

Michael Ancram.

Contents

Chapter 1

Early Years

During the latter half of the nineteenth century new ideologies of socialism and nationalism emerged across Europe. These new ideologies threatened to extinguish older and more traditional notions of Liberalism. At the end of the Franco-Prussian War in 1871, Prussian land owners united a number of smaller provinces to establish Germany. Under the leadership of Bismarck, the unification of Germany prompted a massive population growth and rapid industrialisation. By the 1890s economic growth in Germany had far outstripped the rest of Europe, and a German policy of World Politics was introduced. Germany hoped to gain colonial territory in order to expand economic markets and gain prestige. This aim was thwarted however, by the fact that much of the world had already been carved out in terms of colonial acquisition. A considerable amount of sabre rattling on the part of the Kaiser, particularly in North Africa, ensured that Great Britain and France formed an uncomfortable but politically necessary Entente Cordiale. An Anglo-German naval race increased political tension significantly from 1905 onwards and Europe was engulfed in an atmosphere of Imperialistic, jingoistic militarism, that culminated in the First World War. Although the initial spark for war was provided by the assassination of Austria's Arch Duke Ferdinand, this incident merely lit a tinder box of simmering, nationalistic discontent and Imperialistic rivalry. Under the Treaty of 1848, which was signed between Belgium and Great Britain, the latter was obligated to go to the aid of the former in the event of military invasion. Once German troops marched into neutral Belgium in August 1914 therefore, Great Britain honoured this Treaty and entered the First World War on the side of Belgium.

A few months before this horrific war began, I was born in the ancient city of Bristol on the 8th February 1914. My father Mike celebrated the arrival of a long awaited third son, after four successive daughters, with some exuberance, and initially forgot the necessity of registration until reminded by my mother, the very capable Marie. As I grew up I always considered myself able, thereafter, to celebrate two birthdays the 8th and 15th February. We lived near the Bristol Rovers Football Ground and our road led through Eastville, Staple Hill and into Wiltshire. I was always fascinated by the city of my birth.

Bristol was originally founded as Bricgstowe: "the place of the bridge", and a defensive wall enclosed the city with a church at each quarter. The top of Castle Street ran through the site of Bristol Keep. The solid masonry of each wall was 25 feet thick. "Four-square to the winds of heaven" stood this "noble toure" for more than 500 years. Now nothing of this structure remains, since it was finally bombed to destruction by Hitler's Luftwaffe. But as a boy, ancient Bricgstowe was my imaginary adventure land, peopled by brave men-at-arms, and I loved studying its history. Prince John granted Bristol a Charter in 1188, to mark its growing importance as a thriving city and port. Traditionally it has always been a starting point for many adventures. In 1497 John Cabot set sail in the beautiful and now famous ship the Matthew and discovered Newfoundland. A replica of the Matthew is now moored in Bristol docks next to another famous ship, the SS Great Britain that was built by Isambard Kingdom Brunel. He also designed and helped to construct the city's most famous land mark, the Clifton Suspension Bridge, though unfortunately he died before it was completed.

During the nineteenth century the city continued to thrive under the direction of the Merchant Venturers and its port was crucial for the trading of tobacco and sugar. More controversially, it was also deeply involved in the slave trade. The gross inhumanity of this trade prompted William Wilberforce and the Quaker movement in Bristol to agitate for its abolition. Despite the somewhat dubious trading connections of the early Merchant Venturers they were, nevertheless, largely responsible for the way the city developed over the years. They supported many industrial and educational projects in Bristol, and helped to establish its reputation for educational excellence. They founded a series of schools from primary to private, with foundation scholarships to assist intelligent children of poor parents. The Merchant Venturers also funded the University of Bristol College in 1876, which later became a world famous University. I proudly entered the University of Bristol in 1932, and this became my gateway to the world of which I had dreamed. Whatever success I have achieved in my long life stems from the support of my gracious home town, from primary school through to University.

At the end of the First World War, I was just embarking on my academic life. I attended my first school at the age of four, and was daunted by its forbidding black gates in Milk Street. Those huge, black, iron gates caused me to howl with dismay at the thought of being incarcerated therein. Mother used the age-old weapon of enticement in the shape of a penny bar of Fry's chocolate. I was pushed through the gates as I was contentedly munching. Before I realised her cunning ruse, she had firmly closed the school gates and was out of earshot of my cries of frustration. However, mother had to pay for her heinous betrayal. Thereafter, I refused to enter those fearsome gates without my chocolate bribe. Thus I became a chocoholic and a connoisseur of all Fry's products, nut bars, cream bars and coconut slices. A guided tour of Fry's was a special treat for us schoolchildren, and a day of perfect bliss for me. I wandered through the preparation rooms with their delicious aromas, and tasted innumerable samples. It was chocolate paradise, with gleaming white surroundings and white-clad priestesses. The latter carefully checked each piece on its moving tray, nimbly discarding any imperfects into the containers below. We were assured, to our amazement, that they were allowed to eat their fill of all the "discards", until fully sated. Apparently, on average, this point was reached after only three weeks. I just could not believe it possible that my appetite would ever "sicken and so die."

My lifetime spirit of adventure revealed itself in those early days. First, I climbed the huge black gates in an irrepressible desire to escape. Next I emulated the steeplejack, scaling the local church steeple. I had no problem with the outer wall as there were plenty of good footholds. However, it was rather more difficult when I approached the steeple as I needed knee as well as toe grips. Slowly I climbed until I reached the top of the sloping roof, and was met by a daunting, redstone tiled cover over its length. This was approached on hands and knees. I was doing quite well until I encountered a very bulky turret. My arms were not long enough to encompass it, and I could not edge around. As I sat immobilised contemplating this obstacle a neighbour looked up and, horrorstruck, spotted me perched on top of the church roof. Mother coolly summoned the Fire Brigade, who carried me down their ladder, which I thought a great treat.

Soon after the roof incident, we moved away from Princes Street in St Pauls, to the bracing air of Horfield. I was enthralled by our new, big corner house in Ash Road because it faced the mighty Horfield Common. The open land stretched for miles to Filton and the Bristol Aeroplane Company. This was home to the Bristol Bulldog plane, with a half-section on constant display. I longed to fly in one of those miracles of construction. Our garden was also a source of constant delight as it was full of pear trees, apple trees and strawberries. Now this was the life for me. In a few steps I was on the Common, exploring to my heart's content all manner of trees, flowers, fruits, chestnuts and filberts. A huge stretch of open country with fields, woods, streams, wildlife and hedgerows, my earthly paradise. I wandered freely about that lovely adventure land, often alone, returning home late evening when the light was fading, or my appetite sharpening. Soon I knew every tree and hedgerow with its dog-roses, hips and haws, cowslips, buttercups, dandelions, bluebells, daisies, - chestnuts for conkers ("illy illy onker, my first conker, illy, illy ack, my first crack") - walnuts, blackberries, each day full of wonders and delights. I invented different adventures, happy on my own to play and dream. Time was only a matter of morning light and evening shadows. I would often be discovered by a local policeman, who would escort me back to his small police station. Here I would entertain with a repertoire of my own ditties and songs from my sisters' collection of popular HMV records. They dubbed me the "wandering minstrel", and rewarded me with a glass of milk and a bun. Mother would carry me home, fast asleep. Halcyon days for me, though the world was slowly recovering from the tragedy of that dreadful War. My eldest brother Alfred, had joined the RFC.(Royal Flying Corps), under age, and learnt to fly in those "wire and string" flying machines. They were not securely strapped in and one day, coming in to land, his plane turned over in the wind, and he landed upside down - on his head, and was thereafter "grounded."

To reach my next school, I always turned right from Ash Road into the main Gloucester Road and passed my two favourite shops in the process. The first was a little sweet shop kept by a quaint old lady, who would deftly fold a piece of newspaper into a neat cone, and fill it with broken cuttings of sweets, biscuits, toffees, chocolates. Then she would solemnly hand it to me in return for my proffered penny. Next door was the greengrocer and fishmonger, who was greatly admired by me in his big, blue striped apron, white armlets, rubber boots and straw brimmer. He would greet my "Good morning, Mr. Smith", with a big smile and hand me an apple or a handful of cherries, saying "Have a good day at school young Harry, and don't get up to any of your larks". Such was my early reputation. Then came the exciting part. As I turned right I could see the gates of Horfield Prison with its huge brick walls. Outside there were front gardens that were tended by selected prisoners. They were called 'Trustees' and always greeted me cheerfully. My abiding memory of that school, was drawing circles with stems and tails, and making up words, like cat and dog. Yet those early lessons were well taught and formed the essence of my ability to read and write, clearly and naturally. Shop keepers, postmen, policemen, prisoners, were all my friends and part of my life, and every day was filled with enjoyment.

My big, strong, beloved father was a quiet man with a keen sense of humour. Patient, tolerant, hard- working, he endured the continuous noise of my sisters. He would sit quietly in the evenings in the corner of our living room, contentedly reading the daily paper and studying the racing form. He did not drink, but enjoyed his pipe and Woodbines, the favourite cigarette of World War One. He simply accepted responsibility for our big family, and worked extra hours when times were difficult. His sole recreation was going quietly by himself to the local cinema, to see his favourite cowboy films. Then he would take my mother to see her chosen romantic serials where, each week, the heroine Pearl White was last seen tied to railway lines, with a huge train thundering towards her - then a flash, followed by "To be continued in our next episode". I took special pleasure in the wonderful Sunday walks I had with my father across the Common. We simply enjoyed each other's company and the scenery until we arrived at the Glo'sters' regimental barracks. Their band would play marches, hymns and popular tunes on Sundays to entertain the local people. We both loved their martial music, marching, and open-air Service. Thus began my love of all things military. I would march up and down, trying to keep in step.

My father had wide knowledge, a simple philosophy and a natural love of humanity. He taught me never to lend money, for "that was the surest way to lose erstwhile good friends, who never repaid, but whose conscience then led them to avoid you". Instead, "just give whatever you can spare, with a good heart, and without repayment. In that way you keep all your friends and always remain on good terms." A quiet man, who said little, but what he did say was always to the point. He never argued, especially with my mother whose occasional wrath would simply disappear, with no opposition. He taught me essential truths like "don't be afraid to acknowledge when wrong and, however difficult, apologise sincerely (usually accepted), and thus ease your conscience, and make no enemies."

My sisters often bullied me until I reached the mature age of fifteen. At that point I opened my first Lloyds Bank account with five shillings and took over the family accounts. From then on I was accepted as senior adviser and helper. I gradually cleared debts, whilst putting off collectors of family dues with fair words and promises. I also joined the Conservative Party, essentially for the fun I experienced at election time. In those days elections were more direct and pulled no punches. The orange-box speeches, with robust language, were delivered on street corners, and peppered with ripe comments from the crowd. For me they were sheer enjoyment. They represented the real school of oratory and red-blooded politics, when the Union Jack meant pride in our country, and nobody worried about libel. In 1918 the then Prime Minister, Lloyd George, promised returning soldiers a 'Land Fit For Heroes,' but this promise was never kept. A brief economic post war boom quickly turned into a severe slump. Britain had used all its gold reserves to wage war and was deeply in debt. The situation was worsened by an over production of coal and steel, a war time disruption in traditional world trade markets, an economically weakened Europe, a cyclical down turn in the economy and a disastrous decision to return Britain to the gold standard. In 1923, the Chancellor Geddes was forced to make substantial cuts in public spending, as the country was plunged into a long economic depression. These cuts became known as 'Geddes Axe', and effectively curtailed all house building programmes. There were no homes fit for heroes. Instead, returning soldiers found themselves subjected to a series of medical tribunals that were designed to assess their pension and benefit rights. Victims of shell shock and gas attacks were forced to fight for their pensions, as an economically pressed government administration tried to reduce pension obligations. Political solutions to pressing social problems were thin on the ground, and in the gruelling post war years, life was difficult for most people, particularly women.

Overburdened as she certainly was, my mother had an unbelievable store of energy. She overcame all difficulties, great and small, when dealing with all household affairs, and often discussed details late at night with my father. A supreme cook, she could produce tasty, filling meals almost 'out of nothing,' and her baking was the pride of the neighbourhood. Wherever our moves took us, my mother made immediate friends.

Neighbours often dropped in with their troubles (as if she had not enough of her own) to glean her advice, and to watch her bake in an old-fashioned oven beside the fire.

I can remember her sheer delight at the delivery of our first, polished enamel-faced cooker, from the new Gas, Light and Coke Company. This marked the end of the daily task of blackleading the top, and the ritual scrubbing of the interior. Henceforth, just a wiperound was required. Cooking now became absolute bliss, with final release from the daily struggle with that little black, coal-fired oven, adjoining the fire. How Mother managed to produce all those tasty meals, cottage loaves and delicious cakes and biscuits remains a mystery to me. After the introduction of gas with those delicate, lacelike mantles, that had followed the tiresome problems of candles and lamps with adjustable wicks, came electricity. This miracle of bright shining light totally transformed the 1930s. In those grim post-war days everything was used and nothing wasted. Fruit and vegetables were cheap and plentiful, and grown quite naturally then. Everyone had learned how to grow their own vegetables during that terrible War. Germany was so hated, that schools no longer taught the language. This was not surprising when so many millions of young men from sixteen upwards failed to return home, and even more came back injured and marred for life. This was the lost generation.

The second son of the family was named George and possessed a similar nature to my father. He was quiet, self-contained, thoughtful and observant. He was always ready to share with others, and the only member of our family who was happier at sea than on land. I need to feel my feet planted firmly on the soil, preferring country to town yet happy in both. Tall and slim, George was my hero. He had such intelligence and personality that our solicitor offered to train him without charge. But he loved open-air life, and had made up his mind to do the proverbial, "run away to sea". One day he simply packed his bags and informed our parents that he had "signed on" to serve on a ship at Avonmouth Docks. He went off to sea and we did not see him for a year. He wrote regularly however, and was obviously enjoying his new life.

On his first visit home he had looked fit, bronzed and well, though thin and spare, with many adventures. He kept me enthralled with tales of the ships on which he had served. Sometimes they had been battered by rough storms with brilliant sheets of lightning. These were often followed by long quiet days in the tropics, where there were bright clear skies and stars hung like heavy orbs, and were a sheer delight. We all looked forward to his letters since they were more frequent than his increasingly rare visits. He began to study and pass exams to become third, second, and then first Mate and engineer. His intention finally was to take the toughest exams, because he wanted to become a Captain and own his own ship. He needed to study onshore for his finals. Unfortunately he contracted mercurial poisoning from a tin of meat and tragically died. His Masonic friends dealt with all the funeral arrangements. They also ensured that we received the full details of his demise, and his possessions.

It was the family tragedy. We were stunned and inconsolable. George was the 'white hope' of the family. On his last leave he had bought a Raleigh bicycle to tour the West Country. I remember his many friends, especially girlfriends, begging him to stay and build his career closer to home. He was already First Mate and engineer, and admired by all. Yet he could not forsake his dream of being the Captain of his own ship. Then he was lost to us all and totally irreplaceable. I loved him dearly and longed to emulate him.

Before leaving for the last time, George presented me with his Raleigh bicycle as a reward for winning a scholarship to Fairfield grammar school. It was my best-ever present and I cherished it, cleaning every spoke, washing and polishing, and mending punctures with my John Bull repair outfit. It kept his memory alive and ever present. What joy I had with this newfound freedom of motion and movement. It eliminated any last vestige of my unhappy, asthma years. I cycled everywhere, especially with my close group of friends who all had bicycles but little money. We did odd jobs to earn our independence. Newspapers, errands, anything. I had joined the Cubs at nine, and eventually graduated to 1st Bristol Scout Troop, with our own special yell: "B.R.I.S.T.O.L., Glo'ster, Somerset, County as well. 'Ow bist thee? Where bist goin? Casn't see for dust! One eye open, t'other always in fust."

My father was so calm and self-contained that I never saw him lose his temper. Strangely, it is his quiet presence that I remember clearly, and his strong body shape. Whereas, with my mother, I distinctly remember her beautiful face. I can recall how lovely she looked when she dressed us all, and herself, for a family outing or ceremony. I remember her in old age when her children had departed. Her face was small and perfectly formed, with wide clear brows, a neat straight nose and curved red lips, that never received nor needed artificial colouring. She never used skin creams or artificial aids, saying that her mother, whom she resembled, always maintained that good quality soap and plenty of cold water kept your skin clear.

Both my maternal grandparents were reticent about their roots, but my grandmother, who was English, told me that there had been a dispute within the Coburg family. Consequently my grandfather came to settle in Victorian England, where he was educated and always remembered with great pleasure. They lived in a big house at the top of St. Michael's Hill. I remember the polished wood of the hallway and the horsehair settee, which used to scratch my legs when I was in short trousers. Best of all, I remember Grandmama's big, red, polished sandstone-flagged kitchen, full of delicious smells - and her little greenhouse, in which she grew tomatoes, cucumbers, vegetables, but especially those big geraniums whose smell pervaded everywhere. She always gave me cakes, money and sweet kisses. Her house was ever neat and tidy, clean and shining, just like grandmamma Hannah herself.

Grandfather Coburg was a striking but broodingly mysterious man, with dark hair and a neat Prince Albert-style beard. He seemed to have sufficient income for the upkeep of his big house and three lovely daughters, who were known locally as the three roses. They included my mother Marie and her two sisters, Becky who was tall, serene and dignified, and Rose who never married but cared for her mother until she died. Their elder son, Albert, who became the mainstay of the family, was a sweet-natured, charitable Conservative. He was proud to be a Mason, and told me they did a "lot of good". A wise, kindly man, he was friendly with many people. Indeed I thought he knew everybody. He was the first member of the family to own a car, a Singer saloon. He often took me on his travels around the countryside, where he called on farmers in Somerset and Gloucester to advise them on how to deal with problems. He was always welcomed by these farming communities with great hospitality.

I well remember an old farmhouse in Somerset, where the farmer's wife regaled me with her home-made pie and a delicious cool drink, actually made, to my astonishment, from flowers. It was so tasty that I readily agreed to another tall glass. When it was time to leave I could not stand up, and had to be carried to the car. I slept happily all the way home. This incident marked the first and earliest occasion when I was really intoxicated. The second was on a celebration night in the Victoria rooms in Bristol, with Sam Tucker, who was once Captain of both Bristol and the England rugby team. The third took place in a luxury apartment in Park Lane near the Dorchester Hotel, London. My friend and I sampled everything in the walk-in cocktail cabinet of his absent parents. I then drove back to my flat in Notting Hill, through Hyde Park, singing happily. I parked my car perfectly outside and let myself in. Then sank into a plumped armchair and slept for ten hours, until a friend called and woke me from a lovely, drunken slumber. It was a lucky escape and a complete cure, for I never drank again.

My other uncle, Sam, was a somewhat unreal character. He was tall, slim, red-haired and a complete cynic. He used to tell me about the wonderful country of Communist Russia, where all seemed perfect and life a paradise. Karl Marx was his hero, and looking back, I think he was more of a 'rainbow' communist, all theory, but no facts. When I told him I was a Conservative, he said I was "losing my marbles." I countered with, "Well, why don't you leave this terrible place, where the upper class beat down and enslave the underclass, and go to your Mecca, Moscow?" He would mutter that they had much to do here in terms of proclaiming the truth. Of course he would never dream of leaving England. In fact, he rarely went beyond Bristol, and never set foot abroad. He was popular in his local pub, where they enjoyed his funny stories, jokes, and wild imagination. He never married, just lived in his own dream world where everyone would be equal and experience a worker's paradise. He was a truly good man, simply a harmless dreamer who gave away all his earnings, and then 'borrowed' from his brother.

As a student he introduced me to the Anglo-Russian Club. This consisted of a collection of well known, mainly artistic people, where he said "At least you may be sure of getting plenty of good food, and all for free". With this in mind, I introduced some of my penurious friends to the club, where we enjoyed Russian caviar, vodka, salt herrings and pickled cucumber. We also enjoyed some good arguments with pro-Soviet theorists, before retiring, well-filled. At least it was a costless change from the local pub, and fish and chips. Armed with a view of other cultures, the club simply reinforced our own conviction of British superiority.

Returning to my childhood, our last move was from my beloved Horfield where I spent my happiest years with many friends, to a tall house in Stapleton Road. This busy main road stretched from Eastville at our end, right down to St. Philip's, with tramlines running right through to Market Street, the centre of the tramways system of Bristol. Trams had a tremendous effect on the ability of Bristolians to move about quickly and cheaply to most parts of the town. This was in the 1920's and 30's, when motorcars had just arrived, courtesy of the American Ford and English Morris. Trams were a boon and a blessing. They steadily improved and to some extent stifled the prolific growth of the automobile. They were clean, wholesome, economical and far superior to modern, ugly top-heavy, fuel-consuming buses.

I attended a local primary school known as the Easton Board School. It was a late Victorian edifice of fairly modest size and economic structure. It had one main centre hall running through the length of the building. This was where we all met for Morning Service and important occasions, including Speech days. The hall became four classrooms separated by sliding doors, but the quality of teaching was hardly inspiring. At this stage in my life breathing became a major problem. I awoke one morning to find the family cat lying on my chest. It was sucking in my breath and blowing its own into my nostrils. This developed into asthma from the age of seven, which held me firmly in its grip until I reached fourteen. There was no known cure or remedy then, though our doctor helped ease the attacks. Sometimes they were so bad and left me so weak and breathless, that my father had to carry me upstairs to bed.

At the age of ten, I was entered for a scholarship by my school. I was the first boy that the teachers thought capable of winning the annual contest, which was established by the Town Council to enable free entry to Grammar and Secondary Schools. The carefully engendered school system in Bristol, was divided into four Grammar Schools, four Secondary Schools (slightly lower level), and four Central Schools, that were semi-technical. This seemed to be a very sensible approach to higher education that was available to all, at different and obtainable levels. We were assembled at the Council Offices in Corn Street, and faced iron framed, wooden top desks, which were arranged neatly in rows. Each desk had its own inkwell, pens, pencil, ruler, and blotting paper. Along with a folder containing foolscap writing paper and pages of questions. We commenced at 9.30 am and at 12.30 the bell rang to signal the end of the test. The first questions were on books, general knowledge and written composition followed by simple arithmetic, geography and history. Fortunately I had read many history books at St. Philip's Library, which became my Mecca. My abiding curiosity impelled me to discover whatever lay within that 'Library'. It took my breath away to see all those shelves packed with books from floor to ceiling. They wetted my appetite for wide reading, understanding and knowledge. A kind, motherly lady had greeted me with a warm, encouraging smile and explained the functions of a library, and how all these books were there for me to read. My first borrower's tablet was for the Children's Section. This was a fairyland for me and I simply started reading at one side, and continued to the end. I sat at a corner table and read and read. Fairy tales, books of adventure, romance, history and geography - I read them all.

I can still picture myself in my favourite corner poring over my latest discovery from Dickens, Scott or Shakespeare - all abridged for children's reading. I loved Tennyson's lovely rhymes and Wordsworth's clear word pictures. Gulliver's Travels stretched my imagination. This was a new world that filled my mind with new sounds, pictures, images, and I would return home replete with the sense of adventure. I frequently remained at the library until closing time. It was such a quiet, peaceful and pleasant atmosphere. I became well-known to all the staff. Once I had exhausted all the books which appealed to me in the Children's Section, I daringly entered the Adult Section. The staff pretended not to notice and my friend gave me an adult ticket, with the first book I borrowed. I became the family scribe at the age of fifteen. Noticing how worried my mother seemed when trying to balance her household accounts I offered to help. From then on I became her assistant, and we planned necessary expenditure, cutting down where income did not match. I began to understand the value of money, and the reason for my mother's headaches, and worried looks at weekends. The cost of food and clothing for all our tribe, plus all the regular bills for gas, water, and electricity had been calculated by mother in her head, as she'd had precious little time to spare from her continuous family problems. My father simply handed her almost all of his earnings and relied on her competence.

By the age of fifteen, I had successfully waged war on my asthma attacks with my mother's age-old remedy, which was a mixture of glycerine and honey with lemon juice. It was always kept handy in a small beaker. Soon after my fourteenth birthday I was alone in the house one afternoon, when I experienced a terrible attack. My throat muscles constricted so intensely that I had to fight for breath. There was a pounding in my head accompanied by flashes of light. I gripped the back of a chair and the corner of the kitchen table, as I literally fought for breath. One of my sisters returned and looked at me aghast. I whispered urgently and hoarsely for her to fetch some lemon juice. As she hurried back with the precious juice she tried to unclamp my fingers from the back of the chair, but could not prise loose my iron grip. Finally, she forced a spoonful between my lips. After a few minutes I began to breathe more easily and it was all over. I had won my first battle for life. From that time on I became totally free of asthma. When our doctor examined me he shook his head in astonishment. My breathing was completely normal, with not the slightest trace of asthma. What a joy for the whole family! My father was beside himself and hugged me as though I were still a small child. Gradually my slight frame began to fill out and I launched myself into all the activities that had hitherto been impossible. I was able to run, jump, and play games such as rugby and cricket. I was even able to run cross-country, but was still advised not to swim for fear of water on the lungs.

My physical success was accompanied by some academic success. Completely unknown to my family, I had been entered by Easton School in 1924 for a grammar school scholarship. The news of my success came as a bombshell to the family. A neighbour came into our house one day waving a Bristol newspaper: "Have you seen the paper, Mary? - your Harry has won a scholarship". The situation had to be carefully explained and my name was pointed out in the midst of all those who'd been successful. I had thought no more about it after those exam papers. The Council sent us formal notice that I had been awarded a fully paid scholarship to Fairfield Grammar School. This funding included books but not the school uniform, and there were no free school meals. Easton School was exuberant, because I was actually the first pupil ever to win a scholarship. The whole school was assembled and the headmaster made a speech. This event signalled the end of my last term at Easton School.

Chapter 2

Fairfield School

My new school was reached by tram and on foot. Fairfield Grammar School was an hour away from my home and my asthma attacks caused me to miss many lessons. No help was given to make up the inevitable gaps. One had to fend for oneself as best possible. Consequently I fell behind with my work. I began to amuse myself and developed a reputation for mischief. Only the French teacher, Mrs.Collinson, sympathised and helped. I took to French quite naturally, not yet realising that languages were to become my forte.

The male teachers were mainly ex-military officers who were given a year's training to fill the great teacher shortage after the War. They were generally ineffective and lacked any understanding of children. The geography master gave typically army type instruction. The maths master was nicknamed "Sleeps" as he always seemed half-awake. We rarely saw the physics master's face. In the laboratory he busily chalked up his notes on a double blackboard. His only remark when our work was completed was "Have you finished?" He would rub it all off and then refill the board until the end of the lesson. Then he would stalk out, hitching up his gown, without even looking at us. Once my asthma had cleared I began to enjoy games and exercises in the gym, and even took part in a paper chase. I joined the Cadet Corps, which was run by two of the ex-officers. We wore khaki uniform (with puttees) and learned foot and arms drill with wooden rifles. I was a keen, doughty little soldier and excelled in arms drill and marching.

At the age of 12 my French penfriend offered me an exchange visit to Mulhouse in Alsace Lorraine. I set off with the school party to Paris, where they changed for Dijon. I went on alone to Mulhouse. I walked across Les Halles at 6.00 am through rows of stout ladies sitting at their stalls with huge baskets of fruit and vegetables; they joked in their sharp Paris dialect and gave me fruit for my journey. The journey took five long hours and the wooden seats were uncomfortable, so I was glad to find Charles waiting for me at the station marked Mulhouse/Mülhausen. The German occupation in the First World War had left its mark with all streets and place names inscribed in both French and German. I received an enthusiastic welcome from my friend's family.

His home was a French "guest-house," used essentially for daily meals, with about a dozen regulars. They all talked at once in different languages. The cooking was wonderful and most appetising. I learnt to cook a real garnished French omelette in the big kitchen, and how to toss a pancake made of a mixture of eggs, flour, honey and herbs. Charles guided me around his town pointing out all the places of interest. He was particularly keen to highlight the battle areas, where the Alsatians had put up a dogged fight against the Germans. Strangely I felt quite at home in that embattled town, with its hatred of the German "invaders from hell". I had gained a smattering of odd French, German and Italian phrases from the guest house regulars, along with some swear words which they had taught me with delight. They accepted me as "le petit anglais", "der kleine Engländer", "bubchen". They gave me a Gauloise cigarette and laughed when it choked me. They also tried to educate me about wine. They all came to see me off at the station, as though they were saying good-bye to a favourite relative. I promised to return after Charles came to visit my family in Bristol. Travelling back to England I stayed overnight in Paris, where the 'Exhibition Coloniale' was in full swing. It was such an exciting day. I visited all the stalls and exhibitions with their wonderful displays of Eastern art and sculpture. Most interesting for me, was a splendid Egyptian Stand, with mummies and hieroglyphics, like an ancient pictorial script. In addition there were amazing pictures and photographs of French colonies, exotic robes, jewels and finery, and beautifully dressed natives dancing to their own music. This was all fascinating for an adventurous boy fresh out of Bristol.

Sated with mouth-watering sweets, cakes, fruits and juices I spent my last francs on a huge bottle of Egyptian perfume. This had such a strong, exotic odour, that I was sure my sisters would be delighted. When I eventually reached Bristol without mishap, I considered myself to be a seasoned traveller. I presented my family with the large and bizarre-shaped container, which they duly tested. I can still remember the look on their faces at this strong, oriental perfume! They screamed with laughter and pretended to be slave dancers. "One dab could have lasted a life-time, surviving all washing and bathing". I never lived it down and it became a family joke. Charles had more success when he arrived for the exchange visit. He brought delicious liqueur chocolates and was an immediate favourite.

By this time, continuous exercise on my bicycle had helped me grow strong and healthily active. I had great fun adventuring with my group of loyal friends like Cyril Harwood. He was a brave, courageous lad who had suffered from meningitis as a child, leaving him partially disabled, but never beaten. He would tear awkwardly about the field playing football, and would ride a bicycle that had been specially adapted for his use by his brother who was a local vicar. I admired him for his tough, unbeatable courage. He didn't just avoid trouble. Instead he actively sought it out, just to conquer each challenge. He lived with his parents in a cottage full of brightly polished wood and brass ornaments. I remember sitting around the fire roasting chestnuts and roaring with laughter at their family jokes. They were a poor but happily contented family. The salt of the earth and grain of England. I was to meet their like again, many years later in Yorkshire dales. My friend Ray O'Connor was tall, slim and athletic. He came from a cheerful, hard-working, big Catholic family. He was good at all sports but always quiet, competent and helpful. Cleak and I were known as Bick and Click. He was modest and unassuming, but ever ready to assist whenever needed. Rayner was a quiet, cheerful fellow, whose father owned a pram and bicycle shop nearby. To our immense satisfaction his father always kept his only son well furnished with cash and food.

In the meantime my studies were patchy. My best teacher was Mrs. Collinson, she was a fiery little pigeon-toed Irishwoman, and I became her prime favourite. To her amazement I had even read some French novels. Victor Hugo and Anatole France for example. Clearly she didn't know of my secret haven at St. Philip's Library. Not even my friends knew. I loved the seclusion and was on good terms with the staff, who often fed me biscuits and tea. English was a doddle except for the grammar, which was so badly taught that it remained a mystery to me until Mrs. Collinson explained French grammar, simply and clearly. Then I began to understand English grammar in all its complexities.

History was part of my recreational reading, and I enjoyed stories about the kings and queens of England. The fierce, marauding Scottish Highlanders and their continuous fighting and stealing. To me, the Irish represented fairy folk, their nation was full of songs, magical tales and pretty women. My first real girlfriend was a lovely blue-eyed, black-haired, sweet-natured Irish lass from Limerick, who was training to be a nurse at Bristol Royal Infirmary. I went there for the first time because I had broken my nose in a "friendly" game of rugby. I received cold comfort from my medical student friends who were all rugger players and viewed a broken nose as a trophy.

At the ripe old age of fourteen, I believed that the world was my oyster, and I was enjoying my first romance with Linda. I actually wrote her two "high-quality" poems with rhyming couplets. I thought of myself as a highly romantic, dashing sort of fellow. Until I went to meet her once and overheard her reading my precious inspirations aloud to her friends. They were giggling over my best passages. I quickly ended that affair and others were only fleeting. Much later I met my beautiful Irish colleen Kathleen O'Regan, who was my first true love. Kathleen was seventeen when we met. Matron's rules demanded that she returned to quarters by 6.00 p.m. with one extension to 8.00 p.m. on Wednesdays. I fell in love with Kathleen the first time I saw her in her neat-fitting uniform with its pretty headcap. I remember one most enjoyable night, when we arrived back late and she had to climb on my shoulders in order to crawl over the wall and beat Matron's curfew. Eventually we drifted apart but her memory remains.

By the time I was fifteen, I had become interested in politics and had read the City Council material at the Library. My uncle had a business in Bedminster near the WD & HO Wills tobacco factory. I thought the Wills family must be as rich as Croesus. Yet I never thought that of the Fry's Quaker family. Perhaps because one of their sons was the boyfriend of my youngest sister Eva, and my father favoured Quakers. Though I have to confess that I always found their long silences difficult. There was real grinding poverty in those war and post-war years. The middle classes suffered equally with the working class. Any meagre, available money went on basic family sustenance. People rarely bought new clothes, instead they adopted a "make do and mend" policy. We were all impecunious and helped each other wherever possible. I learnt some of the hard facts of life by being close to people who lived from day to day. They struggled continuously to keep their family housed, fed and clothed. Children often left school well before they were fourteen in order to contribute financially to the meagre family income. We felt the neighbourhood pull together in the struggle to make both ends meet. Somehow most women turned to my mother for advice, as if she were the local oracle. Mother used to say a 'peck of sympathy was worth a yard of advice'. Life was a continuous struggle from hand to mouth, yet never without humour, sometimes raw and earthy. It brought us together in a camaraderie born of shared hardship. The peculiar facility to find odd humour in the most dire of circumstances, has always been very much a British characteristic.

At election times I led my gang carrying my blue flag fixed to an old broomstick. We marched along singing "Vote, Vote, Vote for Johnny Whatsit, and Throw old So-and-So out the land". We were regaled with baked potatoes and roast chestnuts, from street braziers. Tough days with simple, clear, political lines of thought. Present generations have no concept of the real hardship of those post-war years, which just had to be endured. No electricity, gas just becoming available. No television, no radio until the 'cat's whisker' and the first models that were operated by car battery. Childrens' lives were mainly lived outdoors with no money to spare for toys. Yet children were happy enough simply playing outside. Favourite games included hopscotch, rounders, spinning tops, running, jumping and swimming. There were certainly scarcely any fat children to be seen. Nor adults for that matter. Each penny had real value with no inflation.

The Wall Street Crash in 1929 had coincided with my fifteenth year and I was acutely aware of growing poverty levels. Indeed, the real foundation of my life was established during that year. I began to prepare for a crucial matriculation exam. It was compulsory to gain credits in at least three subjects. These needed to include mathematics and a science subject. I chose English, French and History as my primary subjects, with maths and chemistry as "musts". Maths was so badly taught that I had to find my own solution, which I did by learning the principal theorems of geometry by heart. I could already cope with normal additions and subtractions. Thus I passed maths and gained credits in the other four. To the surprise of the staff and myself I duly matriculated.

Chemistry was fun because our Master, Henderson, was a dear old lovable, absent minded fellow. He loved experimenting with odd mixtures and often caused enjoyable explosions, which we encouraged. His gown was in tatters, full of holes that had been made while wiping off liquids, including acids. Notoriously absent minded, he often pushed his wire-rimmed spectacles on his head, whilst peering at some experiment. Then he would search everywhere crying "Where's my glasses?" and of course nobody told him. Yet we all learnt well from him, and enjoyed his enthusiastic, fun-loving way of teaching his beloved chemistry. He was a warm, friendly, tolerant person, a natural teacher, who treated us almost as colleagues. Unlike our cold, precise, unfriendly and inhuman physics master, who did not even deign to look at us, unless excoriating each over poor end of term results. The epitome of a bad teacher, who seemed to care neither for his subject nor his unfortunate pupils.

The best accomplishment "Sleeps" produced and practised regularly, was drawing an immaculate chalk circle on the blackboard whilst facing us, with his back to the board. Try as we might not one of us could emulate him. He never raised his voice but could easily quell a noisy class with a quiet look. He came to life when he was Officer Commanding the Cadet Corps. Immaculately turned out in his Captain's uniform, he taught us that instruction may be delivered and discipline maintained, without the loud shouting and bullying tactics of proverbial Sergeant Majors. He said that in battle you were all part of one family group "in it together", knowing that enemy shells and bullets did not select any particular person. His quiet guide to handling men under command and his sense of responsibility remained with me always. He advised: "Never raise your voice unnecessarily, because it naturally places you at a disadvantage, and you lose respect, which is your best weapon."

He said that outstanding acts of heroism were usually just odd incidents among continuous actions, which just happened to get noticed. Truly brave men, he maintained, were those who carried on quietly in the face of peril no matter how scared they were, and were always ready to help their comrades. Once you were in the midst of battle you forgot your own fears and "just carried on regardless". He had been wounded and his face was heavily lined. I admired him greatly. I learnt much from old Sleeps and from the short, bristly ex-Major geography master, who used to love describing India, the North West frontier and the warlike Pathans. However, his knowledge of Western geography was limited, so I chose history and then added geography as a make-weight, hoping to find questions on India and the Middle East.

Against his will he also taught religious studies, though he fervently believed that the subject should be taught by female teachers. We posed some tricky questions, which he was literally unable to answer. He said that the War often knocked such fairy tales and illusions completely out of you. Yet we discovered that old Sleeps, who had been in heavy action in trench warfare remained, as he said, "a convinced believer," having witnessed "the unbelievable and almost miraculous escapes" from seemingly certain death. He had a quiet faith which he could not describe, saying it was "something beyond us". He may have been a poorish teacher of maths, but I found him a warm, human being, from whom I derived valuable instruction on life.

Now matriculated I was entitled to enter my name for the "Higher School Certificate" which granted free University entrance. My Mecca was Bristol University. This institution was already famous throughout the West Country, and my aim was supported wholeheartedly by my beloved father. He saw in me the realisation of his own dreams. He believed Britain to be the best country in the world. I found it difficult at times to live up to his high standards and unquenching belief in me. But he inspired me, though I fell short at times, and often neglected my studies for other amusements. "Someday you will reach the heights" he would say, "I can see it in your face". When I looked in the mirror at my twice-broken nose and the odd black eye or gash, I wondered what he could possibly mean.

Four subjects were required for University Entrance. English and French were obvious, but none of the other teachers would accept me. I had upset the short, stout Latin mistress, Miss Foweraker who had the peculiar habit of sitting at her low desk with one foot in the waste-paper basket. Pellets would strike her from odd angles as she dozed. I wrote some saucy verses featuring her clearly visible bloomers, which she did not find amusing. The irascible "Miss Fouracres" refused to take me further in Latin, saying I was "incorrigible and doomed to failure," persuading other teachers to cast me forth. I was left with English and French and had to find two further subsidiary subjects. Worse was to come. A summons to the Headmaster's study, meant trouble. Mr. Truscott, in his tweed jacket and corduroys, looked more like a ruddy-faced farmer than a Headmaster as he faced me across his desk with a stern look. However, instead of the dismissal lecture I had anticipated, he bade me sit down. To my surprise he did not appear to be wearing his executioner's mask, but had a slight smile and a twinkle in his eye.

"You know what you are here for, don't you?" quoth he. "Yes sir and I'm very sorry". "Too late to be contrite young man, when most teachers have refused to teach you in the sixth Form, except for Mrs Collinson who alone spoke very highly of you as 'attentive, responsive, a born linguist', echoed to less extent by our English teacher, who said you seemed to produce essays on any subject. Now what do you suggest I should do as your Headmaster, when almost all my staff prophesy abysmal failure if I let you sit the Higher School?" This was not the sort of question I had expected from the Headmaster. Caught completely off balance, I stammered "I really don't know, Sir – but I think I could manage, given the chance." "Tell you what young man - I've checked carefully through your career and noted how well you plunged into games when you recovered from asthma, which seems to have caused some of your subsequent problems. Now most staff say they are convinced of your failure, should I allow you to sit. But I am prepared to back you on two conditions. Firstly that you find teachers for all four subjects and secondly that you promise me honestly, here and now, to work like a Trojan to save me from looking foolish before my staff, who will say 'We told you so.'" To say that I was astonished, relieved, completely bowled over, was putting it mildly. Mr Truscott shook hands with me to seal the contract and made me promise not to leak any of this conversation to my fellows. I left walking on air and refused to answer questions from my waiting friends. All I said was "No more larking about chaps, we must get down to work from now on - just to show 'em and get through" - and they did. All my group passed, to our great relief and celebrations.

But what was I to do? Time was running out and I had to nominate those two extra subjects. It seemed hopeless and there were just over twenty months to go. I sought help and advice from my prime supporter, Mrs. Collinson who came up with one good idea. She had taken German as a subsidiary subject at University many years ago, had passed, but never used it again, as she considered it an ugly and ungainly language, compared with her precious French. If I accepted her offer she would dig up some of her old German books and test papers and get more recent ones to show me the type of questions that were asked. With about a week's preparation she would do her best if I promised to cooperate. I thanked her and said in my impetuous gratitude, "If you will help me, I'll swot it up to get through". A little later she said, "I have a staff friend, Miss Craigie, to whom I told your story and she also has an offer. Many years ago she took her degree at Edinburgh University with Greek subsidiary, of which she now remembers very little. She invented her own system of cramming, and if you are crazy enough to take on these two completely new languages, then she will find time to help you cram Greek "with the Craigie system." What a situation to face! Two completely unknown languages to mug up in twenty months. I just had to take it on for there was no other choice. Mr Truscott signed my application form and I discovered that my parents had a smattering of German. We even managed to find an old German/English dictionary.

My friends at St. Philip's Library, ever my haven of refuge, were very helpful. They sought out language books of instruction, grammar, textbooks, and dictionaries. I never cease to be thankful for my childhood discovery of that blessed library, and the kindly staff who helped me from that first hesitant day, and thereafter treated me like family. They found me a desk in a quiet corner. Then I settled down to my task of Hercules. I was fully prepared to take on this new challenge. I always found that learning a language was more exciting than other subjects and I was keen to start. Mrs. Collinson had produced a pile of old exam papers in German and the "First Steps in German". These included introductory books with constructions, vocabulary and test papers on grammar. We whisked through these without much problem. The dynamic little woman really clarified German for me, calling it an "upside down language". Thus I had mastered the basic principles of German before the redoubtable Scotswoman Miss Craigie, began her stern attempt to "smuggle me through Greek". Like me, she had been required to learn it in a hurry, as a minor subject, during her University of Edinburgh degree course. The set book Homer Odyssey XI, and passages from other authors and the philosophers were a doddle, as she produced perfect English translations for me to learn by heart. There were no set pieces, testing grammar or constructions in the Higher Curriculum - simply translation of Greek texts and a long series of questions of a different nature. Together these tested knowledge of language, grammar and construction.

As Miss Craigie explained: "It is hopeless to attempt to learn grammar and fluency in constructions and language in such short time, but my system depends on extensive vocabulary. If you have mastered literally many hundreds of words and phrases, you can then guess the translation and construction. Learn from slips of paper, five words the first night, to be repeated before you go to sleep and again when you wake. Next day add five more and repeat those ten for a further two days. Then add five more per day until you reach 50. Then a pause for memorising them all for two days. Then continue until you have 100 off by heart, and strongly enclosed in your memory, repeating night and day. Then say to yourself: this is but a good beginning so on to the next 100. But never, never try to do too many, for you won't beat the system. You need to give the gradually increasing numbers space to settle firmly. I did exactly as she said and my Greek vocabulary increased steadily. The family thought I was deranged, as I was now walking about muttering Greek words and German phrases like the proverbial eccentric professor. But it was wonderful training and my memory grew sharper and more retentive. I began to enjoy Greek history and philosophy, and considered those ancient Greeks as having the key to civilised society and wisdom. It marked the rather weird beginning of my real education and self-taught, wide knowledge of many subjects and life interests. I began to think coherently and form clear patterns of thought. Learning by rote clarified my thinking and thought processes. But it was after all, only superficial, quick-fire learning without full absorption. Unless continuously practised and used, it was just as easily forgotten, as with all cramming. Mental absorption needs practical application to firm the memory.

I still kept the family accounts and had already become chief adviser to my mother. My father was working non-stop as usual, and comforted by the new situation, for he believed in me implicitly. When he heard of the efforts of the Collinson/Craigie team, he glowed with satisfaction, and made me promise to thank them for all the time and effort they were sacrificing for my sake. When I did, they said "Nonsense - it's just the sort of challenge to shake us out of our long teaching apathy and bring us alive again.

This is a treat for us but hard work for you, and we are gambling on you". I learnt that the staff were actually gambling on my failure in the exams. Only the teachers of English, Craigie, Collinson, and Headmaster Truscott, were actually putting their money on me. I have often wondered since, what the odds were. Naturally, this made me all the more determined to keep my promise to my protector Headmaster Truscott, and not to disappoint my father, who believed so strongly in me. English and French progressed well and this enabled me to give more time to swotting up Greek and German. I remained in my peaceful spot in the Library until closing time.

In the evenings I cycled with my friends. We discussed our various subjects and gave each other a helping hand, for we were all struggling with difficult subjects that were often ill taught. Imagine trying to study physics when all you saw, was the black-gowned back of the teacher, as he filled board after board with notes to be copied and learnt by heart! Or geography from an ex-officer who concentrated almost entirely on the East, where he had spent his years of service. Or a mathematics master who could not solve some of our basic algebra problems. The quality of teaching at my school was far below average and it was a poorly paid profession. Yet in the Victorian era, the acknowledged leaders of the community were the vicar, teacher and doctor. There were always good people who were prepared to devote their lives to the education and upbringing of mischievous children. It must have seemed a thankless tasks at times. As time went swiftly by, my Greek vocabulary increased immensely, as I mastered and memorised many hundreds of words. Amazingly, my German vocabulary increased well at the same time, though I did not make the same effort to learn set quantities by rote. Greek, with the help of Miss Craigie, took a really strong, sustained effort, to master sufficient of the language in the time available. German was easier with Mrs Collinson, who disciplined and regulated my studies in her own inimitable fashion. I gradually found the exercises viable despite her hard markings. My petite, pigeon-toed, verbose Irish Mrs. Collinson, and her friend the tall, ironic, dignified Scotswoman, Miss Craigie, were my saviours and unforgettable characters. Exam time eventually arrived, and I had to endure three papers of about three hours long in each subject. I actually enjoyed my French and English papers. Then came the struggle with Greek. Miss Craigie had been absolutely right. Just as she had found at Edinburgh, I soon realised that however faulty my knowledge of grammar, my terrific vocabulary helped me translate long, involved passages and allowed me to guess at many of the tenses, adverbs and adjectives.

The German papers were a curious mixture. As I had worked through collections of previous exam papers I found, as Mrs. Collinson had prophesied, several repetitions. However, there were some new questions and passages where my surprisingly increased vocabulary really helped. The Craigie method had sharpened my memory. They should have marketed it, as an indispensable aid to study for all languages. Learning by rote with continuous repetition just as we used to learn arithmetic tables, really did work and train the memory. Though my truly extensive Greek vocabulary began to fade six months after the exam from disuse. I obtained top grade 'A' levels in French and English and actually passed in both the subsidiaries, even gaining a 'Good' in Greek and German, to my amazement. My German Oral was conducted by the University Professor of German himself, one Dr. August Closs, who asked me questions in German and English. Then he asked whether I had ever been to Germany. When I replied "Nein, nur bis Mülhausen in Elsass", he laughed, and asked how I came to learn German in a school which did not have German in its curriculum. When I explained about the concentrated efforts made by Mrs. Collinson and myself, he laughed profusely, and claimed that he had never heard such a story. He offered then and there to accept me as a student, if I agreed to take German as my main subject. I had never had the slightest intention of doing more than scraping through in German and Greek in order to take English and French as my main subjects. Nevertheless, such an offer was extraordinary and I accepted immediately. Thus does fate or our guardian spirit decide our movements, with unseen guidance, sometimes leading us step by step to an unknown, distant future or goal. When he left, I rushed into Mrs. Collinson's room and hugged her in front of her class. She was clearly delighted and took me off to Miss Craigie in the staff room. The tall, dignified, Craigie, actually hugged me in front of all the anti's, and made tea for the three of us in celebration. I was congratulated by the English mistress, but, best of all was my interview with Headmaster Truscott. We shook hands warmly and he stated that he had truly believed in me, and had supported me against the majority of staff knowing that I would keep my promise. He was extremely proud of my solo success.

Thus I have very happy memories of walking on air as an undergraduate student of the University of Bristol. I had travelled a long road against the odds, from my very first infant school, with those awesome great iron gates, to Bristol University. It was an accomplished journey. My father was in his seventh heaven of delight, and took me to his workrooms to celebrate with his friends, many of whom were police officers from Bridewell, who used to drop in on Mike to discuss racing 'form' over a mug of tea.. They all signified their pleasure at Mike's fatherly joy, by contributing toward my impending costs. My father's joy knew no bounds and was my greatest pleasure. He had always believed in me and had urged me on to achieve a golden academic future. Things did not work out exactly as he had imagined however, for the Second World War intervened and cut short my academic career.

Chapter 3

University Life

I began my undergraduate studies in the September of 1932. Before then, there were months of sheer pleasure, free from work and study, free as the air. My group of close friends had all passed. We had our bicycles and camping gear, but precious little money. Therefore, we pooled our resources and decided to continue camping at Brean Down, Berrow, that homely little Somerset village, which we had discovered by chance some miles from Burnham-on-Sea. There we lived in that glorious, cloudless, sunny summer and it was the only truly carefree time of our lives. Schooldays were over and the future was unknown. We rented a field from Farmer Hicks for half a crown a week (12.5p), with a big dray, holding a large can, that drew real fresh spring water. Mrs. Hicks supplied us with fresh eggs, fresh milk and their own thick bacon rashers, along with plenty of fruit, including cider apples. We dug a pit and lit our fire with wood gathered from the sand dunes. Soon our large frying pan was bubbling, filled with sausage, eggs and bacon and the kettle boiling merrily on the primus. Tea bags were unknown. We had a giant teapot and enamel mugs. A supremely happy time with no pressures. We were able to run across the sand dunes and plunge into the sea. Then we chased each other around the dunes until we were dried by the warm sun that shone benevolently. Those were healthy, halcyon weeks of perfect freedom, with not a shadow across our horizon. The tiny, quiet village boasted one pub and one general shop that doubled as a Post Office. We were welcomed at the pub, where we drank local cider and played darts and shove ha'penny. As students fresh out of school the locals took us to their hearts and we soon adapted to their broad 'Zomerzet' dialect. Even the solitary local constable joined in, for there were no other visitors in those days. The campsite in Farmer Hick's field and the quiet, friendly village became our summer holiday base thereafter. We helped at the farm and enjoyed free fresh fruit and vegetables.

When September finally arrived we were all fully rested and eager to begin our studies. My friend Cyril Harwood had decided to study economics. The University of Bristol had just opened a Department of Economics and, as the first and only student in the department, he had logically reasoned that he was unlikely to fail the course! As I began my studies, I quickly realised that Professor August Closs was a delightfully absent-minded scholar from Vienna. He was not very interested in the history of language and could not understand my deep interest in philology. However, he was a powerhouse in German literature, from Old High German and the first poem extant,"Ich sass auf eyne steyne ...." (I sat on a stone,) to his all-time favourite Goethe, closely followed by Schiller and all the poets, authors, philosophers, playwrights and musicians of the Romantic period. For him, Goethe was the German Shakespeare. I actually enjoyed Goethe and his poems, but I considered English and French authors to be far superior. Language always held a peculiar fascination for me and I studied its origins; Sanskrit to ancient Classics, to Old and Middle, then the ever-changing modern English; then Old and Middle High German and much more slowly towards Modern German. Closs had to agree that the English language had developed at one giant step ahead of the German. I was absorbed in philology, fascinated by the whole shift, movement and formation of language and sounds. The gradual changes of word-endings, vowel-sounds and pronunciation. These were affected primarily by laziness of speech and lip movement, and by breath and sound formation over the palate. Also by the effect of differing forms of labour and occupation, geographical position and even the climate. I found it all absorbing, whilst Closs thought I was in danger of losing my soul. Closs would drift away from the set subject towards odd philosophical theories of Hegel or Nietzsche. I enjoyed a really happy relationship with him despite our arguments on the 'soul of German literature.' When he propounded that a man's soul and spirit could only be truly found in his literary, musical and artistic work, I would reply that it was man's gift of speech which lifted him above the animals. I was of the opinion that man's development was to a great extent governed by his progress first and foremost in speech and much later in writing. He would smile and say: "I fear for your soul."

Professor Boillot was the complete opposite. Accurate to a degree, his timing was perfect. If a lecture began at 9.00 am, we had to be in our places before time. As the Great George bell boomed out the hour, he would enter precisely at the fifth stroke. His upright frame was held in place by firm corseting, and on his desk he would place a neat pile of small pads, saying "one thought to each leaf." Then he would take the book, poem or play for that study period and proceed to analyse it in his precise French, completely accurate in word and phrase. Unlike Closs he was a devotee of words, meanings, roots and derivations. He produced his own books of words, and explained the significance of their derivations under his assumed title of "Felix de Grande Combe", to indicate his close association with his adopted and truly loved areas. He was a completely Gallic Englishman with an impeccable accent, and three attractive daughters.

Boillot soon discovered his serieux (serious) students. He quickly spotted my love of language and presented me with some of his books. They'd been published in France in a characteristic heavy paper cover with rough-cut edges. "Ah Beck" he would say, "We are twin-souls in our search after the meaning of words and language". It was true and I never tired of French language, literature, poems and plays. French writers like Molière and Corneille had a lighter touch and a finer use of words than German writers of the same period. Writers like Anatole France seized one's attention immediately. Boillot's detailed analysis was like a rose, since he carefully removed petal after petal for scrutiny. Whereas Closs was concerned only with the whole view and its philosophy.

We scholarship boys had no money to spare and scarcely any pocket money from our parents. We worked our way through the University years by finding odd jobs at weekends. I worked as a shop-assistant, odd-job man and a poorly paid theatre attendant, but I did get to see good plays. My greatest success was with E.S. & A. Robinson, papermakers and printers, where I became assistant to the Head of Department of paper seals. We held musical evenings and dance nights where, for a shilling, we could dance the night away. These were great fun, removing some of the tensions of work. Sport was my preferred relaxation and Rugby my favourite outlet for pent-up energy. Though I did achieve success as a table tennis player, and became a leading player for the Student Union. I also joined the Theatre Society and enjoyed both acting and producing. I gained a certain artistic reputation and even produced German plays, which pleased Professor Closs, and French comedies that were graced by the presence of Professor Boillot and his family.

All students were automatically members of the Students' Union. I thought the Victoria Rooms were magnificent, and was quite happy to be put forward for election as Union President in my last year. I came top of the selection but a close second was K.C.P. Smith, who was a large-framed medical student. He boasted that he was in his fifth "First" year, having failed his previous attempts at exams. His father was a wealthy dairyman who paid his fees and seemed content for him to be a University student. KCP not only had plenty of money, which made him many friends, but he was also an inveterate gambler. His close friend was a dental student named Lee, who was as thin as KCP was large. They gambled on horses and dogs, went regularly to race-tracks and were known to all the bookmakers. They gambled on anything - a fly crawling up a wall or window, the weather, the name of a new ship, but especially on snooker and billiards. Unfortunately, Lee lost so heavily on the horses and dogs that the bookmakers informed his father, who was a successful dental surgeon. He bailed him out, but swore that henceforth he would refuse to pay. Instead, he would let him be taken to Court, possibly imprisoned, but definitely dismissed from the University. Smith's father dealt similarly with his son. Both immediately turned over a new leaf perforce, studied seriously and began to pass their exams.

Our daily coffee breaks in the Carwardine restaurant opposite the University were forums for a myriad of discussion. We would discuss contemporary events, gossip, weekend plans, meetings, expeditions, games and affaires. None of us seemed to be attracted to the teaching profession, even though the university had opened the first Teacher Training College nearby. There was still a shortage of teachers and we were offered an extension to our scholarships, with free tuition plus a bursary if we signed a guarantee to teach for at least five years after our two-year course. There was one momentous general meeting, wherein opinion was sought concerning this offer. By a big majority, students voted against being tied down to a period of five years teaching 'without the option'. Nevertheless, the same majority finally accepted the offer of free places with a grant and a secure job at the end of the Course. The economic depression that dominated the 1930s had curtailed job opportunities, and they soon realised that the prospect of getting a decent job elsewhere was very poor. I preferred to seek an assistant tutor's post at Bristol or some other University. It more or less guaranteed a year, although the pay was only about £250 per annum. However, one could be dismissed arbitrarily at the end of the trial year if judged unsuitable. I found myself alone in such venture, since it was regarded as being "too chancy" by my friends. Yet I enjoyed the challenge of lecturing and active academic discussion. I might well have developed my chosen academic career, but for the unhappy intervention of Hitler and his bloodthirsty Nazi Storm Troops.

As part of my course, I was required to spend some time in France and Germany. I only made short study trips to France as I was lacking in funds. Nevertheless, I always enjoyed Paris, and used to sneak off to the Left Bank with my fellow students. Since German was my main subject, I had to study at least one Semester in Germany in my first year. I chose to study at Freiburg University in the Black Forest and was well impressed by that clean little town, with streams running through the wide gutters that kept the streets fresh and clear. A delightful rural area that was spoilt by the Nazis during the War; since it became a military training centre, and a hidden storage base for heavy weapons.

Germany had also been plunged into economic depression after the First World War. Germany's humiliating defeat in war, the territorial losses conceded under the subsequent Versailles Treaty, coupled with heavy reparation payments, caused extreme bitterness and resentment throughout German society. Most of the German people were starving in 1918 because naval blockades had prevented the importation of essential food supplies. Left and Right wing factions fought openly with each other on the streets. Post war epidemics of venereal disease and tuberculosis, and an influenza pandemic, all combined to form what became known in Germany as racial terrors. Government officials, scientists, biologists and doctors all began to question the health and fitness of the German race. Positive and negative eugenic policies began to infiltrate public health administration, as social problems increased. The newly formed democratic Weimar government, under the leadership of Gregor Stresemann enjoyed some years of stability, mainly due to American loans and a re-negotiation of war reparations. Unfortunately Stresemann died a few weeks before the Wall Street crash, and political extremism surfaced once more. After some diverse and complex political events, right wing politics eventually gained the upper hand. The Nazi Party, under the charismatic and forceful leadership of Hitler, was gaining ground rapidly. Their political rhetoric exploited the public discontent that surrounded the Versailles Treaty, and blamed the Jews for an economic world conspiracy. As the historical expert in this field Ian Kershaw has noted, Hitler was saying the same things in 1920 as he was in 1930, namely that the Versailles Treaty was an injustice, and the Jews were to blame. In 1920 however, nobody was listening, whereas in 1930 they were. Indeed, Churchill often referred to the Second World War as being merely a continuation of the First, with a rest in between!

The University that I attended was an attractive sandstone building. Unfortunately in 1932/3, its Rector was the philosopher Heidegger. German students swarmed at first to hear his lectures and discourses. He was a prime favourite of the Nazi Government at that time, because he endorsed Nazi ideology. I stood with a crowd of students and listened to him, but soon became bored and turned away. Fragebogen (questionnaires), were thrust at each entrant and these were considered to be of greater importance than the usual Studentenkarte (Student's Card). Unless these questionnaires passed muster with the Nazi staff, entry to academic study was impossible. Details were demanded of birth, circumstance and ancestors. My mother's name Marie Coburg caused some astonishment, and I was treated with surprising civility. We were constantly watched however, so I took precautions. Some of the staff were already wearing Nazi Brown shirt uniforms, and strutted about in their boots and breeches, looking like caricatures. We chose the lectures to attend, mine being philosophy and early Germanic language. Though it became increasingly obvious that academic studies were taking second place to Party rallies.

We were invited to the Sportplatz to see a demonstration of 'physical prowess'. This event was devoted entirely to military manoeuvres, marching and counter marching by uniformed students who were throwing wooden grenades and bombs. Finally, we stood to attention as the band played Deutschland Uber Alles, their aggressive anthem. Then came the Nazi "Horst Wessel Lied". We stood quietly still, while a forest of hands were raised in Nazi salute around us. As a result, we received many long stares and muttering. Then, as we began to leave, we were pursued by Nazi uniform-clad youths who surrounded us menacingly. Fortunately we had our distinguished blue British passports so they left us alone. It was a narrow escape. We were also invited to parties and fancy dress affairs. One was at the house of a well-known Graefin (Countess), who, I was warned, was elderly, wrinkled and severe. I was advised by her grand daughter to take some flowers for our first meeting. I duly presented her with a bunch of roses, which caused her to shake with laughter. "Young man, do you know the language of flowers?" She explained that red roses represented a declaration of love, to my utter confusion. Nevertheless, because I alone had brought her flowers, I became her favourite and received further invitations to meet her daughters, one of whom was a doctor. I discovered that the family was totally opposed to the Nazis and longed to get to England. However, they were also scared of the Nazi regime, and warned me not to get involved.

I began to spend more time in the Black Forest with a trusty group of British and Germans. One night we climbed a steep hill towards some lights that were shining from a dwelling at the top. We found ourselves in a pretty little village called Muggenbrun. The lights emanated from a large, wooden, peasant cottage, where we were received somewhat suspiciously, until we explained that we were hungry, penniless students. Whereupon they provided a hasty meal of thick vegetable soup, home made bread and wine, that tasted like elixir. We became so friendly with the family that we stayed two nights. They showed us lovely, hidden spots and a miniature waterfall, which we all used as a shower, splashing about with glee. At night they produced an accordion and we danced and sang for hours. Once accepted by the village folk, we learnt how they lived and joined in with chopping wood and helping in the fields. Thus we earned our sustenance and became fluent in German. On my return to Bristol, Professor Closs had a long conversation with me about my studies. When he heard my answers he roared with laughter, saying "I know where you improved your German. In the Schwarzwald, rather than the University. You have the broadest Schwaebische Southern accent I have ever heard from one of my students. You obviously spent more time fraternising with the villagers". When I explained why, his face grew troubled. He respected Heidegger as a well-known philosopher, and could not believe the extent to which Nazi ideology had already permeated the academic world.

On my next visit I was offered the post of Lektor (assistant lecturer) in the English department, with more time in the University. The post gave me the opportunity to study philology and ancient derivations in more depth. The exam largely consisted of vivas with the Professor of English and the Head of Language Studies. These two good academics were solidly pro-British and anti-Nazi. They were not fooled by Nazi bravado and pressure, and managed to survive along with many members of the intelligentsia. I heard Hitler's first speech that was broadcast all over Germany when he gained power in 1933. Standing outside the University in the midst of a hushed crowd, I learned that the old Chief of State Hindenburg was near death. He was mentally unbalanced and had relinquished his great power into the hands of a little known, demented fanatic called Hitler, who had earlier outlined his nightmare policies in his book Mein Kampf. He had written this book in prison and the title translated to English as 'my struggle'. The text essentially contained a variety of rantings that reflected his distorted world view. This view was based on a mixture of anti-semitism, social Darwinism and his own bizarre adaptation of eugenic theories.

Later I witnessed the burning of books in the Marktplatz (market place), and managed to rescue three books by Thomas Mann and the much-loved poet Heine. Fortunately, my foolish, heroic and almost suicidal act went unobserved by the brown-uniformed louts who, doubtless, had never even read a good book. It was a brutal, shameful scene and it made me very angry. I wrote articles to British newspapers and journals to inform them of the situation. Those editors who bothered to reply stated that they were "well covered by their local agents". Nobody in England seemed to want to hear the truth about German military preparations for war. At that time Winston Churchill was the Chancellor of Bristol University. He sat on the dais in the Great Hall, wearing his gold brocade gown and mortarboard with gold tassel, in his throne-like chair. When my name was called, I marched up the steps. He clasped my hands in his and murmured the Latin phrase as I said "just back from Germany." After the degree ceremony he stood up and made a great resounding speech, for which he was dubbed as the "Voice in the Wilderness". During this speech he stated things that I had sought to reveal, but with far better eloquence and depth of knowledge. He was magnificent, and I became his devoted follower thereafter. He encouraged me to continue my efforts, and said that we would all be needed in the near future. His was the warning and defiant voice of Britain.

At University I joined the Officers Training Corps, which followed my training in Fairfield's Cadet Corps. I duly took Certs A & B, pledging my services as an officer in time of war. By 1936 I was sure that Hitler was intent on war. The German people at home and abroad, including a strong colony in America, were firmly behind him. He had provided work for the unemployed by introducing a series of public work schemes, which included the building of a mighty Autobahn circuit and new bridges. Vast newly constructed luxury liners helped to spread Germany's aggressive message to the world. His propaganda machine flourished under the guidance of the evil genius Goebbels, who was crippled in mind and body. Bribery and corruption were rife in Germany, but also abroad. Even peaceful, neutral Switzerland played a part by providing a financial haven for Mussolini's and Hitler's ill-gotten blood money. The latter had hoped to demonstrate the physical supremacy of the German race, when the Olympic Games were held in Berlin in 1936. However, he was totally disconcerted by the sporting success of black Americans who won most of the gold medals, and an American, Jewish supreme athlete, who won a world record of seven gold medals. By 1937 Hitler had begun his far-reaching secret plans to take over areas of Europe. Areas that would provide Germany with much needed sea ports, and Lebensraum (living space) for the German people. The secret 1922 Treaty of Rapallo between Germany and Russia, had enabled Germany to use Russian territory for rearmament purposes. By 1937 there was no need for such secrecy. Hitler's dictatorship was secure and he began confidently and openly to step up the pace of rearmament.

Chapter 4

London, War Office and Juliska

In 1936 I found lodgings in Coptic Street near the British Museum, and became a Londoner. I lectured, coached and wrote. I enjoyed getting to know London since it was a world in its own right, after the confined limits of Bristol. Then, in 1937, I brought my parents to live with me in a big Mews flat in Cambridge Gardens, which was off Ladbroke Grove in North Kensington. We all enjoyed the colourful Notting Hill district and the busy shopping centre of Portobello Road. It was time, I thought, for my father to retire. We settled in a large, comfortable flat, but my father soon grew bored with idleness and found new friends and interests. I inherited his tireless energy and continuous desire to be actively engaged. Mother loved shopping in Portobello Market. The butcher, baker and greengrocer all addressed her as 'Duchess' and exchanged their latest gossip and colourful views.

As political tension mounted in Europe, I was convinced that Hitler had to be stopped abruptly, or war was inevitable. In 1937 I gave up lecturing and work generally to write articles for journals. I wrote to the War Office to offer my services. An official replied: "No necessity at this time", then: "No imminence of war". The Intelligence Service replied that they were at full strength, although this was patently untrue. The Service, like the rest of Britain, was generally unprepared. I tore up the reply in anger, and temporarily joined a newly-formed Rescue and First Aid Unit, which was based in the Convent of Sion off Ladbroke Grove. There I met a young Canadian with a great fund of stories and a love of travel, but no desire to "get shot or disabled just when I should be enjoying life!" He offered me a job as his assistant and to introduce me to the Windmill girls, because he played the piano part-time at the Windmill Theatre.

True to its motto "We never close," the Windmill theatre kept going all through the Blitz and played to full houses day and night, under the clever management of Vivian Van Damm. The Windmill shows at that time were regarded as "shocking and sexsational". In fact, they were fairly innocent. The girls, supposedly bare, had to stand perfectly still, waving huge ostrich feathers. Those moving and dancing, wore imperceptible finemesh body stockings. Decency rules were strictly enforced, and there were never any completely naked bodies on view. They were a happy-go-lucky group, and would gather round the piano after each show to sing popular songs, in different versions. They accepted us as being engaged in war work, with me waiting to be called up. They certainly completed my education and regarded me as a young innocent 'from the sticks'. I enjoyed every moment of their company, especially their stories and racy jokes. London was a completely different world from conventional Bristol.

The open-mouthed audience entranced by the sexy shows, never knew the down-to-earth attitude of those attractive, lissom girls. They often received messages in bouquets with money or gifts enclosed. They had their own moral code that helped them to avoid trouble, but they all loved the excitement and fame of being one of the renowned, dancing Windmill girls. There was continual pressure from stage-door Johnnies, who used to hang around hopefully, clutching boxes of chocolates, flowers, stockings, jewellery. One fellow had a crush on Susie, a vivacious redhead and simply would not take no for a definite answer. We sought help from our friendly Soho police, who discovered that he was leader of a well-known mob. Susie had to appear at Bow Street to give evidence against him. This situation generated great interest and press speculation, which almost depicted the Windmill as a haunt of iniquity. It was nothing of the kind. Everyone worked very hard staging six shows a day non stop, with revues and scarcely time to pause and draw breath. Many famous comedians and performers literally owed their fame to being spotted by the Van Damn genius. These included Peter Sellers, Harry Secombe, Bruce Forsyth and Benny Hill.

We were accepted as mates, and allowed to hear about all their many adventures. We were also privy to the 'weapons' they used to deal with the over-bold admirers. These included long hatpins, needles, pointed shoes, heels and fingernails. For many years the Windmill provided the most popular shows. It was also home to the best and happiest gossip-shop, with the most outrageous stories. They rarely stopped during the day for a proper meal, though they had specific hours off for rest. Then some days off, that were allocated by rota. We became used to a late night 'scratch' meal at a local café. Local girls "on the game" would join us and add their sometimes grim adventures to the wealth of existing stories. They told their own tales with fits of laughter, even against themselves. They accepted each other without question, no matter whence they came. This time of my life was lively, vibrant and exciting, a world away from quiet, sleepy pre-war Bristol. I shudder to think of how my friends might have reacted to all my "goings on." Sunk into the mire of iniquity, and lost forever in those terrible haunts of London!

Soho took on a different face from midnight through to early morning. Characters in full evening dress and fancy costumes filled the cafes, coffee shops and milk bars that were open all night. I learnt much about 'the inside secret world of Soho', since I was accepted and trusted everywhere as 'one of the Windmill crowd.' Yet most of those who lived by illegal dealings and petty crimes were loyal to England, and ready to defend her when the time came. When war eventually broke out, it was astonishing to see men who had spent most of their lives carefully avoiding the police, with 'no known address', suddenly emerging at police stations and recruiting offices, to be given a service number and uniform. Many were released from prison eager to play their part in a just war. Love of country is born in us, though the seeds sometimes develop odd forms.

Soho's area lay behind Tottenham Court Road, and at the back of Piccadilly and Leicester Square. It was like the reverse side of a coin. We used to enjoy lunch or dinner at a small Italian restaurant in Cecil Street called Bertorellis. Our three course meal usually began with my favourite minestrone, that was sprinkled liberally with Parmesan cheese. Though it was almost a meal in itself, it was followed by some excellent ravioli. Finally we ate some ice-cream and drank coffee or tea. All this for one shilling and sixpence, which is less than the cost of a cup of tea today.

Next door was a small building where I met Charles Forte. He was originally Carlo to me, but, much later, became the famous hotel owner Lord Forte. He was busily making tasty sandwiches, and cutting up blocks of fruit cake, for his original Milk Bar at the corner of Oxford Street and Shaftesbury Avenue. It became the most famous Milk Bar in the country and was immediately copied all over the UK. Once he had satisfied himself that I was a genuine academic, he proved to be a most pleasant acquaintance. However, fate prevented me from forming a closer friendship. I chanced to walk into the Lyon's Corner House at the corner of Oxford Street, to take tea. Lyons had chosen the best sites in Piccadilly and Oxford Street for their very popular Corner Houses. These usually contained three separate floors, each colourfully decorated in different styles. One floor was entirely Spanish with guitar players, another was Italian or Mexican and accompanied by appropriate music. Yet another was decorated in a pleasant English style, with an orchestra playing popular tunes by Ivor Novello and the Master, Noel Coward. He was one of Lyons' inspirations.

Tea was served by Nippies. These were young girls who worked as waitresses in the Lyons Corner Houses. They were always dressed in traditional Lyons neat black dresses with white headbands. As I sat in a corner enjoying tea and toast, I suddenly felt impelled to look up, and there, right across the room in the far corner sat a little angel - or so she appeared to me. Slim, with blond curls and a petite oval face, I was sure she was smiling at me. As we made eye contact, I felt the urge to talk to her. Despite my friendly association with the Windmill Girls, personal relations were taboo. I always seemed to be too busy with my multiple activities, to devote much time to any one person. Moreover, my anxiety about the impending war had driven me into an endless whirl of activity. However, this chance meeting in a tea shop was how my truly deep, and lasting heart-felt romance began. I fell completely in love with this slim blonde the moment I saw her, and she responded equally. An instantaneous revelation! Juliska Hepp (nickname Czibi) as she was called, was an exchange student from Budapest, who was visiting London with a group of girls to improve her English. Working primarily as a companion to an elderly lady, she also attended English classes at a language school in Notting Hill. I offered to teach her English, but she was too cautious to accept immediately. However, she did agree to meet me when she had an afternoon free. At the same time she was testing me, wisely seeking assurance that I was telling her the truth.

Czibi was a slim, slight, slender figure with a strong mind, absolutely forthright. She was willing to show me her passport, agency information card, and pictures of her home in lovely Budapest. But demanded proof of my identity and credentials in return. Czibi had a good working knowledge of German and French, and we became really close companions. Soon Czibi grew quite proficient in English. She was a serious student, and sought perfection in her writing and speech. Most of all, she loved to visit the countryside in my car. Eventually, we found a reasonable flat in Notting Hill, which she immediately began to transform. Despite her slender body, she often moved the furniture about unaided, including a heavy wardrobe and cupboards. Her angelic looks disguised her strength and resourcefulness. Her Hungarian goulash was "out of this world". There seemed to be nothing that she could not do. She even made her own clothes from material bought in the market, and she was entirely at home bargaining with the street traders in Portobello Road.

For well over a year we lived a blissfully happy life, though not in the least domesticated. Czibi was full of bright ideas and never still except for our visits to the new, well-built cinema. She would sit in rapt attention, loving every moment of the films and entertainment. After the show Czibi would give me a big hug and dash back to the car, in an effort to hurry home to our carefully prepared supper. I never stopped loving her for a moment, and would have cheerfully have married her had she accepted. For the first and only time in my life, I was completely absorbed in this one beautiful girl, and nothing else was of any consequence. I should have known that such exquisite moments rarely last in this troubled world.

The element of doom arrived in the shape of a letter from her brother, who was then lecturing in America. He had been offered a senior position at Budapest University and was coming to England in a few months to take her back to Budapest. Since their parents were dead, he expected Czibi to look after him. Selfish? I thought and said so. Czibi said she did not want to go back to Hungary, especially as I had warned her that war was imminent. Hitler was already making his first moves. But for some reason she seemed afraid of her masterful brother, and dared not refuse his request, as he was her only relative. Much later, I divined from a letter that her brother had fallen under Nazi influence. If only I had known, I would have refused to let her go back with him. He should have remained safe in America, without making selfish demands on his sister.

Czibi promised to keep in touch and return to me, if all did not turn out well in Budapest. When her brother arrived, she was packed and ready, against my steadfast opposition. Except for one small hand-case that held her combined Hungarian/ English, French/German dictionary lace table cloth and mats that she had made herself, along with a few other small possessions. I was inconsolable and utterly despondent. I wandered about in a depressed daze, until a small but significant event broke the spell.

The manager of a local food shop in Ladbroke Grove sought my advice. I shopped there for my parents and we were on good terms. On this occasion he called me into the back room, to discuss the possibility of his taking over the shop. The owners wished to sell and move out of London and had given him first option, since he had served them well as manager. In fact, he was hardworking, energetic and effective. He had always stocked a wide variety of groceries, and kept the accounts accurately. However, he did not have the money to buy the business, and with a wife and small baby to support, he was at his wits' end. The shop was a real success and popular within the community. Our discussions led to my accompanying him to my bank, Lloyds, where, for years, he had deposited his takings for his trusting employers. The Bank Manager agreed that he had conducted the business and himself well. It was clearly a "going concern". I said that he was a first-rate business man and suffered only from lack of funds. The Manager asked for details of the offer before ascertaining that it was reasonable. The proprietors were making a genuine offer to a good employee. There was no mortgage business in those days, so we persuaded the manager to agree an overdraft and conferred in his back room. John was still worried about his ability to pay off the overdraft, so I made him sit quietly with his wife, and assess his weekly and monthly takings, against his costs and expenditure. He quickly discovered how much profit he had been making over the years for his employers, whilst his wife was attending to their baby. Consequently, they fixed an overdraft at reasonable rates with the bank, and began to realise their potential.

I called to see him the following week and was transfixed. They had cleaned the whole place from top to bottom and had begun decorating, working over the weekend. They were proudest of all to show me their names, now painted in clear block letters over the door. I laughed and said "You will kill yourselves at this rate. Now fix yourselves set hours. Close as usual on Wednesday afternoons, and use the weekends to do your accounts, and find time to relax and rest on Sundays. They promised to fix working hours and arrange some leisure time. They were so proud of their ownership, and grateful to me for inspiring them. I enjoyed watching that business grow, and the new owners increase in stature and confidence. Often on my way to the Underground in Ladbroke Grove, I would be hailed and called in for a chat and a joke. They had become my firm friends and I enjoyed many a supper and celebration with them thereafter. Their friendship helped to distract me and soften that dull pain, which had caused me continual sleepless nights. I received only one photograph from Budapest but no address, and afterwards simply silence. Many years later, my wife discovered that carefully hidden little case with Czibi's lace and filigree work, but I refused to discuss my brief period of true happiness. It was too precious a memory.

During this time I attended Conservative Party and general meetings. I voiced my opinions, to little effect. But the general public was growing uneasy. The Government were following a policy of appeasement towards Hitler, and failing to take proper action. Chamberlain had reassured the nation that everything was under control. Notting Hill was truly cosmopolitan at this time, and there were many left wing trade unionists, socialists and communists, along with right wing fanatics. Mosley and his Fascists were making trouble in the East End. I witnessed the frequent verbal battles of ordinary citizens against the Fascists and felt restless. Mosley and his Fascists in their Blackshirted insignia, essentially had the same motivation as Mussolini and Hitler. They were all lusting after power and used the Jews, blacks, Asians, gypsies and disabled as handy scapegoats. At this point, the clear prelude to World War Two was already under way in the shape of the Spanish Civil War.

Chapter 5

Meeting the Donners and the Foundation of
The Wakefield Shirt Company

In 1938, Britain, under the leadership of Neville Chamberlain continued to pursue a policy of appeasement towards Hitler, along with Deladier of France. Moreover, the Munich Conference of that year, appeared to quell any immediate threat of war. Hitler had made territorial demands in respect to the Sudetenland. This was an area that Germany had been forced to relinquish under the terms of the Versailles Treaty, and it was heavily populated by Germans. Chamberlain and Deladier both perceived appeasement as being the most sensible course of action to pursue, given that neither country was prepared for war. Thus the Sudetenland was duly and peacefully handed over to Hitler. Chamberlain appeared to be politically naive, and referred to Czechoslovakia as being a 'far away country of little consequence.' When he returned to Britain from the Munich Conference waving his now famous slip of paper, that supposedly offered 'Peace in Our Time,' he was cheered as a hero by the British people. Less than six months later, when Hitler invaded Czechoslovakia they were singing from a different hymn sheet! Poland was clearly the next German target. An embarrassed and contrite Chamberlain, or 'Chamberpot,' as he was nicknamed by the British public, offered a military guarantee to Poland. This move effectively sealed the British path to war. Once Hitler invaded Poland on September 1st 1939, and ignored British demands to retreat, Britain declared war on Germany two days later. The much berated appeasement policy, had merely given both Britain and France more time to prepare for war.

I had written strongly worded articles warning of the Nazi re-armament, and the menace close at hand. For some timenewspapers were not really interested until it was clear that appeasement failed. As a result of the Austrian Anschluss, a large number of Austrian refugees had flocked to Britain. When I heard that our Council had welcomed some of these people and provided them with a row of houses off Westbourne Grove, I offered them my help with their language problems. Very few spoke English, and I found that it was more difficult to teach English to the Viennese, than to Germans. I set up classes, and deployed those with some knowledge of English as assistant teachers. Soon they made progress. I met Mr. and Mrs Donner from Vienna. Their family owned a company making men's collar-attached shirts. These were unusual and unique, since each shirt was supplied with a spare collar. The cleverly designed, attached collars, bore a small loop on the undercollar. When the collar became worn, one pulled this loop, which released the stitching so that the collar came away completely. The neckband was a double gusset into which the spare collar was sewn with a single line of stitching. Behold! Each shirt had double life with a fresh new collar. Donner had a burning ambition not to impose upon British charity, but to begin work by establishing a factory in London. At this time however, nobody was permitted to open a factory in London, or indeed elsewhere.

Donner persisted in his desire to begin work, and my further enquiries discovered that Wakefield, in Yorkshire, was prepared to provide him with rooms for a factory, on condition that he employed local labour. The Donners would not venture into this unknown area called Yorkshire on their own, and begged me to take time off, to accompany them. Thus it was, that Isi, Herma and I, set off from Kings Cross station on the long, exciting journey. Although war had been declared by Chamberlain, it was the phase known as the 'Phoney War'. The German bombing of Britain did not begin in earnest for almost another year. At Wakefield we emerged into a grey station with cobblestones, and sooty flakes to emphasise that this was a mining town. It was cold, dark and drizzly, but there was a warm welcome awaiting us from the town's representatives. Wakefield was ending its long mining period and was experiencing growing unemployment. Therefore, we were doubly welcome, for the area desperately needed new industries.

We all shook hands heartily, and went straight to view the rooms that were being offered in Kirkgate. They had just been vacated by a Spiritualist Society. The Spiritualists had obviously left behind a good aura, as the Donners were immediately impressed. There was one main, large, long room that was just right for the principal workroom, and two smaller rooms, with an office. Gas, electricity and water were all connected. A little plumbing work and the installation of heavy duty plugs for the sewing machines, was all that was needed to convert the rooms into a working factory. The representatives promised to fix everything, and we discussed workers' conditions over lunch. Next we were shown number 49 Ruskin Avenue. This was a conventional, but well-built two storey, red-brick Council house, situated just off the Bradford road. Finally we discussed terms. The rents they quoted for the rooms, all facilities and the house, were extremely reasonable. I had explained Donner's circumstances to them, which they duly considered. They seemed happy with the thought that these were their first refugees from Nazi Austria. I was very grateful to them. This visit marked the beginning of my love of Yorkshire and especially of Yorkshire folk.

We departed, giving them assurances that we would consider their offer and reply soon. The Donners busily discussed prospects, firing questions at me in German, to ensure they understood all details. We parted at Kings Cross after arranging to meet next day. My mother was convinced that we had found the right place, and laughed at my fears of all the problems the Donners might face in the wilds of Yorkshire. They were agreed that Wakefield, with its warm welcome and plain-speaking "down to earth" councillors was the right place for them. They were amazed at the consideration, willing co-operation and courtesy of the Yorkshire people, after their brutal experience of the Nazis. I offered to write again on their behalf, accepting their terms and raising any other points. "Yes, Yes" they replied. "But we have one remaining problem - You". "Me? Surely I am doing everything to help you." "Oh yes," they replied, "You are so good and efficient, you arrange everything so well and all the people respect you and discuss everything with you. We cannot begin on our own. We cannot speak or understand the language or the people. How can we go to work, catch a train, or even live from day to day without your help? Nobody there speaks German or understands us like you. We cannot go to Wakefield on our own with our baby son, we would be lost without you."

This was a crazy situation. Here was I, still waiting to be summoned by the War Office. I explained this to the Donners, who, after their own unhappy experiences, were anxious to create a successful shirt production business. Could I not at least go with them for a short time, just to get started? Was my presence in the Army so vital? Not apparently to War Office, who obviously thought me of little importance, despite my own sense of urgency. My mind was set on playing my part in the War. They went to seek advice from my mother, who, of course, was on their side. Though not just for their sake. Later she confessed that she thought it might keep me out of the War. The memory of the First World War with all its heartbreak and misery, was still fresh in her mind. A time when it seemed that all her neighbours had lost fathers, husbands and young sons. Her eldest son Alfred was wounded out of the Royal Flying Corps, and her foolish husband tried to join up and leave her alone with young children. Now her youngest son was seeking to join up. I assured her that I would be no less liable than anyone else to be called up when my time came. "Well, you might at least help them start." As usual her argument prevailed, and to the delight of the Donners I agreed to go with them to Wakefield and stay until they were properly established.

Without any knowledge or experience of establishing a completely new industry, and in an unfamiliar area, I should have quailed at the tremendous problems ahead. I was their full-time guide, companion and mentor, interpreter, planner, manager and book-keeper. I lived and worked with these absolute strangers, foreigners who could not even speak our language coherently. Workrooms and offices were set up and skilled seamstresses employed and trained. There was a myriad of other problems that needed to be resolved, for I had to begin everything from scratch. Mr. Donner could only express himself in German, so all naturally turned to me. Yet everything came together with our joint will to succeed. I made plans for the future with layout drawings and notes. I calculated the number of sewing machines that were needed, and discovered where to buy them second-hand. Then I obtained shirt material, cottons, threads, needles, canvas and extra equipment. The Donners had brought patterns, designs, and some important equipment with them. I consulted representatives of Wakefield for their advice, including workers' pay and conditions. What wonderful people they were and so genuinely helpful! We appreciated their prompt replies and practical guidance. They found us, from their own stock, a long hardwood table, that was necessary for laying and cutting material, with work-tables, benches and chairs. They understood that we had slender capital. It would be many months before we were ready to turn out properly finished products. Where could you find a Council today, that would be prepared to search amongst its old stocks of furniture and equipment for our many needs?

Council members not only found the requisite number of tables, chairs and benches, but also supplied us with both hard and soft brooms, buckets and mops, and other necessities we had not thought about. They advised us where we could find second-hand sewing machines and equipment in Leeds Market. Then we turned our attention to costings. I had no idea how much money the Donners had managed to bring out of Austria. They had recounted heart-rending stories, of how Jews and others trying to leave Germany or Austria were made to wait for weeks and months, and give bribes, before their requests might even be considered. Usually they were robbed and beaten if they failed to answer questions satisfactorily. Personal treasures were promptly confiscated.

The Nazis controlled police officials and tough emigration authorities, who often subjected people to strip-searches. The Donners had shown great courage, or perhaps foolhardiness, by hiding some jewellery and other valuables, including gold coins about their persons. I believe that Herma was more adept at this and took greater risks than her husband, and used her baby's wrappings to good effect. They had managed to smuggle out £3,000 through relatives and friends This was enough capital to start the business. They knew that they would have to stretch this like elastic, to make it last the distance. Donner put a proposition to me. If I could match his £3,000, he would make me equal partner. I was really touched and flattered that they should think so highly of me. After all, I was really an academic, with only fragmentary knowledge of the business world and its methods. I did not even have £300 to produce as a possible investment.

Therefore, partnership was out, but he said I would be co-founder and general manager, and receive the princely sum of £4 per week. He would oversee factory production, and I would be responsible for just about everything else. Once this was all amicably settled, it was agreed that, of necessity, I would live with them. Firstly, for economic reasons, for we had to count every penny. Secondly to utilise our time effectively, for every evening we would sit down, after a hurried meal, and go over all details of the day, and make future plans. In fact, we worked well together, and I helped with young Ricky by arranging his education. It was tremendously hard work. I had entered a bustling new life, that was completely different from my previous existence. But I was young, strong, and keen to enjoy these fresh experiences in the North's biggest county. I certainly slept soundly at the end of each full day.

Sewing machines were duly lined up, and sample shirting material hung on the fierce curved hooks that were embedded in the wall. I helped Donner carefully remove the material that was neatly folded in layers on the hooks, and laid it across the long table. Then we set the shirt patterns on the material and chalked around them before cutting with the electric machine. As we had no ceiling power plug connected for this purpose, it fell to me to join the cable to the ceiling plug. Warning Donner to switch off the current, I placed a chair on the table to enable me to reach the ceiling. Carefully I prepared both sets of wires and started to join them. There was a bright flash, and I received a major shock. I regained consciousness with my back against the far wall, which had broken my flight across the room. Donner had switched off the wrong fixture! This was my second escape from death. First the dreaded asthma and then a major electric shock. I was saved by my fashionable crepe-soled shoes. Naturally I had cuts, bruises and a severe headache, but I suffered no real harm. In fact, I felt more alive and energetic than before. Not that I would advise such electric shock treatment for health.

During my next visit to the Labour Exchange, I met the young, witty Scottish manager. He had been struggling to understand the local dialect, and was delighted to find that I, at least, spoke intelligibly. When I copied his own Scottish brogue, he laughed and said "Ah weel." I produced some of my native Bristolese with vowels before final consonants, and always before 'l' as in "A good idea-l." After that we enjoyed a good understanding and friendship. He selected six needlewomen from a long list of names. Donner set them to work and soon, most were discarded. Following numerous visits, almost enough to exhaust his list, the manager asked whether we would ever be able to find suitable seamstresses, who could work to our high standard. "Of course we will!, I said, "Just have patience and within a year, you will be wearing Wakefield Shirt Company products."

We had agreed on that title out of respect for the good relations that were so quickly established within the town. Donner gave me German literature to translate. This explained the wonderful extra value that was given by their shirts, which were unique in the whole of the Austrian shirt industry. Before the war, almost all English shirts had a plain neckband, with separate white collars attached by studs. Only Van Heusen made collar attached leisure shirts in England at that time. The extra collar made our shirts unique. They were supplied with each shirt and pinned across the shirt front. The German version was named Doppel-Kragen (double-collar), which I changed to "Double-Two." This highlighted the fact that the collar served two purposes, and the shirt had two lives. I then translated the remaining instructions into clear, simple English. This was a most enjoyable exercise, since it used my language skills and imaginative ability. The translation was fully praised by the Donners, whose English was now improving fast. My inspiration of 'Double Two', became our internationally famous and lasting trademark.

About this time we began to run short of funds. Although I had kept a close watch on all expenditure, even our bus tickets to and from Ruskin Avenue or Leeds. One day Donner came to me looking troubled, saying, "Read this, Harry." It was an offer from another refugee called Fritz Meyer, who had owned a ladies' garment business in Berlin. He had managed to escape Germany in the early 1930's. His influential brother-in-law was a banker, and had been able to transfer most of his money and Meyer's out of the country. Meyer wanted to buy into Donner's business, and the banker had drawn up terms and submitted them to Donner for approval. I studied the offer, since it was written in English legal phrasing, and was obviously beyond Donner's comprehension.

Cleverly included, was an intricately worded paragraph which belied the apparently innocuous remainder of the agreement. Had the Donners signed that contract, Meyer and his brother-in-law would eventually have owned over fifty per cent of the shares. This would have left the Donners, the real owners and founders of the company, with a minority share holding. Obviously at some future date they would have been subjected to a takeover, or forced to accept a minor role. I was furious at such dirty, underhand connivance by a fellow refugee. The Donners took my advice. We crossed out the offending paragraphs and rewrote them, giving Donner a good margin over Meyer. Thus they would never have to fear a future attempt to buy them out, or risk being overpowered. I could not bear the thought of going into the Army, and leaving them at the mercy of such people. Meyer had perforce to accept our version of the agreement and I was rapidly learning how to guard against such 'tricks of the trade'.

Unfortunately, when Donner met Meyer and his brother-in-law for final discussions, he revealed that I was the person who had re-written the contract. Meyer never forgave me and did his best to cause me problems. Much to the amusement of the Donners, who would tell me all about his latest moves at home. Meyer knew nothing about our factory production. He preferred to sit his stout framed body in the best office chair, and question Donner or me about the business. Donner had no time to spare so I had to suffer. Meyer examined my account books, and clearly had knowledge of that side of the business. He could never find fault however, for I checked everything and entered every detail of our slender resources. There could be no income until we obtained orders, despite his grumble that all the money was going out. He was effectively a non-working partner! Donner called him a "kibitzer," he never took part, but always offered unsolicited advice, which none of us heeded.

Herma was a highly skilled seamstress and made the old Singer sewing machines sing. She produced the first samples and taught the girls. We eventually had a well selected team of between six and eight girls, two changed every two weeks, so that we had two skilled reserves. Donner had extensive expertise in shirt-making, and Herma could sew shirts right through at top speed. The girls soon learnt to be punctual and exact. He was a hard taskmaster, but would show them by active demonstration and worked continuously harder than everybody else. Therefore they learnt to respect and obey him. They even copied his broken English, word for word, including swear words. They would also teach him theirs.

There was a happy atmosphere on the factory floor, and gradually samples began to take better shape. Now we had to visit the wholesalers to buy material for the first sales plan, in safe plain colours blue, white and brown. Boxes were also sampled for despatch, with well designed labels. Pins were everywhere. I never knew that so many pins were needed to secure a shirt, once it was skilfully pressed and folded. Finally, we included a matching card-holder for the spare collar, stamped 'Double Two,' and the instruction pamphlet. All in all, it seemed an enormous operation to produce just one shirt, neatly and accurately folded and enveloped in its individual see-through bag.

Our reserves were now running down, and I was urged to visit our Bank Manager, Mr.Capstick, to plead for an overdraft. Fortunately he knew me from the time the account was opened with Donner's capital, and he received me courteously. He was a thoroughly nice man, always polite and courteous and we became good friends. He kept two kinds of cigarettes, ordinary Players, and the much superior Royals. It was my privilege to be offered a Royal with a cup of tea, as I did not drink alcohol. He enquired about my background and how I came to be acting on behalf of Mr. Donner. We couldn't have found a better or more cooperative Bank Manager. Personal relations were so much better in those pre-war times. War seemed to diminish good manners, politeness, and general good behaviour. Mr. Donner may have been short in stature, but he was tall in strength of personality and determination. He could brush aside obstacles or trample over them, whilst I preferred a more diplomatic, circuitous route. But he was a self-possessed, strong, silent man, whilst I was a social animal. I always liked people, especially the very young and old. The Army taught me how to deal with men of my own age, whilst we were living in close packed company. It was now 1940 and we were getting daily news of Hitler's sweeping victories. Following the hasty Dunkirk retreat Neville Chamberlain had been replaced as Prime Minister by Winston Churchill. The Donners were trying to hide their fear of a Nazi invasion: "You don't know the power or terror of Hitler. He is the devil incarnate." I did not tell them of my fears as I did not want to alarm them further.

The first samples were now ready and I was urged to go out and get the first orders. This was something new to me. But Donner insisted. "So who shall go then? If I could speak English I would go." Off I went, with an old luggage case containing samples, and an order book that we had devised, based on collar sizes. I mustered up courage and walked into an outfitters in the centre of Wakefield. When I explained that I was from the Wakefield Shirt Company, he laughed and said, "Oh yes, I've heard about your efforts in the Kirkgate. Are these your first samples?" Well come on lad, let's have a look. Mmm - collar attached. Sorry, we have no call for these in Wakefield. They wear their shirts all through the week and just change their collars." Undeterred, I went into my song and dance act about this wonderful spare collar, and how it gave the shirt an extra life. "How does it work - can you show me?" Fortunately, intelligent, clear-thinking Herma, had thought of this possibility and had made some sample collars out of ends and cuttings of cloth. The tabs were partly pulled and the stitching loosened for easy removal. I silently blessed her perspicacity, for I was able to demonstrate to his satisfaction and obtained my first sample order of a dozen shirts. I went all round Leeds, Halifax and Huddersfield by bus, bravely marching into outfitters shops, and telling my story of how we had started this shirt factory "In Wakefield of all places." I received a sympathetic hearing most everywhere. In fact I was amazed and encouraged by the pleasant reception I received. No wonder I became more and more endeared to Yorkshire and its people.

It was a hard slog, knowing that the Factory and workers depended on my orders. I had to sell shirts in the material I knew we had in stock, choice of four colours. At the same time we had to remedy the first faults. Fortunately, our customers had understanding and patience, and seemed to enjoy my humorous stories of our efforts at Wakefield. Our anxiety gradually decreased as we began to receive regular, repeat orders from satisfied customers. I had discovered my ability to sell, and the pleasure of receiving warm welcomes from regular stockists. Many of their boxes I had packed myself. At my invitation, some came to visit the factory and were well impressed, especially by Mr. Donner. He was the hard working new Yorkshireman with the odd, quaint Yorkshire accent.

One day I was walking down the High Street in Leeds when I saw a queue of men outside a Royal Air Force recruiting base. Without a second thought I joined the queue and was soon being interviewed by two RAF officers. They questioned me closely, especially about my academic language background. "Just the sort of chap we're looking for" said one. "There is a new development. We need men like you urgently." They took all my details and said, "Be prepared to be called up within a few days." I later discovered that it was the beginning of the early warning radar detection systems. Sure enough, I received a quick recall. They said that my recruitment process had been blocked by War Office officials, who had informed them flatly that I was listed for the Army. The War Office did not even bother to inform me, send a card or phone me. I was upset and miserable. I was not prepared to wait any longer, I would join up willy-nilly.

Chapter 6

War Service

The very next day in Huddersfield, I visited the Army Recruiting Depot. I simply entered and said, "Here I am! Just sign me up." "Welcome!" said the Sergeant. The Army doctors found me A1 and my orders were to report to No. 2 Royal Engineers Motor Transport Regiment, based at Ripponden near Halifax. The Donners were devastated, but they always knew I was determined to fight Hitler and his Nazis. I was leaving them with a thriving, and steadily growing business. Meyer should have taken over as the salesman. Instead, he continued to grace his favourite chair, and moan about the financial situation. Donner was now fluent enough to call on customers, which he did successfully, until he later engaged an agent.

My Regiment was stationed in old derelict Mills, broken down, neglected and long since empty of everything except grease, oil and rats. Our Identity Numbers (I still remember mine: 2122428) were stamped on everything. Issued with bulky loads of uniform, kit, blankets and boots, we had to dress for inspection, and an odd-looking bunch we were. Finally we had to gather straw to stuff into palliasses for our beds. There were no sheets or pillow cases. By morning old oil had seeped through the floorboards and covered our beds. We then collected double supplies of straw, after we had scraped up the oil with iron scrapers. A fine beginning! The NAAFI and canteens were in underground cellars that were damp, rat-ridden, and in need of a good clean. Not a cordial welcome for us embryo warriors.

Most of the recruits were Yorkshire miners who'd been looked after and 'mothered' by their wives. They usually went off in mining gear with their 'Snack Tins', in the morning, and returned to a hot bath by the fire in the evening. All prepared by the missus, who scrubbed away the coal dust, prepared warm towels, had their slippers waiting for them by the fire, and a hot meal on the stove. No wonder some big fellows cried themselves to sleep in the first week. Many could not even write home and I became their scribe. We were allowed two days to recover from the multiple vaccination injections that were pumped into us. Then fully dressed, buttons, belts and boots polished we were lined up "On Parade". The Non Commissioned Officers strode along the rows of recruits, bawling insults: "What an 'orrible lot. Stand up straight, chest out, chin in" and off we marched, some unable to swing their arms in accord with their legs. Next came our arms drill, with ludicrous results, described by the Sergeant as "wrapping their rifles around their necks." Child's play to me after my training in the Cadet Corps and University Officers' Training Corps, as soon became obvious to the drill NCOs. I was given one stripe as a Lance-Corporal Drill NCO, and put in charge of my section's training, to much ribald comment. I marched them down the road to Triangle, where I found a quiet square. I explained to my 'intake' that I could teach them the tricks to make drill easy, .

This proposition was eagerly accepted and I taught them the drills, counting aloud by numbers and repetition. We treated the process as a game, and they soon became united and supportive of each other. Mistakes were laughed at sympathetically, and it was surprising how quickly those awkward Yorkshiremen became a close-knit unit. "All in t'muck together." I made them practice arms drill on each other, which caused roars of laughter. They did not realise that they were becoming fully competent. Within two weeks they were marching in unison and singing the songs that I had taught them with enthusiasm, especially the bawdy ones. I was really proud of my section.

At the end of the first month came the "Passing out Parade," and, after inspection we recruits were allowed out of barracks. Happily, my section came top of the Parade, and celebrated in the NAAFI by presenting me with a tin of Players cigarettes. I found the Women's Voluntary Service canteen at Sowerby Bridge. For sixpence they served well-cooked meals of sausage, eggs, bacon and fried bread with thick slices of tasty bread and butter, and a large mug of tea. All went well until some of "our lot" ventured as far as Halifax, where they met opposition from infantry units in the local pubs. Soon the trading of insults turned into fights, and we had to gather NCOs and rush to the rescue. Surreptitious visits were made to the Quartermaster, accompanied by explanations concerning lost, damaged, or missing bits of uniform. They were reluctantly re-issued on the reassurance that "our lot" had "knocked hell out of 'em." Our new R. E. Transport Regt. was now fully 'blooded' as a virile, fighting unit, ready to take on anybody. A few cuts and bruises were simply marks of manly heroism. Taking part in a 'rough-house,' was another new experience.

There followed courses on transport, car, truck and lorry driving, and engines. I learnt to draw accurate designs of the Internal Combustion engine, but the course I most enjoyed, was the RSM's Cadre Course for NCOs. He was the Regimental Sergeant Major, who looked more like an officer than most officers, wearing a polished Sam Browne belt and officer uniform. He was nicknamed the Panther because he was always on the prowl, and regarded with awe by recruits, NCOs, and junior officers alike. Naturally I enjoyed his Course, for I could 'swank' with my foot and arms drill, and knew all the tricks. My early training paid off handsomely. I came top of the Cadre Course, to the cheers and satisfaction of my section, and the Panther actually smiled and said approvingly, "I'll be keeping my eye on you." Unlike the Cockney Sergeant Major, who as a Londoner, looked down on what he called "those wild Yorkshiremen, straight out of the jungle." On learning that I was a "University toff", he had me scrubbing out his office with a tiny brush, over worn flagstones, "taking the micky". "Not used to hard work are you, Becky? Well, I'll larn yer to be real 'andy with propa clarning, me old cocksparrah". I didn't rise to the bait, though my mates threatened to 'do him.'

To my surprise he called me into his office in my third week and said, "So you live in London. How would you like a visit? "You know I can't get a Pass for months." "Well, I can fix it for you on condition that you call on my wife and hand her my wage packet. I have a Pass but can't go yet and she's waiting for the money. I daren't let her down." Of course I seized the opportunity and shot off immediately. I arrived home that night to the great enjoyment of my family, who'd not seen me for months. We celebrated with all our news. Then the alarm sounded and I was led to an Anderson shelter on the pavement. It was only a one-brick construction, not much protection against bomb splinters and falling debris. When the bombs began to fall in Ladbroke Grove, I could feel myself shaking in time with the shelter. There was I, a real soldier in uniform, quaking inside, whilst women and children sat calmly knitting, chatting or playing in that fragile shelter. My father preferred the comfort of his own bed, so they all followed him, and took shelter under our stout tables. Fortunately they had no direct hit.

Next morning, I set off for the East End, Bow dwelling. To my surprise the door opened to reveal the smiling Sergeant Major. "My wife swore me pay packet had 'gone for a Burton'. But I knew you'd turn up, Becky. He invited me in to enjoy a cup of tea and door-step sandwiches, with his cheerful wife, who kept our fierce Sergeant Major in close check. When the sirens screeched, she led these two brave soldiers down to the depth of the nearest Underground, where large numbers of families had bedded down in what they assured us, was "the safest 'ole in London, which the Jerries could never reach." Those suffering families produced an amazing amount of Cockney humour and caustic wit, all in the midst of heavy bombing and terrible tragedy. Their spirit remained unbroken despite smashed houses, physical damage and surrounded by death. I greatly admired the indomitable spirit of our people, which I was to meet again in action.

Back at Ripponden I was on guard duty, in charge of the sentries. The condemned old, grey stone, forbidding-looking Mills, with their deep steps, worn concave thin by the pounding of workers' clogs, stood cheek-by-jowl along the road. Our transport was all lined up at the roadside, as we had no normal Parade Ground. Sentries had to mount guard on our vehicles day and night on the street. It was an eerie experience being alone with one's rifle on a dark night, completely blacked out. We had a guardroom, and I was NCO in charge. On my first normal weekend Pass I returned to Wakefield, having already visited the Halifax area and been cheerfully welcomed, with approval, by all my Double-Two customers. One presented me with a handsome hunting crop, saying,

"Use this on parade instead of your drill-cane and you'll be a sensation." We all shook hands and they wished me luck and a safe return, promising to support Double-Two, in my absence. The Donners gave me a warm welcome, and admired my uniform. They said that they were surprised I was not an officer, as expected. I replied that I was 'tired of waiting for War Office,' so had decided to start at the bottom and work my way up, just as we had done with Double-Two. Meyer looked down his long nose in disapproval at my one-stripe, a low-grade common soldier. I told him cheerfully, how glad I was to have his support in going forth to defend him and his family. At which point his disapproval subsided.

The girls in the Factory gave me a really warm welcome. They were led by Mrs. Forsythe, who was a down-to-earth, plain-spoken Irish woman. Best of the first batch we had engaged, and duly made charge-hand. Her council house was opposite ours in Ruskin Avenue and she lived with her children and humorous, cheerful Irish husband. I helped her with the children, so we were good friends before, during and after the war. I assisted them with their education and they were successful in school and careers. One girl qualified as doctor. They were all delighted to see me in uniform, regardless of rank. I was their factory hero and they actually wrote to me and sent me khaki shirts. I said good-bye to Wakefield customers and, of course, Mr Capstick at the Bank, who presented me with a tin of his Royal cigarettes and a gold sovereign, saying "I'm sure you will find good use for this." I gave it to my mother to assist with her meagre Army allowance, as I had no wife.

After about four months my Commanding Officer sent for me, saying, "Your record states you are an academic, qualified for a Commission. What are you doing here?" I explained and he was very angry. "We lost so many good officers before Dunkirk, the War Office delay is inexcusable. I must remedy this without delay." When I said that I was happy where I was, he laughed, and said, "So I hear. In fact the RSM has put your name forward for Sergeant's rank. But you must go straight to the Officer Cadet Training Unit.

Outside was the RSM "What happened?" he asked. I told him and he said, "Don't take it. You don't have to go. I can promise you I will see that you are moved up to Sergeant Major, and eventually RSM." Then he gave me a lecture on the power and value of RSM, which is the highest non-commissioned rank in the Army. It was all a great revelation. All uniforms officer type, supplied free, quarters free and the RSM is number one boss of all, and head of the Sergeants' Mess and all functions. He is treated equal to the rank of Captain. The Commanding Officer seeks his advice and, under the OC, his word is law. "Of course it is a tremendous overall responsibility, but you are just the chap for it and I would like to bring you on personally. So think it over carefully".

Looking back I can remember how tempted I was to say "Hang the Commission - who needs Officer's Rank?" There I had real friends and the support of the RSM himself, who'd spotted me as top material, while War Office had turned a blind eye. The feeling of comradeship, at the prospect of going to war with a well-knit unit of stout Yorkshiremen was clearly stronger in the 'Other Ranks', than between officers. Once commissioned, it was possible to create or build loyalty, but on a different level. Had my C.O. not checked my record, I would have been happy to have remained with my Royal Engineers. Strange sentiment to find in War! There was no time in all the years that followed, when I felt as much at home and amongst real friends as right there in Ripponden, Yorkshire. I would have cheerfully gone into battle with them at my side. It is that feeling of comradeship, loyalty and trust, which makes the British into great soldiers. At Catterick RA Officer's Training Unit I learnt how ill-equipped and unprepared we were for war. This major Officers' Training Course on Gunnery concentrated on the new 25-pounder, but had only one new gun. How can you train over a hundred men of all ranks to be Artillery Officers, without the guns to give them the most important practical experience? In fact we became theoretical gunner officers, schooled in theory without firing a gun.

The C.O. was an elegant Lt. Col. who interviewed each of us, noting any recruit who might not fit. Thus the wrong accent or previous occupation (he hated journalists for example), could target you for Return To Unit. His son was at Clifton College, Bristol, so I passed muster as an ex-academic of Bristol, with an acceptable accent. We spent the first month on repetitive foot and arms drill and pistol shooting, as if we were raw recruits. It was a sheer waste of time. Then during the second month we began gun drill, with our only gun. After long practice sessions the first live shell was loaded carefully and fired. It exploded in the breech, causing it to swell like a massive, huge balloon. Fortunately for the CO, instructors and cadets, the British steel withstood the tremendous pressure, for it could have killed us all. A tribute to good well-cast British steel. We were left with theory and algebraic workings and logarithms, plotting projected curves with carefully worked out charts of rise and fall, sweep and search. Good training was then needed on actual gun firing, to check the parabola and fall of shot so that, in actual combat, such things were almost done by instinct.

There was a general air of unrest and mistrust amongst the remaining cadets. Our group of friends, who had worked as a team and enjoyed each other's company, felt that we were treated like prisoners, confined to barracks. We were only allowed out on special occasions. Then only to Richmond where, as official Officer Cadets we were easily recognised by our white cap bands. We were not allowed to drink in any of the pubs frequented by our Officers. We were especially upset when we heard news of Alton Towers RA OCTU, presided over by a genial C.O. who never dreamed of RTU for anybody. News was that he treated all alike as gentlemen, and he and his wife gave parties and dances. They invited local girls to these functions and even indulged in match making.

We were green with envy, so paid unusual attention to a missive from RA.HQ., explaining that the Artillery had now been chosen to head new anti-tank gun operations. Special anti-tank courses were being set up immediately, and applications were invited. These new anti-tank units were to be regarded as the "crème de la crème" - heroes who would be well trained with these easily manoeuvrable guns. They would go 'in front' of the infantry, in order to be well placed to destroy oncoming enemy tanks. Highly adventurous and dangerous, since artillery guns were normally placed to the rear of infantry, firing over their heads. This was just right for us we decided. Therefore, the whole of our group of about a dozen, immediately put in for transfer to R.A. anti-tank Regiment. Within a week we were off to Larkhill in Wiltshire.

Senior Artillery instructors explained this new branch of Artillery in the shape of light-weight anti-tank guns. They were manoeuvrable in front of the Infantry. Our remit was to lie in wait for enemy tanks and hit the leaders with solid shot. This would penetrate the tank, killing or wounding all inside. But we were not to wait to find out. Our orders were to leave the guns and run, before remaining tanks could aim at us. Now this was new. Hitherto gunners were ordered to stand by their guns and fire to the end. But your guns were your flag and your lifeline! You never left them. So what's the new idea? Just poop off your little peashooter at the nearest tank, then run away as fast as your legs will carry you? It was just not on!" But it was on, as we learnt. Unfortunately even then, in 1941, Larkhill had not a single gun carriage or barrel to show us. How could we learn the drill and handling? Some triangular gun carriages had been roughly fashioned out of pig-iron, with a solid iron bar shaped like a gun stuck forward. On these we learnt to drill, hoist these 2-pounder guns, and carry them across ditches and rivers. "Don't grumble, its good for your muscles. You are gunners now, not just rifle toters." Well, at least we each had rifles and ammunition - "Oh, but we have the gun-piece and solid shot to teach you".

Two stainless steel pieces and magazines, the all-important mechanism of the gun, were produced. Instruction was carefully given on taking them apart, cleaning each section, then reassembling - BLINDFOLD, in case we were caught in a sandstorm! It was a most enjoyable experience for about 30 of us who were supposed to be "the cream of the cream." The guns and carriages were light enough to be carried by hand, once you became accustomed to them. We learnt to get up close to the enemy on miniature motorcycles, so small, nippy and quiet, you could get right up to a hedge, unseen and unheard, and peer through to make out the enemy line-up. We had a good chief instructor who was fairly new himself, and we all entered into the spirit of the Course. The two pound solid shot was supposed to penetrate the German tanks and whirl around inside, killing all the crew. I had my doubts. Churchill had ordered the first supplies to be mounted on our Churchill Tanks - to bash the German tanks - which they failed to penetrate, until six pounders were made. Best joke, it was our new 25 pounders which smashed through all German tanks in direct action, and became our best anti-tank guns, as well as first-rate field guns.

We were duly commissioned, and my friend Stewart and I departed for Northampton, weighed down by our 'heavy' single pip on each shoulder. Stewart's marriage was arranged, and I was to be his best man. The large Church Shoe family made us very welcome as superior high-class officers. We did not disenchant them. My own family was most impressed, and my father admired my new uniform. He thought it very superior, set off by my highly polished Sam Browne and shiny shoes, that were a present from Messrs. Church. I managed a quick visit to Wakefield, where I had a very happy reception, Meyer now quite in awe of this smart officer.

Back in London my greengrocer friends were making progress and profits, in their smart well-stocked shop. At a ball I met a charming girl named Margaret Scott, who was the daughter of a famous builder. We enjoyed each other's company and met often. Trouble was that I was short of money, and I found that Margaret was used to high living. My lasting memory of her, was her desire to dine at a select, expensive restaurant in Lower Regent Street. I had not anticipated Margaret's choice of exotic dishes and began to worry at my sorry financial situation. But Daddy had insisted that she "go Dutch" and pay half, so that she should be under no obligation. I warmed to him, settled the bill and parted lovingly, promising to meet next evening to be introduced to him. However, I found an urgent order awaiting me, to join my first new Regiment at Romsey, immediately. I travelled overnight with only time for a hurried phone call to Margaret, who was not best pleased, since she had anticipated further meetings.

Chapter 7

India, the 8th Army and Code Breaking

I reported next morning to a new R.A. Anti-Tank Regiment that was quartered on Lord Mountbatten's Romsey estate. I met him one morning as he was striding across the grass with a gun dog. He returned my salute, smiled and said, "Good morning". I was lodged with a director of Strong's Brewery, and every night on returning from duty, I found a bottle of Strongbrew, tea, chocolate and biscuits placed on a little table outside my room. They were my best quarters of the whole war, housed in such a lovely peaceful area, a quiet haven of English countryside.

I was assigned my troop, and training finally began with real two-pounder guns and carriages. My first Regiment and the experience of an Officers' Mess, made me feel that I was at home at last. Commanding my own troop with full equipment, convinced me for the first time, that it was all real. In fact, the War was going badly, and only my hero Churchill succeeded in holding the nation together. He continually hurled defiance at the Nazi menace. Within a few weeks we received embarkation orders. However, one of my men, Wilson, was missing, and eventually returned forty eight hours late from embarkation leave. This was a Court-Martial offence. Under old King's Regulations he could have been shot. A rumour went round that I was a lawyer, and I was appointed as Defence Officer for Wilson, against his most serious charge of Desertion. I found the poor fellow in a cell, in shocked state. I sought first to calm him and then gradually make sense of his actions. His father was in the Merchant Navy, and his ship had just returned. It was due to sail again from Ireland in a few days. Wilson had used his embarkation leave to make a dash for Ireland and had just managed to catch his father before he sailed. Then he rushed back, but had arrived forty eight hours late.

I began an intensive study of King's Regulations. This was the legal guide book on all Service conduct. Eventually, I found that extra time was allowed to cross to another country and return. Therefore, his forty eight hours could be discounted if his story could be proven. I had his father's ship traced and a message signalled for confirmation. Travel vouchers in his kit provided vital proof of his crossing to Ireland, so I was able to prepare my case in time for the Court Martial. I also prepared my gunner, and we went over the dates and timings. I told him to stay calm and to answer every question firmly.

It was my first experience of a Court Martial. There they sat, Senior Officers and the Judge Advocate General, at a blanket covered table. The Prosecutor spoke first and outlined the details. Then the prisoner was asked sternly if he was "Guilty or Not Guilty?" He looked at me and answered clearly "Not Guilty" to each charge. They then called the Defence, and I admit that my heart was thumping as I rose. With permission to read from factual notes, as dates and timings were of the utmost importance, I outlined my case. Then I quoted days and hours, and the reasons for Wilson's actions. He was an only son and his father in the Merchant Navy had not been seen by his family for many months, and was soon to sail again. I produced tickets, vouchers and the corroboration of his father via the Navy.

I finished by claiming that he had returned to his unit within the time allowed. They thanked me and asked us all to retire. Shortly after, we were recalled. The verdict was given "Not Guilty. Gunner Wilson you are free to rejoin your regiment. You should be grateful to your defending officer, who has gone to great lengths to prove your case. Prosecuting Officer dismissed." They asked me whether it was true that I was a lawyer. When I explained my background the J.A.G. smiled and said: "I think you have missed your vocation." They even asked for a copy of my notes. My sergeant gleefully informed me that they had all bet on my winning. Some months later I received a grateful letter of thanks from Wilson's father, which I have treasured ever since. From then on, whenever there was a serious case I was chosen to be the Defending Officer. It was an onerous duty but I became quite skilled. Fortunate release came via a message that sought volunteers for the Middle East. I was soon on my way to a hidden destination somewhere in the North, with time only to dash to London to say goodbye to family and friends, and phone Margaret, who had not forgiven me for disappearing the day after our dinner.

Off we went at night, heading interminably North, until somebody peered out and said "It's Scotland." We loaded up in blacked out ships, and slipped anchor before dawn. As the sun rose, we saw our big convoy, and suddenly we were zigzagging with our armoured escort of long, slim grey shapes, darting to and fro. They finally left us when we were way out to sea, warning us not to show lights or much movement. It was a long and difficult voyage, and we seemed to cross and recross the oceans to escape the dreaded U-boat submarines. I never learnt how many ships we lost on that long, desperate voyage in 1941. Certainly our Leader ship containing the Vice-Admiral, had disappeared when we anchored, first off Freetown, where only boats went ashore for provisions, then Durban to dock. We had been forced to change course and direction several times, yet there stood a big woman's figure, clad in flowing white, singing us a welcome.

As we stepped ashore, we were met by a line of cars that stretched all around the harbour. I was taken to a lovely villa and fed as if I'd been starved for months. It was a wonderful, memorable reception. Mrs. Brown, the Mayoress gave a magnificent party. But the heat was terrific and we soon dressed down to shirtsleeves like our hosts, and enjoyed some carefree dancing. When I questioned Mrs Brown about the size of Durban and the area, she actually lent me her big black limousine and big black chauffeur. He drove me up to the sugar plantation and showed me the green hills, forests and farms. It seemed like semi-paradise. Alas we were allowed only four days in Durban, and left behind our good hosts and friends, along with the tropical fruit, exotic plants and flowers. One lucky unit remained to guard Durban. Some married those lovely girls of Durban and eventually settled there after the War. We, however, pursued our new course through the Indian Ocean to Bombay, the Gateway of India. I had volunteered for the Middle East expecting to land at Cairo. Yet here we were in the blazing heat of India facing the delights of Bombay, with immediate invitations to Clubs, dinners and dances. But we gunners were sent straight to Deolali, miles north of Bombay. Deolali was a famous Artillery Transit Centre during the First World War. We heard the story of the last unit that was left behind and forgotten. Years later they were found, suffering from 'Deolali tap' madness. We were warned "Don't stay long in Deolali. They all go mad." Proof was forthcoming.

As we piled off the train at Deolali, native bearers met us and offered to carry our bags and light metal trunks. All the tents were in orderly rows at that interim transit staging post. The O.C. was a certain Captain Balfour, who obviously had been there too long in that forsaken place and drank too deeply. He considered himself quite a potentate, waited upon by the local Indian suppliers with obeisance, compliments and precious gifts. He had literally precious little to do, as we were all independent and simply awaiting posting orders. There was an old-established Officers' Club in the village, where senior retired officers met. Their favourite game was bridge and they recruited me when one died. Those were quiet, enjoyable evenings with good conversation and humour. A cold bug suddenly affected many of us, taking us by surprise. The Medical Officer said that we just needed to rest for a week, so we were temporarily confined to quarters. Just then a unit of Queen Alexandra's Royal Imperial Nursing Service passed through Deolali from Bombay. They were given a tremendous welcome, since they were the first white women we'd seen since leaving Durban. A ball was hurriedly arranged with escorts assigned to each. Mine was an attractive redhead, a green-eyed, merry widow, and our date was fixed for the following Saturday, when we would be out of quarantine. The MO gave us verbal clearance, and off we went for a most enjoyable evening of dancing and merry-making.

Returning late to my tent, I was surprised to find two officers waiting for me. "Come to tuck me in?" I enquired. "Oh no, you are under arrest." "Its rather late for jokes." "No joke, the O.C. has ordered your arrest, confined to quarters." "But this is ridiculous. I haven't committed murder or been in a fight. So what's the charge?" Grinning, they read out the following unbelievable charge: "Subject to arrest because, on the 5th December 1941, when ordered not to go to a dance, they went to the dance." "This must be a joke. We were cleared by the M.O." "Ah, but you did not seek clearance from our lordly O.C.Transit Camp."

We had no need of clearance from Capt.Balfour, who was not our O.C. We were in transit, awaiting orders to our allotted Regiments and needed only the M.O.'s clearance, which had been duly received. But there I was, imprisoned for the first time in my life, charged with the heinous crime of escorting a visiting Q.A. to a dance. Others were similarly charged by Balfour, in the most palpably ridiculous charge ever trumped up by this drunken half-wit, puffed up with his own pride and self-esteem as the great, powerful O.C. of a transit camp. "Deolali tap strikes again" said my bridge friends, who had devised a scheme to secure my temporary release for the bridge evenings. They gave assurance that they would escort me back to my prison quarters. It was a real joy and relief to hear their private views. They made a copy of the charge and promised to take the necessary action at higher level. They considered it their duty, in time of war, to prevent the busy Judge Advocate General, and senior R.A. officers from being called to little Deolali for a court-martial. It would go down in gunner history, as Deolali tap, if it were not hushed up at source.

In the event, my friends prevailed. I was summoned to the nearest Army HQ. driven unofficially by my senior friends. This was a good sign. I was marched before a General who stared at me with a quizzical look and what seemed like a twitch of a smile. "Well, what have you got to say for yourself?" "I have done nothing wrong Sir, - broken no military law." "But the charge is, that you were ordered not to go to a dance, yet you disobeyed and went to the dance." "Well, I had to keep my promise to escort the Q.A. to the dance and I had received clearance from the M.O." "Yes, I had a note to that effect from your M.O. who pronounced you fit. But Captain Balfour claims you failed to obtain his clearance". "There was no need Sir. He is not my C.O. I am, like the other officers, in transit. It was the M.O. who confined us for seven days and released us on the morning of the dance." "Hmmm, I hear you, and your statement corroborates the other officers' stories."

He looked at me searchingly and said: "I have read your record which has been clean until now. Are you prepared to accept my judgement here and now, or would you prefer to defend yourself before a court-martial?" "Good heavens no Sir, I would not waste the Army's time. I will accept your judgement." Then he hit the desk with his baton and said "Case dismissed." I saluted smartly, much relieved, then he added with a smile, "See you in the Mess in ten minutes when we will have a celebratory drink together" - which we certainly did; while other officers slapped my back and laughed their heads off at such an idiotic case. My senior bridge friends were delighted. They had brought me all the way in a staff car and drove me back to Deolali triumphant, but complained that they were now going to lose their bridge and poker companion. They had prior knowledge and told me that, though cleared and found not guilty (the papers would be destroyed as a non-active case, non-recorded), I could not remain in Deolali. Sure enough, sealed orders were awaiting me. I was instructed to join an R.A. Regiment at Quetta at the far northern end of India. My friends told me that Balfour had already been quietly removed from Deolali, "and put out of harms way."

Quetta seemed to be the opposite end of the earth from Bombay and Deolali. Overlooking Afghanistan, it was a thoroughly British Army town, firmly under Artillery control with a good atmosphere. We even had clean streets and a Service population with all conveniences. These included the only officially registered brothel in the whole of India and Africa. An institution that was kept under strict supervision by the Army M.O.s. In all of my travels, I have never met a more contented, and quietly disciplined set of soldiers, than those who were stationed in Quetta, in that northernmost post. Whilst there, we had the terrible duty of going out in boats to rescue the natives from flooding. A nearby area, which had suffered terrible floods from rivers swollen to bursting by unusually heavy monsoon rains. Bodies were floating everywhere in the muddy waters. Many had escaped, but others had to be rescued from the tops of tall trees. It was an eerie, distressing sight and had a profoundly, depressing effect upon us. Our troops made valiant efforts and saved hundreds of lives, but it left us with a grim memory of the terrible power of nature. The force of nature inflicted far greater wounds on mankind, than all the mayhem we managed to cause by our own stupid acts. Facing the stark strength of nature, not only with floods, but earthquakes, volcanic eruptions, great storms of lightning, thunder, rain, snow, hail and hurricanes, reminded me of the Greeks' portrayal of the wrath of their Gods of nature, war and sea. These portrayals came closer in fantasy to mirroring the suffering of humanity.

My Regiment in Quetta was Heavy Artillery. This was completely strange to me. I was trained at Catterick on twenty five pound field guns, then transferred and trained at Larkhill on small, two pounder, solid shot anti-tank guns. I was now faced with massive guns that required entirely different training. The C.O. called me and said : " I could send you to Staff College for training as a Staff Officer or, I have just received an urgent secret message 'for the eyes of C.O.s only', concerning some secret Intelligence Organisation. They need German specialists urgently. You have the essential qualifications. So which would you choose?" Without hesitation I chose the latter and packed the same day. I was then driven to Abbottabad, high up in the mountains on the North West Frontier of the Punjab. There I reported to a R.A. Regt., which contained a secret section mysteriously named 'Intelligence School B,' deep inside the grounds. Inside that mysterious enclave we were greeted by the Bletchley instructors, who made us sign the roll, and swear an oath never to reveal to anyone what went on in Bletchley Park Intelligence. This included parents, wives, husbands, girl friends, boyfriends or relatives, throughout the war and for thirty years after the conflict had ceased. We were assured that the roll had been signed by Churchill, Generals and all concerned. From then on we were 'The best-kept secret of the War.'

We were immediately set on a crash course on code-breaking, with unremitting concentration. We learnt about the mighty efforts at Bletchley Park to break the German top secret ciphers, that were transmitted through complicated machines like Enigma, which the Germans regarded as totally unbreakable. Those who succeeded in passing this course would disappear to Bletchley Park, or turn up at some odd, distant battle zone. Thus began four weeks of strenuous instruction and training in the mysterious art of decryption. We learnt about 'boxes' and other methods, using different formulae, seeking 'clues,' and inspiration. Hour after hour we studied a confusion of letters and numbers, searching for hidden keys to decipher secret messages. It was an ordeal that had been suddenly sprung on us without notice or preparation. Yet gradually, after intense thought and experiment, recognisable shapes began to appear that made sense of the methods demonstrated by these wordcrafters. If the strain became unbearable, we were allowed out, within a confined area, to wander about and clear our minds. Some people gave up and returned to their units after repeating their oath of silence. I was enjoying the struggle, and the process of learning code breaking techniques reminded me of my earlier memory exercises with Greek vocabulary.

Whilst we strove to master these extraordinary but gripping mental exercises, we knew nothing of the life around us. We had our own quarters and shared huts with separate rooms. Awaiting me was a tall, fierce-looking Pathan with a deep black moustache, who had already unpacked my kit. My quarters were extremely well furnished. Some days later while hosting a party, it was discovered that Ibrahim had removed choice pieces from other huts to make mine the best of all. Most enjoyed the joke and, as I would not be there long, they agreed to leave all in place. Ibrahim was a good valet. He cleaned and pressed my kit fastidiously. He was also a mine of information. His fierce Pathan tribe were allowed by the British to own their own rifles and long sharp, curved knives. His code of honour allowed him to steal from others, which he did regularly, but not from me, for he was the guardian of my 'honour' as well as his own. He did not just serve me, but looked after me better than any other servant, valet or batman I have ever employed. When we eventually left I presented him with a gold sovereign extra, which to him was of magical value.

There were sudden storms in that Northern hill country, and it was awe-inspiring to see the magnificent great streaks of lightning flash across the high peaks, and hear the huge peals of thunder, which threatened to crack open the mountains. We seemed so close to the bright sky that was lit daily at dawn by the huge ball of the rising sun, that one could almost reach out and touch the woolly nimbus clouds overhead. The dawns were like shining red spheres across cathedral towers, and the evening sun descended without notice from a beautiful sunset to sudden eerie darkness. Very different from the lingering dawns and sunsets of my English West Country.

We were a round number of twenty on the course, and were taught the secret methods of code-breaking by keen instructors. We began with simple codes. We learnt the universal Morse Code, and about its contribution to our winning the first World War. A time when Captain 'Blinker' Hall and his team deciphered top grade German codes and ciphers without the aid of machinery. He thereby revealed to the over-trusting American President Wilson, the treacherous deceit of the German Head of State, Zimmermann. The knowledge that the latter had sent a secret signal to Mexico, to declare war on the Americans, with the aid of the Japanese, effectively brought America into the war in 1917.

We progressed to learning the complicated methods that were used to decrypt the German high-grade ciphers, and Rommel's own army secret ciphers. Without the aid of the machinery of Bletchley Park, that formed the basis of our secret cryptology HQ, and eventually broke even the most 'secure' of Nazi ciphers like the Enigma, we had to rely upon difficult processes, using intuition and various aids. We called these aids, 'clues' that we had picked up, of German habits and errors. We used a system of double 'boxes,' with which we developed some of our deciphering methods. These enabled us to break into and solve German secret ciphers. However at that stage of the war, we could not rely on mechanical means to assist us. We were forced to rely upon imagination, experience, luck and inspired guesswork. Clues were often forthcoming as a result of German operator mistakes and by transmission frequencies. These all combined to make the code breaking course the toughest I had ever experienced. Of the original twenty only two passed, a Lt. Kirk and myself. We were immediately flown by Short Sunderland Flying boat to Cairo via Basra. En route we landed on the Shatt-el-Arab river and enjoyed a night in a luxury hotel in Basra. From there, untouched by war, we set off the next morning to Cairo and landed smoothly on the Nile. We were quickly escorted to our secret unit, which was some distance from Cairo, and hidden in King Fuad's unfinished palace outside Heliopolis.

We were linked by short wave listening units of Royal Signals and Intelligence Corps who were in concealed positions 'in the blue' (slang for desert). They took down Morse signals and messages at speed, with as much length as possible. These enabled us to find frequencies of the letters e, t, n and other repetition. We collected these regularly and concentrated on deciphering and unravelling them into the original German 'plainspeak,' then translated them for urgent delivery to Generals Alexander and Montgomery, who visited and encouraged us. I reminded Monty that he was my CO. in Southern Command but his reply was: " You are much more useful here." He used to tell his troops "I can read Rommel's mind," but of course, we were doing the reading.

Nevertheless he made good use of our information on Rommel's battle strengths and weaknesses, positions and intentions, in close communication with his Generals and their Forces network.

A close watch revealed that King Farouk was in close touch with both Italians and Germans. He even planned to meet Mussolini, who had boasted that he would enter Cairo in the very near future. Farouk's refusal to cooperate with the British became so serious, that our Ambassador decided on drastic action. Farouk awoke one morning, to find the square in front of his palace in Cairo, full of British tanks and guns all aiming point-blank at him. He was so scared that he signed the agreement placed before him by our Ambassador, on the spot, and behaved correctly thereafter. Our arrival in 1942, was marked by a nervous reaction to Rommel's latest push toward Cairo. Hurried preparations were being made for a retreat to Palestine and top secret documents were being prepared for burning. Many Egyptians had been collaborating with the Italians, and were caught sending emissaries to welcome Rommel's imminently expected triumphant entry into Cairo.

They even brazenly attacked some of our soldiers in the streets and bazaars of Cairo. Consequently we were ordered to move about in armed pairs. Fortunately, General Auchinleck, 'the Auk', stopped Rommel's onward rush in a trap that was neatly laid in front of Alamein. Then Monty arrived and issued an immediate order, "Stand Fast, we are not going anywhere but forward, so let's get down to hard training." This he did to good effect. He welded the eighth Army into a tough, fully trained, competent force of fighting strength. They were hard, strong, determined. Churchill visited North Africa and insisted that with Rommel reputedly held up by a lack of fuel and supplies, the time was now ripe for a confrontation. Monty sent him home, stating that he would not move until he had received fully trained reinforcements along with the new, stronger armoured tanks, guns, ammunition and supplies. He also demanded full RAF coverage. Only then would he attack and defeat Rommel and his Afrika Corps.

Churchill went away satisfied that here was a man who knew his business. Clearly he could be relied upon. As weeks of hard training went by we were all absolutely assured that victory would be ours. In the meantime we worked in shifts day and night, 'breaking' all possible messages from Rommel and his Generals. These revealed their position, order of battle, full strength in detail, and dispositions. Monty's staff were then able to divide the whole desert area into defined sections that were occupied by Rommel, with each General and his forces, strengths and planned movements. This information allowed Alexander and Monty to chart future movements and make due preparation to deal with them in the intricate game of war.

We became quicker at decoding messages as soon they arrived. We spotted clues, signs and repetitions that enabled us to recognise individual German radio operators. We were a small mixed group consisting mostly of academics, German specialists from Universities and Bletchley. They had a peculiar semi-mufti, semi-uniform dress. Our rooms had long tables with tilted desk tops on which we spread the messages and sought to match any from the daily intake. The longer the message the more hopeful we were of finding the beginning, with German habitual exact details carefully encoded. The quantity and sequence of letters and numbers revealed recognisable addresses and dispositions. Also the ending, messages were usually signed off with the General's name. We compiled a list of Generals, Commanding Officers and their Commands, to make it easier to break into the code with such 'clues'. Best of all was to find messages and signals from Rommel to his Generals 'in the blue,' and especially reports to his Chief, General Kesselring at his H.Q. in Italy. We were able to pinpoint that location for the RAF, who bombed it successfully, though unfortunately Kesselring was not there. Such messages were a great triumph to pass to Monty 'in clear,' and we often jumped on the tables and danced a jig in the middle of the night after successful efforts. Hence our nickname 'The Madhouse.' It was exhausting work all day and sometimes far into the night! We unpeeled layer after layer of code to arrive eventually at the original 'plainspeak.' We were left to our own devices and took turns, either to go into the desert to collect messages and deliver supplies - or to take time off to visit Cairo for a necessary break. There were no 'normal' hours. We broke off only when the strain became unbearable, or we had successfully broken a whole sequence of signals.

We would climb aboard the long tramcars from Heliopolis to Cairo, which were always overflowing with natives hanging on roofs, sides and jutting fixtures, like a swarm of galibeah clad weirdies, shouting, singing and cursing. We avoided the popular Officers' Club, looking with disdain on what we called 'lounge lizards.' Of course we were 'holy righteous,' for our work was completely secret and invisible. Thus we enjoyed visiting the bazaars, drinking muddy semi-solid coffee or sweet tea with the stall-owners, who seemed to enjoy our visits, and we learnt the art of haggling. Courtesy demanded long and enjoyable haggling: "I beseech you. It is so beautiful, I haven't the heart to part with it. But for you, effendi, I will make a special offer, for I can see you admire our beautiful objects" (quite likely stolen from a tomb, or pyramid to be sold to dealers in the bazaar).

I was determined to make my own research into that early age of civilisation, which fascinated me above all others. As for the Sphinx, nobody studying it closely could ever forget that awesome stare, seeking to penetrate the unknown. Another symbol of a secret existence, but doomed to failure and semi-oblivion, as with all other kingdoms and states, even the glory of Solomon. It was there I met an Egyptian scholar, one of the accepted authorities on early Egyptian civilisation. He was a doctor of philosophy who, remarkably, spent half the week in the family wool shop in Cairo. A curious combination, necessary he explained, to earn his living, for he gave the rest of his time in voluntary work to the museum and the study of Egyptian history. A completely honest intellectual, a rare person with whom I enjoyed interesting discussions. But he could not explain how those ancient Egyptians were able to calculate, in minutest detail, the exact measurements of a massive pyramid. Each stone carved, dressed and then moved by unknown means into its exact prepared position. How long did all this finite preparation take? How many years did it take to make one pyramid, with its carefully structured interior? How did this ancient Egyptian civilisation fit into the framework of the East, and the first records of our ancestors?

Oh, to be able to visualise the dawn of our civilisation! To see the truth behind our accepted stories of Creation and the birth and development of mankind. We can verify the existence of that highly civilised and progressively fascinating people called the Sumerians, and calculate the tremendous population growth over 6,000 years ago of mankind on the banks of the rivers Tigris and Euphrates in Mesopotamia. But our previous ancestors remain shrouded in mystery. We have scientific proof of mankind's existence, and progress, but some still believe the mythological tales of the birth and development of religions. From the worship of the Sun, to the many man-made gods, to the final worship of the one God by our Hebrew ancestors. But religion then engenders slaughter, assassination and torture. This violence has undermined the fact that we are basically members of one family, no matter which gods different faiths may worship. These problems have haunted me ever since my fateful wartime journey there, from England, via India, to Egypt to join the 8th Army.

One other spectral image remains in my mind concerning a chance visit to the 'City of the Dead.' My friend Kirk and I were exploring different areas of Cairo, when suddenly we found ourselves in strange, uncannily silent surroundings. Empty streets, silent, grim crumbling buildings and rows of tombs. It was like a ghost town, grey, grim, silent and menacing. The sun was blocked out and we shivered in that still, chill air. We became lost in its silent, empty, unmarked streets. Not a sound stirred, not a dog barked. It was truly the City of the Dead as it was called. I have seen ruined and war-smashed cities in Germany, France and Britain both during, and after the War. But never anything like that dead, deathly still area where nothing moved, not even a stray dog. Obviously it was a place avoided by all, but it had an uncanny effect as we walked noiselessly through its tomb-grey streets. We emerged in unhappy state, blinking and still shivering in our thin tropical uniforms. It seemed ages before we felt normal again in the heat of that Egyptian day. Nobody had an explanation. Clearly, it appeared that this area of the city had been set aside many years ago, as a burial place for the dead. It was simply a part of the city that became a funeral area, which gradually became isolated and avoided. It was left untouched, although we were told that cleaners were supposed to brush the streets on rare visits. There was no evidence of any dirt or rubbish of the kind that would conventionally be left by visitors. Only grey dust which seemed to settle on streets and buildings alike, advancing that shroud-like appearance.

We had gradually extracted a list of Rommel's Generals, so it was useful to find the position of the name at message end, and check whether the Morse letters fitted the number of letters in each name, whether Schmidt or Faltinghausen. This process provided valuable clues when deciphering other parts of the message. Our main efforts however, were focussed on discovering Rommel's total Forces. We sought to learn his Order of Battle, state of arms and armaments, number of tanks and guns, shells, ammunition and especially fuel, without which his tanks could not move. Eventually we were able to reveal his plans of attack and defence, and the layout of his Afrika Corps, including the strengths and intentions of each General. Thus we were able to furnish Monty with up-to-date information. We then transcribed Rommel's personal messages to his Chief and even to Hitler. These usually outlined his situation. Towards the third quarter of 1942, he was pleading urgently for much needed fuel for his tanks. By this time the Bletchley Park team had broken the Enigma code, and full reports were being brought to Monty, by R.A.F. special messengers. These confirmed our deciphering results. We were able to inform Monty that Rommel's terrific advance at speed would never reach Cairo as he planned. German supply ships were being sunk in the Mediterranean. The lack of fuel, as well as our determined resistance with the heroic stand of the 8th Army, brought Rommel to a halt, and his tanks to a standstill well before el Alamein. Our defence fortification was on an elevated ridge, that was first developed by Auchinleck.

This information enabled Monty to plan his famous attack at Alamein. He had time to lay mine-traps for German tanks and cement blocks and fortified sites, from which British guns opened a devastating twenty four hour barrage that numbed and froze the enemy. Preparations that opened the way for Monty's daring attack. I still remember that terrible opening barrage, which split the night sky like bolts of thunder and lightning. The continuous roar of the Gods of Battle. It went on solidly hour after hour, paralysing the German troops, and allowing our first attack forces time to move forward and crush the enemy. Our code breaking techniques ensured an element of surprise which greatly contributed to the British success. Along with the wonderful heroism of all the troops, British, Commonwealth, Indian, Ghurkas, who were all part of the glorious 8th Army in which I am proud to have served. The 8th Army spirit was irrepressible, and chased Rommel over 1,000 miles through the desert to Cyrenaica and then on through Italy. We were busily packing to join the move when our OC. Lt.Col.Jacobs called me over, holding a signal. "Sorry, Beck, you have been recalled to India. Intelligence needs you there." Argue as I might, "orders is orders." I was certainly furious at being torn away from the 8th Army and that great victory drive, but off I had to go. I hitched a ride on an American plane to Bombay.

Chapter 8

Return to India

The course of the war had changed considerably by this stage. Britain had experienced the Phoney War, the Blitz and the Battle of Britain. The amazing RAF victory in the Battle of Britain, was crucial in preventing Operation Sea Lion, the planned German invasion of Britain. Without air supremacy, Hitler had no chance of staging a successful invasion and he was forced to turn eastwards. In June 1941 Operation Barbarossa was implemented. This was the German invasion of Russia and a tactical German error that effectively turned the tide of the war. Later that year on December 7th, the Japanese attacked Pearl Harbour, and the United States of America entered the war on the side of the Allies. Despite the objections of American Generals, who wanted to pursue the conflict in the Far East as soon as possible, Churchill insisted that the defeat of Hitler remained the primary objective. Once the war in Europe was over, he argued, there would be plenty of time to focus on the Far East. After Monty's victories in North Africa, Churchill decided that the best strategy was to attack Europe from its 'soft under belly.' Thus British troops prepared to enter Sicily. Furthermore, thousands of American troops were taken to North Africa at this time, in order for them to gain some experience of battle conditions. By 1943 the Italian government had abandoned Mussolini and fascism and joined the Allies.

I had played a supportive role in the North African victories and was due some well earned respite. At Bombay, the embarkation officer said: "You are to report to Intelligence HQ Delhi. However you are entitled to leave, so where would you choose?" "Kashmir." "Why that's thousands of miles away. What about a Hill Station?" "No thanks, just make my leave pass out to Kashmir and notify HQ." "OK, but you will suffer for days in burning-hot trains, followed by miles up the mountain side." He was absolutely right. The train had plain carriages, no air-conditioning, and only a huge tin bath on the floor that was filled with blocks of ice to keep it cool. I soon fell asleep, and only awoke when we arrived at a station that was full of vendors offering hot tea, cakes and fly-blown sandwiches, with passengers pushing the sellers away. Two officers joined me and ordered more ice. But the train left before delivery and the ice gradually turned to water. Then it simply dried up in the heat. As it became hotter and hotter, we discarded our uniforms.

On reaching my destination, I was glad to dismount with my kit, only to find a dilapidated bus full of peasants, who were carrying all manner of live poultry. The Indian driver saluted, asking "You go Srinagar, Sahib?" The old bus lurched forward and climbed the narrow mountain paths. My heart was in my mouth as large stones clattered down the steep cliffs. They sloped sharply downwards to some lovely green valleys far below. The driver kept turning his head to chatter. "You go first time Srinagar, Sahib?" "Do look where you're going," I pointed to the sharp curve ahead. That journey took hours for we had to stop halfway because the engine overheated. The driver had recourse to a big water tank. "Sahib, drink pani"? "Not likely!

Arriving at last at Srinagar, the capital of Kashmir, I was delighted. It was as beautiful as my geography teacher had described. A broad square with finely carved wooden buildings, an Indian version of an English village. It was surrounded by lakes, with lovely water lilies floating peacefully in the clear sunshine. Everything was bright and welcoming. The shops even more so, with their displays of handsome rugs and carpets that were characterised by intricately woven designs. The shinar leaf (Indian oak) was carved on lovely, hand-made furniture, boxes, and jewellery by workers who used only small chisels and a hammer. By custom, I was offered cups of tea and sweetmeats, to accompany the bargaining.

One large shop was named 'Habib the Thief' and it competed with neighbouring shops that were entitled 'Ahmed the Robber', and 'Ram Singh the Crook'. I was fascinated by the display of locally made carpets that were all handmade in ornate designs. Habib assured me that he had dealt with British Royalty, Statesmen and Generals and produced ornate-lettered, hand-scribed documents as proof. Of course they were all forgeries. I rented a houseboat on the lake and was visited daily by narrow boats laden with a huge variety of fruit, vegetables, soups, jam and marmalade made in Kashmir. There I lived like a pukka 'sahib' awaiting my orders from HQ.Delhi. None came for over three weeks, so I enjoyed climbing the mountains with a fellow Bristolian, who was also on leave. We travelled mostly on foot but used donkeys for the heights. It was so still; clouds came ever closer, and the huge, pale peaks of the Himalayas looked as though they were beckoning us towards a fairy world. For the first time, I understood the magnetic attraction of these mountains to great climbers. It must be such an enormous thrill to stand atop these pointed peaks. But for the War, I might have ventured myself. Unfortunately, I was fast running out of funds when my recall arrived from Delhi.

The Western Wireless Intelligence Centre (WWIC), occupied a hill-top above Anand Parbat village, miles from Delhi. Yet the tall aerials, reaching heavenward clearly exposed the true nature of the enterprise. There were rooms full of Hollerith and other machines, which gave the place the appearance of a hive of industry. We were supposedly breaking Japanese ciphers, to communicate to General 'Bill' Slim, the Commander of the 14th Burma Army. Intelligence was culled from Japanese messages and signals, but there was a shortage of Japanese scholars and trained code-breakers to supply Slim's urgent demands. Operations were supposedly conducted by specialists from British Universities who'd been flown out, some with their wives (which was unheard of in wartime), at great expense. They were reputed to be experts in Japanese. They occupied comfortable quarters and were well attended by servants and suppliers. They were also cared for by a Captain Quartermaster and his wife, who ministered to their every need. Indeed, so well that he soon received promotion to Major as a reward.

To my surprise, I was forbidden entry to the machine rooms and all Intelligence work. I was told to join the Service Officers in administration and training duties. I asked why I had been taken from my real work as a code-breaker with the 8th Army, only to be told that I was needed to complete their military strength. My request for transfer back to the 8th Army was refused. The QM offered me a position as his deputy, saying it was a 'peach of a job' and carried a Captain's rank. His magnificent offices were full of fine carpets, luxury stores, food and quality drink in profusion. The Indian suppliers treated him as the great Panjandoram-their Lord and Master, and showered him with gifts in profusion for his gracious orders. I politely refused his offer saying that I was a code-breaker, not an admin wallah.

Money seemed to flow unceasingly on expensive drinks and luxuries. It was an executive's paradise that appeared to be totally unrelated to the war and the economy. Accounts seemed vaguely recorded.. The situation was an elaborate sham that was carefully concealed by declaring the cipher rooms out of bounds. I reminded them of my valid contribution with the 8th Army and my Bletchley training and experience. To which they replied, "Ah, but you have no Japanese." "Then why drag me away from doing my real job?" Leading members would disappear in staff cars to Delhi clubs and for shopping, claiming that they were conferring with Army HQ. Days were burning hot, but whilst they enjoyed the comfort of huge electric air-cooled fans, we 'old sweats' had to endure the heat. Then, in the cool of the evening they would gather in their closed family circles. There was no proper control or discipline, as there would have been in a normal service unit.

Apparently the site had been chosen for its lofty position, reception of radio signals and difficult approach. They lived in splendid isolation with a seemingly endless supply of rupees. They spent these royally as if they were pukka rajahs. It was an artificial semi-civilian existence, with uniformed officers expected to serve these intellectual masters. I was itching to get at those machines, but they were carefully hidden behind locked doors. I tried to discover if there had been any progress in breaking Japanese messages, but was allowed no access. I sent a report to Bletchley Park to acquaint them of the situation. I was aghast! To have endured the rigours of the Desert Campaign with Monty and brave fighting men, then to be confronted with such laxity and complacency. I was now watching British taxpayers' money being freely poured out for no valid purpose; in great lakhs of rupees, with no proper accounting, whilst General Slim was complaining of lack of intelligence information.

Eventually, a senior Service Officer was appointed and necessary changes were made. These including the dismissal of that QM, who must have benefited well from looking after his civilian masters and their wives. In the meantime, we Service Officers, who were heartily sick of the pseudo pretence of being an effective Japanese code-breaking unit, kept our own company. We performed the tasks we were given and bided our time until we could escape. How I longed for the real down to earth activity of the 8th Army. There was no shambolics in that unit. We were small, effective and completely self-sufficient.

Captain Bradbury, Royal Signals, with whom I shared a small hut, was a decent, pleasant companion and engaged to a Q.A. Eventually the wedding date was fixed to be held in Delhi and I was invited to be best man. I accepted, with some hesitation because I was hoping for a transfer to an active Intelligence unit. But I enjoyed arranging a highly successful wedding. Our quarters were unbearably hot and infested with white ants, and they demolished everything. Furniture legs stood in pots of water; clothes were kept in covered bags and mosquito nets hung around our beds to protect us against the mosquitoes that carried malaria.

A senior officer there was a 'Regular,' Lt. Col. Stevenson of Frontier Force Rifles. A tall, lean, sunburnt figure, he was a real hard, genuine British soldier and not taken in by WWIC. I respected him as a straight, truthful man of few words, who had lived most of his life in India, and married into his Regiment. His wife was an elegant lady and a true 'daughter of the Regiment.' He told me thrilling stories of his mountain campaigns against the wild Pathans. He could speak their language fluently, and had even dressed as one. He grew a long moustache, and dyed his body dark brown. He was tall as most Pathans, and a keen sportsman. He was also a good sport and adept with a knife. As a spy, he could advise his Regiment on how to prevent ambushes in the hill defiles. He was a fine English soldier, and he, too, had felt lost in such odd, pretentious company. Moreover, the costly unit had produced little of value to General Slim's 14th Army, so we planned to escape.

His plan, to take a unit of soldiers, men and women, for defensive military training, was accepted. He argued that this training was necessary in case the Japanese should ever break through and threaten our area. The soldiers were mostly English speaking half-castes, delighted to be serving the Army in tropical uniform. He demanded me as his Captain Adjutant and we moved our motley collection of soldiers down to the pleasant green plains of Bangalore, where we pitched our tents. Oh the pleasure of that cool, green countryside, that was almost like part of England. Trees, green grass, sweetly flowing rivers, flowers and birds. It seemed like home.

Col. Stevenson then revealed his real plan. General Slim was complaining of lack of real forward Intelligence. He needed regular direction on Japanese operations closer at hand. This was where we were to play a part. There were two unused Bletchley units outside Calcutta and Barrackpore. When working properly, these units were supposed to set up radio operators in forward areas and record Japanese signals. However, they had not been functioning properly, so messages were not getting back to decrypt. What a mess! Stevenson was the only man capable of restoring order in that area, using his Army contacts. He knew nothing about code-breaking, but was aware that I had been an active code-breaker with the 8th Army. The plan was for Lt. Col. Stevenson to establish his HQ at Barrackpore, and myself as OC in the Calcutta area. My unit was just outside Calcutta, with well-made, modern large bungalows that were equipped with electric fans in every room. In our primitive quarters in Anand Parbat we had ceiling fans but they were operated by a native punka wallah (fan-mover), who sat against the wall with a cord from the fan attached to his big toe. Throughout his stint, he would move his foot up and down, turning the fan until his replacement arrived.

The Army Regulation Contract for my unit, which was called 'Intelligence School C,' was well guarded, to keep out strangers and renegade Indian Army spies. It had a complement of one Lt. Col. O.C., two Majors, three Captains, junior officers and Army personnel, truck drivers, vehicles, equipment and furniture. Sadly it was lacking in all of these, except for some vehicles lying empty and unused. The unit had clearly pursued none of its originally planned duties of Intelligence gathering. I took over as O.C., and they sent me one junior RAF officer Smart, who was an ex-bank clerk and fresh out of England. Otherwise I was in at the deep end, with full responsibility for a major Unit which existed so far only on paper. Anand Parbat begrudged any expenditure outside their secret hideout. For them Calcutta was dangerously close to the conflict. I literally had to start from scratch and was absolutely delighted to do so, as Col. Stevenson had conjectured. My first action was to use his knowledge and connections in India to send a 'round robin,' asking C.O's to select men for a most important secret mission. I requested highly trained, skilled and trustworthy drivers to work in jungle areas. The C.O.s did exactly as Stevenson had warned me they would do, ruthlessly clearing out their worst trouble-makers and dumping them on me.

In the meantime I took over the previous owner's staff, for my new quarters and Messes for officers and other ranks. As I could speak their language, I soon elicited their previous rates of wages, and gauged that the butler was extremely capable in terms of supervising his staff. I had a long conversation with him and clarified his duties. All staff were to be courteous, polite and helpful at all times to all British officers and ranks. We reached a good understanding, and I increased his salary and promoted him to major-domo. I knew that the baksheesh (bribery) system worked here as it did elsewhere in India. The lowly sweepers belonged to the lowest 'untouchable' caste and they dared not let their shadows defile that of a Brahmin or any upper caste. They had to pay a small amount of baksheesh to the gardener, he paid the next rank a little more and so on up to the butler. Under the auspices of the butler, they became a well trained family group of servants who learned how to deal with all Sahibs. We achieved such a good understanding, that I could leave for a visit to forward regions, knowing that the butler would conduct his duties with scrupulous efficiency.

The bungalows were divided into my HQ, office, a control centre for secret Intelligence operations, and accommodation for me and the other officers on the schedule. The latter never arrived, despite constant reminders. Nevertheless there were many Army and RAF officers along with a few American liaison officers who passed through continuously. They were either on their way to or from Burma. Some stayed just for one night; whereas others prolonged their stay. All appreciated the comfortable benefits that I had gradually introduced. They were able to enjoy a proper bath, shower and toilet facilities, and a breakfast that was served English style. This was luxury when compared with jungle hash and mud quarters with no facilities. After the sweat, mosquitoes, flies, leeches and other insects, the continuous wetness of the jungle, and the constant threat of sudden Japapanese tactical moves, the bungalows were like a paradise. I expanded the transit hospitality as it provided good camouflage for the intelligence activity. As our reputation spread I even gained some regular customers for my unmissable Mess. The bungalows soon became known as Beck's Hotel.

Officers exchanged many stories of adventures in the jungle. These included some from the American fighter pilots who were serving with General Stilwell's Force with the Chinese. The bar became a news and gossip shop for many who were glad to have a little relief. They were able to relax in good company after a spell in tough jungle conditions, fighting against a Japanese foe, who simply decapitated officers who surrendered, instead of fighting to the death like the Japanese. The officers' mess served regular meals, which included the all time favourite, Indian curry. The bar was like a small English club that served a variety of cool, soft drinks, real Scotch whisky, gin, liqueurs and tins of beer. All with plenty of ice. Whisky and gin were well nigh impossible to obtain elsewhere by 1943 and severely rationed in Delhi clubs. Since many ships were sunk en route they were restricted to carrying absolute essentials. Luckily, I had found a warehouse that was owned by a Parsee, although I became so engrossed in learning about their Persian faith, that I quite forgot my purchases. My new friend reminded me and offered a wide variety of drinks. He also recommended a red fruit juice for me. I arranged to deal with him regularly, and as I was about to leave, he produced a bottle of

Haig's whisky. He smiled at my astonished look and presented it to me as a token of friendship. I left with this precious treasure, not knowing that it presaged future similar bounty. In fact, my new friend had a considerable store of well concealed whisky, gin, liqueurs and cigars, including genuine Havanas. He carefully locked away his stash of supplies to keep them secure from the many thieves of Calcutta. His store was like an Aladdin's cave. He quoted me fair prices with the sole condition that the source remained a closely guarded secret between us. Otherwise he would not have been able to cope with the incessant demand. My Mess became more popular as the news of my well stocked bar spread. Many found it their 'duty' to pass through Calcutta to spend at least one night at 'Beck's Hotel.' And why not? I knew the experiences that so many had to endure serving within the fourteenth Army and RAF air operations. Hair-raising adventures were almost the norm, according to the tales which were being told nightly in my Mess.

Naturally with such continuous demand, whisky and gin had to be rationed to one or two chota (small) 'pegs' each. The atmosphere was wonderful, all 'rank' was dropped and everybody shared their experiences, told stories, cracked jokes and witticisms and sang service versions of popular songs. A wounded RAF friend who I had originally met in Bangalore, was a good pianist. He could make our battered old piano produce a fantastic mix of tunes. I could breathe freely again, as Lt. Col. Stevenson had foretold. I simply enjoyed having the full responsibility of running my own 'Show', under such good, enjoyable cover, as a training school.

In the meantime, my transport drivers had arrived from Army units who were delighted to be rid of them. Twelve men lined up in the yard before my garages, trucks, and petrol and oil supplies. Nondescript was too mild a description. I was appalled at such a collection of throwouts. They all seemed hopelessly ill-equipped, for the tough secret task that lay ahead. But I could not just send them back to their previous units, no matter how sorely tempted. I was stuck with a band of outcasts, who were completely unsuitable for the secret tasks awaiting them. I felt total despair, until I spotted an artillery badge belonging to 'Tiffy' Jones. A 'Tiffy' was the name given to a mechanical wizard who was in charge of the guns. He kept them in perfect condition both before and after firing. Lives depended on these oddballs who lived in a world of their own. They were excused parades, except for very special occasions, because they always had 'sumfink to do' whether it was with guns or transport. They loved crawling around engines or in and out of guns, they took the latter to pieces, pulling the firing mechanisms apart and putting them back together to demonstrate their expertise. Their overalls were always stained and holey with the odd patch. They were the despair of the QM and instructors and carefully hidden away.

However, they kept the guns and transport going and were 'excused darn near everything'. They would even sleep with their guns as though they were favourite horses. Fortunately for me, Jones had become estranged from his Regiment, and hence was in trouble. He looked at me, saw my R.A. badges, stiffened and then grinned. I grinned back. From that moment I had an ally, and devised a plan of action. I paraded my blacklisted soldiers, stood them at ease and explained their duties. Essentially they were in charge of transport, which had to be kept in running order at all times. Their main mission was to visit our radio units in forward positions, quietly and secretly, without noise or fuss. They were required to deliver important material and collect and bring back secret consignments safely to me. They were not to talk to anybody outside about us, or what we were doing. All missions were strictly secret and they needed to swear an oath of secrecy. They were now special soldiers who were entrusted with secret assignment, and different from normal Services.

There were no drills or parades, unless for some crime, trouble or a 'brass hat' visit. There was no uniform inspection, but they had to be 'in clean order', and ready on time for each trip. All transport had to be kept in perfect working order, ready for emergencies with no danger of breakdowns, especially on jungle duty trips. There needed to be back-ups ready, especially when I was on board—since I was their most precious cargo! They had to keep to their rota, to ensure that each truck was fully manned and ready on time. They were responsible for their own quarters, upkeep and condition. I or my junior officer would visit quarters regularly, to check vehicles and any incoming personnel on leave or in transit. All such personnel would have to report to my office or junior officer on arrival, and leaving, but it would be their duty to look after them whilst in their quarters. I then left them with their mouths open, to discuss this surprise speech with Tiffy Jones, who I had appointed as being nominally in charge. There was a long, narrow building which lay just off the transport yard, that had been unused for some time. I allotted this building to these new outcast recruits. Then I left them to chew over the situation. It was a shrewd gamble, designed to bring out the best in them, and they willingly accepted my terms and conditions. I think that they were intrigued by their entry into the realms of Intelligence, and pleased to be regarded as trustworthy.

I visited Area HQ and reported my arrival to the O.C. He stared at me and said "What is an Artillery Officer doing with this set of spooks?" I explained over lunch in the Mess and tea in his quarters. I gave him my record leaving out my Intelligence experience, which he had already guessed at. "I envy your luck in getting posted to 8th Army," he said, "but sorry you've got yourself mixed up with this lot." He explained about the grave situation of reinforcements for the 14th Army. They had trekked from Rangoon over 1,000 miles through Burma to join General Slim. Then I explained that my mission was to look after my forward radio sections. Our real enterprise remained a close secret. Hence my development of Beck's Hotel as a cover for an Intelligence training school. He thought the title of my special Unit a rare joke! We were obviously peculiar, typical

Spooks! But of course there were many strange units with the 14th Army, like Wingate's marauders. It was the same with the 8th Army, we had the Long Range Desert Patrol units from which sprang the Special Air Services. Mine was just another oddity.

He promised to help as much as possible, first with furniture and equipment requirements, then with welfare. We received games, books and parcels from the Red Cross, and even the Salvation Army and other aid sources. These provided some comfort for my forward listening posts, existing in their miserable conditions. I returned highly delighted with my visit to the Area CO, who was responsible for the whole military area. This responsibility included the continuous training and movement of units that were fully equipped for the Burma operations of the 14th Army. He was cool, competent, unflappable and cheerfully resolved all impossible problems of forward movements, or hastily relieved them from action. Out of necessity, maturity develops quickly in war conditions.

My Officers' Mess was now fully equipped and the drivers' quarters furnished. All was coming together quicker than I had anticipated. I avoided visiting my OR.'s quarters. I wanted to give them time to settle in and also demonstrate some confidence in their abilities. They were going to have to carry out special secret missions to their comrades in the forward jungle areas. I was in command but my Pilot Officer would be keeping a discreet eye on them too. They were used to being holed up in some strongly disciplined regiment, and their new situation was entirely different. I left them alone to appreciate the changes and adjust. I hoped my different approach would work, because so much depended on them.

My sole assistant Pilot Officer Smart was a rather indrawn, conscientious man. He was not used to handling army personnel, but very good with accounts, documents and bills. He balanced Mess accounts, bills and officers' payments and kept them scrupulously up-to-date and accurate. He enjoyed the paper work and kept meticulous records of transport movements. This alleviated me of burdensome administration, and allowed me to concentrate on essential intelligence work. With only a smattering of Japanese, obtaining useful information for General Slim was difficult. Intelligence was built up by tracing unusual growth of signal traffic in a particular direction. This growth clearly indicated preparation for action from that area, and gave General Slim time to prepare his defences. For example, thanks to such information, the final buildup of Japanese forces for major onslaught from different directions simultaneously, came up against Slim's famous 'Box' defence. Unable to penetrate this defence, the Japanese were forced into a headlong retreat that eventually resulted in their defeat.

We ensured that all small forward listening units had at least bearable quarters, with secure equipment and acceptable conditions. Some were sadly lacking in coverage, though whether in tented huts or dugouts, they needed better facilities for rest and welfare. The army was not often in a position to provide these. Some of the jungle conditions were almost impossible to endure. There were continuously wet, dripping trees and bushes, and attacking insects, especially mosquitoes and leeches. I did my best with the help of the Area OC. to provide welfare parcels. These consisted of sweets, chocolates, games, cards, chess, draughts and quoits, for which they were most grateful. Anand Parbat scarcely acknowledged our existence, but we managed well, and Tiffy Jones and his gang never failed me, whatever their 'adventures' in Calcutta.

Pilot Officer Smart preferred to live in a tent near my bungalow. He wanted to be within earshot of the field phone in case he was needed. The field phone was a wonderful contraption in a large box, with a handle needing vigorous winding. Coming from his first job in a bank, he seemed to regard me as a father figure even though I was only twenty nine years old. He sought my advice because his bank was paying his salary regularly into his home account, but the RAF India Paymaster was also sending him RAF pay regularly. As a conscientious bank clerk, he felt that it was wrong to accept double pay. I wished that I were in such a happy predicament! I warned him never to argue with the Indian pay clerk. They were taught to stick rigorously to written instructions, and they never deviated and had no flexibility.

How different was my Lloyds bank. Cox's and King's branches! I could draw cash at any branch anywhere in the world, at any time, without question. The clerk simply entered my details in his ledger in red ink, as overdraft for the bank's safety, to be adjusted later. They provided information wherever you might be. They even addressed me as Lt. Col. on my Bank Statements, before publication, and before the modern communication systems that were developed through Bletchley. Smart accepted my advice to leave well alone. He was the acme of perfection, but I did discover one weakness. I caught him once in the act of blissfully licking a spoon of thick, sweet Nestle's Condensed Milk. The tin had just arrived in a parcel from his mother. I did enjoy watching an expression of heavenly ecstasy, flicker across the normally expressionless face of that acme of bank clerks.

I decided that now was the time to discover the result of my gesture of freedom to my inherited bunch of oddments. I was met at the door of their quarters by Tiffy Jones, who was clad in clean khaki shirt, shorts and sandals. Gone was his greasy cap. His face was expressionless as he held open the door. Inside was an astonishing sight. There were pale green cool looking walls, fresh white window frames and rush mats on the scrubbed floor. Ceiling fans were working fast and noiselessly in a cool temperature. The biggest surprise was an unknown artist's wall paintings of Disney characters. I was staggered by their sheer beauty and accuracy. "Who on earth did this?" "Don't you like it, Sir?" "Like it? I'll have it cut out and transferred to the Officers' Mess." "Not bloody likely," they said. Now, fully satisfied, I sat in an easy chair, noting the radio and gramophone, card tables and games. Two men were playing on a repainted table tennis top.

Their quarters were now much better than a Sergeants' Mess, and for sheer artistic ability they excelled them all. As Jones explained, this was the first time that they had been trusted and considered capable of arranging their own affairs. Consequently they had all vied with each other to produce something special. There were neat lists of names and rotas of trucks, dates, times and units in order of visits. These were handed weekly to Pilot Officer Smart. From that time on they were left to their own devices. They only came to me with special requests or leave applications. They were always polite to Smart who had befriended them. I wisely asked no questions, although I did hear snatches of gossip when visiting Area HQ. or friends in Calcutta about some of their adventures around the town. They became a united force, and carefully separated such activities from their duties. My lovable rogues never failed any consignment trip to control units, and guarded me safely at all times. We had a special, unspoken bond of trust.

One of my best sources of news and gossip was a group of monks. They quietly carried out wonderful work amongst the many poor and outcasts in Calcutta. The pavements of Chowringhi, the main street, were strewn day and night with bodies of destitutes, and were stained with red juice from the betel nut, that was continuously chewed and spat out everywhere. Bullocks, cows, donkeys and other animals went unhindered through the streets. Nobody dared molest them and car and garry drivers waited patiently until they moved away. The monks invited me to their simple residence. Cool, stone washed walls and scrubbed plain flagstone floors, with a long, plain wooden table in the middle. No tablecloth, just rush mats under polished wooden fruit bowls. They served Indian vegetable curry with fruit and cool drinks, knowing I did not drink wine. They did not ask pointed questions but cleverly extracted information. They were wise to all the news of Calcutta but failed to draw me on my secret operations.

We enjoyed some pleasant evenings discussing all manner of themes, from philosophy to philology, books and life in general. They knew about the activities of my staffs' dealings with merchants, gambling joints and the Calcutta racecourse. They had apparently won a considerable quantity of rupees. I learnt with astonishment that jockeys who did not agree to fix races were whipped whilst riding, and finished with torn shirts that revealed great weals across their backs. But my men were discreet and watchful, as I learnt during a visit from Staff Officers. I was asked to escort them during their visit and we finished the day at a well known restaurant. I had parked my jeep behind their staff car and instructed their driver to keep careful watch. He left the vehicle for a few minutes and returned to find my jeep propped on its hubcaps, with all wheels gone. He called me out, dismayed at the inquest that would follow. Just then a familiar face appeared around the nearest corner saying, "Trouble, guv?" I pointed to my jeep, and he simply said, " just go back and leave it to us." So I kept the Staff Officers entertained for as long as possible, and eventually emerged from the restaurant with great trepidation. But there stood my jeep balanced on its four wheels looking as trim as ever. I drove back mightily relieved. I never discovered how it was done, but obviously my men knew the thieves, and won back my original wheels. A neat and efficient job all round. My respect for my staff grew since they were clearly familiar with the inner workings of Calcutta.

Any Other Ranks from forward units always headed straight for those famous quarters, but were only admitted after due inspection. First, they had to strip off their uniform, then shower and place their laundering in the washing machine. This was rigged from a large drum attached to a battery unit. A real laundry section. Tiffy Jones lived up to our RA ubique motto; solving problems everywhere. Personnel on leave said their greatest pleasure was using the lavatory chain, after their jungle experience of being close to nature. Then the exquisite feel of the cold shower, clearing the sweat and grime. These were simple pleasures for which Beck's Hotel grew in fame and popularity. I have retained many of the thank you notes that were often scribbled on odd scraps; for paper was scarce. All Signals ranks were grateful for our regular, duty visits, and the welfare supplies that accompanied every truckload. The Area O.C. always referred to us as Beck's Place. It was he who pointed out to HQ that I was entitled to the rank of Lt. Col. According to King's Regulations I was entitled to that rank after holding and serving in that position for over six months. I had actually served as O.C. for over two years. Anand Parbat were ignorant of Army Regulations and most annoyed at this ruling. They belatedly put through my Majority after reminder by Stevenson. But they had to admit I had done a solo job of running the whole Unit, with only one junior officer, Pilot Officer Smart, for whom I also requested an overdue promotion.

Lt. Col. Stevenson was now promoted to full Colonel and appointed O.C. Anand Parbat. He wrote to me indicating the existence of many problems, and requesting my help. I had done a good job in Calcutta between early 1943 to 1945 and they were about to hand over my Unit to another organisation. My seniority as Major was backdated to 1943 with my proper promotion as Lt. Col to follow. I was reluctant to give up my solo command because I had enjoyed real success under General Bill Slim. I was proud to be with the 14th Army. Protests came from our forward units and many visiting officers. I also received many pleasant tributes, including one from Bletchley, who were now sending Japanese decrypts direct. Full translations of Japanese messages and signals were now being sent direct to Bill Slim. WWIC had no viable role, it was never worth all the vast sums that were poured into it, since it had no real purpose. I still feel shame at that terrible, unnecessary extravagance. The ill-serving QM had been removed along with many of those costly civilian pretenders, but some still remained. Alas, my Unit and all our good work had to come to an end. We had a final farewell party. None of my team wished to accompany me to WWIC so I arranged transfers for them, as they requested, to the new Unit. I even managed to get two of them returned home because of family problems. Years later, I met one of them in London. He was the proud owner of a grocery/café which he had named 'Beck's Store.' What better tribute?

The remaining civilians spent more time in the Officers' Club in Delhi. To my amazement, the entire huge Western Wireless Intelligence Unit had all been moved, in my absence, to the maidan (meadow) at the bottom of the hill. My old friend Captain Bradbury explained that there was a rumour that the whole operation might be closed. They might be sent to more dangerous zones like Australia, which was now being attacked by the Japanese. Scared? These were merely delaying tactics, they were holding out to the end since they were now redundant.

Millions of rupees were simply wasted by moving the whole establishment down to the valley, only to be besieged by mosquitoes, flies and insects. It took literally months and for no valid reason. Everything and everybody was moved, at enormous cost and labour. Now they had cunningly arranged to move the whole, enormous operation back to the top of the hill. It really annoyed me to see those mountainous costs. I did my best to curtail luxury purchases and stop the enormous waste. It was enormously costly, compared with our successful operation at Heliopolis. We broke German codes with a small group of ten and did everything ourselves. We took turns to go out to the desert radio units, collecting and delivering. We did our duty without fuss and treated each other as colleagues, whether in uniform or civilian dress. We were an economic and highly successful unit when compared with this huge elephantine; the most costly enterprise in our whole Intelligence operation. It made me ashamed to think of my erstwhile comrades sweating it out in dangerous forward posts, taking down messages to be transmitted for deciphering.

I was relieved to receive orders to return home at the end of my overseas duty towards end of 1945. The war was over! We could sun ourselves on deck and relax without fear of U-boats. Soon after docking and reporting to our Units, we were allowed home. No red tape. Everybody was celebrating, so we were scarcely noticed. I had a lift in an army truck and duly arrived home with my trunks and gear. My family scarcely recognised me. I was burnt as brown as a native, and weighed under seven stone. Only my tropical uniform fitted me. The war against the Japanese was not yet over, and I felt guilty at leaving before they were finally defeated. The four years I had spent in the East had been an exciting adventure, which had made a marked difference to my life. I was now more mature and experienced, but somehow not yet ready, nor willing, to face civilian life. I was eager for more adventures, with no desire to return to a conventional humdrum life. I would have happily returned to Calcutta, to continue my best war years.

Chapter 9

Foreign Office (SO1):
Mission to German Universities in the Rhineland

Once the dust had settled, the Royal Artillery assigned me a Command over a large area of Germany, with full armour and troops. It felt strange to be wearing full uniform again with a polished Sam Browne belt. However, the Intelligence Service warned off the War Office, to my delight, since I had old scores to settle. I was advised to take some well-earned leave, and report back later for a new assignment. I was therefore able to relax at home after nearly five years abroad. The Smiths, who had remained proud owners of their smart shop on Ladbroke Grove, welcomed me back and suggested I stand for Parliament. Instead, I visited my home city of Bristol to see my relatives and renew old acquaintances. However, I suffered a tremendous emotional shock when emerging from Temple Meads railway station. I almost wept at the great catastrophe of disaster and dereliction before me. The whole of the centre of my beloved great city had been flattened, as though a giant hand had crushed a doll's house. I wandered about like a complete stranger, unable to recognise previously familiar streets. I was completely lost in the heart of my own, ancient city. All my world had vanished and been replaced by a pile of rubble.

The University was fairly intact, with Mr. Treasure, Chief Porter, still on duty. It was such a pleasure to wander about the main building and lecture rooms. They seemed smaller than in the early 1930's, when the University had a total complement of less than 1,500 students. Those were carefree years, with the odd threatening cloud from my experiences in Germany. My brave town of Bristol had survived all German efforts at mass destruction, and repairs were well underway. I found Grandmother Coburg, now 90, ensconced in a little apartment over the Christmas Steps. These connected Park Row to the Centre Gardens. Grandmother had the same bright eyes and rosy cheeks and was still living with Aunt Rose, my mother's younger sister. They were remnants of the age of gentlewomen and refinement. Both greeted me with great joy as the last surviving male, and always a favourite of my grandparents.

When my leave was up, I reported back to the Intelligence Service. To my surprise I was now under the jurisdiction of the Foreign Office. I was promoted to Senior Officer,

Grade 1. My remit was to supervise the denazification and 'resuscitation' of German Universities in the Rhineland. My headquarters were in the University of Cologne, with Bonn University some distance away, along the Autobahn. Cologne had been bombed, shelled and its centre completely smashed during the British Army's progress across the Rhine. All the bridges had been destroyed, principally by the Nazis themselves, to cover their hasty retreat. The Americans had crossed the Rhine here and General Patton had built a strong, temporary bridge across the Rhine for all traffic. The Americans were the first to enter Cologne, but only briefly. They had re-appointed the previous Oberbürgermeister (Lord Mayor) Konrad Adenauer. He was famous for establishing a green belt around Cologne. As Catholic Head of the Christian Democratic Union he had been imprisoned by the Nazis on the borders of Italy, and was later rescued by the British. Nevertheless he'd been sacked soon afterwards by a newly appointed British General, who'd lacked experience, competence, and proper briefing. This had been a stupid act that was never totally forgiven. Obviously, this situation had serious consequences. In one foolish move, the inexperienced General had destroyed carefully crafted diplomatic relationships.

Adenauer had bitterly resented the indignity of dismissal out of hand by a junior officer. He had received a curt phone call ordering him to clear his office immediately, and get out. Despite the fact that he had been rescued by the British, he never forgave this affront to his dignity. He later plotted with General de Gaulle against the British. I did remind him, that as Leader of CDU, he might gain a far more important job as Chancellor of Germany. As an academic he talked freely to me. After all, I had the honourable task of helping the recovery of German Universities. He had no inkling of my Intelligence background and certainly helped me with useful introductions. There was no denying that I needed these, since I had considerable problems tackling the hopeless state of repair, and re-establishment of German Universities.

Adenauer loved good coffee, which was virtually unobtainable post-war. German ersatz (substitute) Kaffee was reputedly made from trees! His first visits to my office in Cologne University early 1946 therefore, were more for my fresh coffee than for welfare of the University. I also had the only genuine heating, so my office was doubly welcoming. I gave him use of a room when he needed one, and this established friendly relations. It was a relationship that paid good dividends and helped me to obtain building materials, which the Town Council could not provide. I also met some of his close friends, who were pleased to be lubricated by my good coffee! I was primarily interested in University politics, and they were complicated by the petty dictator Rector Kroll. Adenauer had been instrumental in the appointment of his successor, Lord Mayor, Herr Pünder, who copied him so closely that he was called Herr Pündenauer.

I came to know the Adenauer family, and it was clear that Bonn was chosen as the seat of the first post-war German Government because the family home was situated in the town. Adenauer's brother was Professor emeritus of Cologne University, and his sister was married to the Town Clerk. I met her often at meetings that were held in the temporary Rathaus, since the old Town Council building had been completely demolished. I was invited to Council meetings as an honorary member to advise on Cologne's restoration. I tried my best to resolve the labour and material shortages. I even persuaded our local Army Unit to lend a hand. They were truly grateful for this help, particularly for the services of the engineers. But when I mentioned the University they threw up their hands, saying it was almost bottom of their very long list of essential reconstruction priorities.

The Americans had demolished Cologne while they were busily chasing the fleeing German Army, and they had hastily accepted the offer made by Professor Kroll to resume control of the University. He had been the previous Rector, hence I was greeted by him when I arrived early 1946. He quoted his American authority for assuming official command of the University. He could be very persuasive and used what I came to recognise as his 'honeyed approach.' He tried to convince me that without his authority, nothing could progress within the University. This was patently untrue of course. The University was badly damaged and inoperable, but so far he had achieved nothing whatsoever.

I reminded him that Cologne was within the British Occupation Zone, and he clearly came under our jurisdiction. He could make no decisions without our permission. There was no life in the empty, broken University. Furthermore no staff or students could be accepted until I had reviewed, checked and questioned each one of them, including the Rector. Everyone had to be screened, to ensure that they had never given support to the Nazis or been a member of the Nazi Party. The Rector was a self-appointed official, without office or support. I showed him my authority to assume total control of the University, and assured him that he was unable to make any appointments of any kind, without first consulting me and obtaining my permission. Once he recognised my authority, he climbed down from his assumed height and, perforce, agreed with all the terms and conditions I had laid down. At least he did on a superficial level, but he was a cunning man, and did his best get his own way by employing underhand methods. He produced documents and academics for my inspection. What he failed to realise, was that I was already in possession of their Fragebogen, Nazi style questionnaires. These were discovered by my Intelligence colleagues. Thus I was able to study the true history of the university staff, before hearing their current versions of the truth. They dared not lie to the Nazis for fear of their lives. I had yet to learn Kroll's overpowering desire to become permanent Chancellor of Köln University, and his cunning manoeuvres to assume absolute command. He would go to any lengths to maintain his self-assigned position as Supremo, rather than return to teaching.

Sifting through the records became a long and wearisome process. I worked continually throughout the nights preparing each day's interviews with staff candidates. My first priority was to ensure that the senior appointments of Deans and Heads of Faculties were 'clean' and trustworthy, since they had to bear the responsibility of creating a sound infrastructure of lecturers and students, to promote the organic growth of each Faculty. Then I made a careful inspection of the structural damages that had been caused to university buildings, to assess the possibility of partial use. It was immediately obvious, that reopening the university would be impossible without a great deal of outside help. There was considerable damage to infrastructure doors and windows. It was a desperately cold winter, and electricity and water were unavailable. The whole complex was in sorry state and needed extensive interior and exterior repair. Many sections also needed to be totally rebuilt from scratch. Kroll just shook his head helplessly. He had an overwhelming desire to be Supremo, but lacked the mental strength of purpose to command and control. He simply used cunning to get his way. He was a man of words, very wordy! He enjoyed making long speeches on every possible occasion, but real action was left to others. Outside the University he was powerless.

I informed Kroll that his first duty was to seek material and physical help, in order to get the University up and running as a viable academic institution. This displeased him. He did not regard such hard labour as being within his remit as a lofty academic. He, of course, sought the easy way out and appealed to the already overstretched Town Council. He received a curt reply. The university was very low on their long list of priorities and he was told to seek help elsewhere. He had to admit total failure. He was useless beyond his academic duties, and I came to suspect some of his activities in this area, when I carried out my detailed survey. Thus the University remained closed, in a semi-derelict state, until I was free to take a hand with repairs.

My official Foreign Office contact to whom I sent my regular reports, was a charming, raven-haired senior lady, Principal Officer Grade 1. We enjoyed a good working relationship throughout my years in Germany. I sometimes made amusing comments on my monthly reports about Rektor Kroll's peculiar behaviour, and other matters of interest. As a result of my work with German universities, she asked me to make a lecture tour of Swiss, Dutch and Belgian Universities. These institutions were all interested in the restoration work in the British Zone. Thereafter, I gave lectures to British Universities, including Bristol, to explain our work. This task was extended to include other areas of higher education; as well as those of an Intelligence nature. My original remit was thus widened considerably. I was entrusted with queries from other Universities, mainly British. They all wanted information about academia, and possible contacts with Professors, and other notables, including Members of Parliament.

My primary task of ensuring the denazification of academic staff, was completed with the aid of the Nazi Fragebogen. I then concentrated on the students. On the whole, the academic staff had not been pro-Nazi, nor suborned. But there were exceptions. It took months to check all the staff and then every single student application. There were thousands of the latter, including ex-service personnel, who were all carefully screened for a Nazi background. The majority of staff remained quietly aloof and feared snoopers. I had the support of a quorum of good academics who had suffered under the Nazis. They had confidence in the British and soon accepted me in good faith, since I was intent on restoring the University and their positions. I arranged for some of them to visit British Universities.

One of my worst cases was that of a notorious Cologne Professor of Philosophy. Records clearly showed him to be a well-known and prominent Nazi sympathiser. He'd even written poems praising Hitler, and lectured on the benefits of Nazi creed. Of course this made a travesty of his philosophy lectures. They were worse than Heidegger, whose lectures I'd heard in Freiburg in the 1930s. This pro-Nazi, Professor Bertram, was decisively refused entry to the University; a decision that had the unanimous backing of all University staff. He wrote angry letters threatening to lead his former students to attack me! He never ceased his considerable ability of string-pulling. He actually caused a question to be raised in Parliament, concerning this young officer who refused the renowned Professor of Philosophy his natural right to return to his department in Cologne University. Members of Parliament questioned Foreign Office officials, who referred the matter to me. I quoted senior members of university staff who were ashamed of his pro-Nazi conduct. His behaviour was unbefitting a Professor, especially one of Philosophy. In my report I enclosed one of his poems praising Hitler, along with other primary evidence of his career during those Nazi years. This information silenced all questions in the House.

The task of checking student applications was again assisted by Intelligence reports. My Intelligence colleagues discovered many Fragebogen. But there were many others, especially those who were returning from the German Forces, whose applications had to be carefully examined. These were followed by personal interviews. There were thousands of applications, and we hoped to admit those students who were most likely to benefit from a university education. Once I had completed initial screenings, I set up a Board of trustworthy senior staff, to vet all remaining applicants according to age and academic qualities. They were instructed to select the maximum possible for first and second year admittance. My Intelligence colleagues kept a close watch. The following primary questions were considered:

1) Age of youngest applicants circa 18. Were they active members of Hitlerjugend, wearing Nazi uniforms, heavily indoctrinated with marching and propaganda parades and war exercises, excused school activities, leaders of local or regional or

national groups? Or whether refrained from taking any part in the Nazi movement? Family reaction?

2) Over 18 to 25. Were they Nazi members, active or non-active? –details of type of membership and activity. Blackshirt SS or Brownshirts, rank and responsibility. (SS members were generally eliminated, since they were Hitler's bodyguards, his elite force and guilty of the vilest crimes.)

3) Service experience: Length of service, rank, decorations, where, when and especially whether taking part in holocaust, mass murder or massacres anywhere. Essential to discover the truth of their activities – often supplied by Intelligence. Check for concealed identities or failure to report essential facts

4) Because of the huge demand, careful screening of older applicants most necessary. Only small part of the University was usable, so we had perforce to limit the number of acceptances, for sheer lack of space and facilities, including lack of suitable academic staff, with many missing.

It was astounding how many obvious lies were told, how many influential strings were pulled, how much obvious and surreptitious bribery was offered. Most seemed to expect the British to adhere to a continuation of the old Nazi system. We had an amusing case of an old farm woman with her son. He had spent most of his life working on the small family farm, far away from Nazi influence. Yet his education had been carefully monitored by his mother's compelling desire for a better life for her son. Consequently, she placed a large parcel before me with the plea that I look kindly on her son's application. The parcel was unwrapped to reveal a large chunk of raw meat, still dripping with blood. This was her obvious sacrifice of food, since meat was especially scarce and almost impossible to obtain in Cologne. Taken aback by this gory, yet somehow strangely innocent and clumsy attempt at bribery, I just had to laugh, especially at the look of horror on the faces of my staff. They expected me to whisk her off to prison. Instead, I told her to rewrap her offering. I explained that unlike the Nazis, we sought justice without bribery or coercion. Her son would be judged solely by the same criterion as all the others. Her son then came forward and apologised for his mother's mistake. They had lived an isolated life on their smallholding, and had kept away from all the troubles. I then reassured his mother that we were really human beings, and not monsters like the Nazis. According to my list, her son had a good, clean record and would be admitted.

There were, of course, academics and students who had resisted Nazis. Timorous, gentle, little Professor Jachmann, Head of Classics had shown great courage. Nazis had demanded that all academics join the Nazi party, or suffer expulsion from universities. He, along with a small group of friends had held out against all intimidation. He showed me his radio that was hidden carefully in his cellar, with which he'd listened with his wife and friends, to BBC broadcasts. Such behaviour was strictly forbidden by the Nazis and there were dire threats of punishment. Extreme courage and bravery for that timid little man, who earned my respect. His next-door neighbour and close friend, was a more colourful character. Professor Rumpf was the internationally famous Head of Archaeology. He had spent many earlier years digging and exploring in Egypt. He and his wife, another sterling character, refused point blank to join or have anything whatsoever to do with the Nazis. He'd even refused to give the Nazi salute. Somehow they left him alone.

As an example of his strength of character, I learnt that as the Allies advanced towards the Rhine, the University staff were all ordered to the barricades, to erect fortifications. Kroll, then Rektor, made academic staff march with spades to the ramparts. Rumpf was always missing. He was ordered to turn up under Kroll's threat of reporting his defiance to Nazi authorities. He arrived late, armed only with his umbrella, on which he leant whilst entertaining his colleagues with stories of his adventures. He would rather have sallied forth to welcome the British, who were coming to free them from the Nazi barbarians. They were a bonny pair who would not submit to Nazi threats. Their house was full of trophies from digs all over the world. They genuinely loved England, and viewed it as the land of freedom. They hated the Nazis as barbarians, but as Rumpf explained, the Germans were lost without a leader (Führer) of real strength. Before the madness of Hitler there was the vanity of the Kaiser, and before him, the brutality of Bismark and his Prussians.

My local Intelligence Group were most helpful in discovering records and background information. But they too, could make mistakes, and make judgements on circumstantial evidence. One outrageous case, was a demand by Intelligence for the immediate dismissal of the Professor of Clinical Medicine, Knipping, who was famous for the development of the Iron Lung. He had a small room with special apparatus which could take over a patient's breathing completely, for lungs and heart treatment. My trustworthy friends laughed to scorn any suggestion that Knipping had been a Nazi. Yes, they knew he had been awarded a gold medal by the Nazis, but in odd circumstances, as they related. Knipping belonged to their anti-Nazi group and had never joined the Party. He concentrated on saving lives and almost lived inside his department, seeking new methods of lung treatment.

Working alone one day, he was confronted by black-clad SS officers carrying a severely wounded man; they demanded an immediate operation in strict secrecy. Knipping initially refused, saying that he needed assistance and had to keep exact medical records. But they demanded absolute secrecy and claimed that they would assist. Knipping could not refuse. The patient had suffered severe bullet wounds in his chest and abdomen. Knipping warned them that the situation was nigh on hopeless. But they knew his reputation and insisted that he operate immediately. He did so successfully, then stitched and bandaged the patient and the SS officers carried him out. Knipping was persuaded to take an oath of silence and did not reveal anything of the incident.

About six months later, a ceremony was held in the University by leading Nazi officers. They praised the University, and especially the Department of Medicine, for the work they did for the hospital, which was attached to the University. They publicly thanked Knipping for saving the life of an important Nazi leader, and awarded him a gold medal. Subsequently, Nazi supervision of the University was withdrawn and academics were more or less left in peace. Naturally, colleagues were astounded by this affair, of which they knew absolutely nothing. Knipping explained how he had been sworn to secrecy, in fear of his life. I asked what would have happened had he failed to save the leader's life. He replied "they would have ensured my eternal silence." I presented the details to my Intelligence Section who were convinced by the evidence placed before them. Thereafter they visited him often. Knipping had a great sense of fun and frequently held weekend family parties with colleagues and friends, to which the two Intelligence men were invited.

I first heard about these parties from Knipping's closest friend, Dr Lewin, a Jewish gynaecologist who had survived Concentration Camps. Knipping had a big, strong, robust frame with strong surgeon's hands and a tremendous fund of witty stories. Lewin was the opposite, he had a slim frame, dark oval face and long, slender fingers. They looked complete opposites, yet they would drink, sing and make music together. Most of all they enjoyed their new found freedom to work unhampered. Dr Lewin had a curious history. His father was a famous Professor of Gynaecology at Berlin University, and his son had followed in his footsteps. The father died in a Concentration Camp, but his son was made to assist the brutal surgeons who were conducting medical experiments on prisoners. Many of these became victims of the Holocaust. Lewin could not bear it and fainted. His life was saved because he lanced a huge boil on the warder's neck, and he became cook for the prisoners. He foraged among leftovers from the guards' meals. Somehow he survived and was finally released. He made his way back to the British Zone, but he still looked like a skeleton.

The University advertised urgently for a Lecturer in Gynaecology, who was also required to work in the University Hospital. The number of patients was increasing rapidly and the current hospital staff could not cope with the work load. Lewin's application was turned down repeatedly. After the third rejection, a colleague advised him to seek help from the British Officer in charge of the University. Finally he plucked up courage to seek an interview, and I offered him a cup of coffee. He looked at me as though I were some strange creature. I was dressed in mufti, sports jacket and trousers. I did not resemble any of the officers he had met before. He had survived several Concentration Camps, and simply sought a normal life working within his profession. I could not understand why he had not been snapped up immediately by the Faculty, who were urgently seeking a gynaecologist. There were no other applicants, but an overall shortage of good gynaecologists and doctors. Lewin was also a trained professional lecturer, he had been brought up in the University of Berlin under his famous father. Gradually I extracted the reason. Even now, despite the good atmosphere I had managed to engender in the University, despite ridding the institution of past Nazi members and restraints, there still existed this unhealthy and inexplicable anti-Jewish feeling. Nazi rhetoric had been so persistent and all pervading, that even the Medical Faculty had become indoctrinated. Indeed, some of the earliest members of the Nazi Party had been newly qualified doctors.

I attended all Faculty meetings where staff, department and student problems were discussed. I discovered their real needs, and was often able to obtain help from different sources. I had not been aware of the slightest tinge of anti-Jewish feeling anywhere. There was not a single Jewish member of the academic staff, but this was not surprising, for the Nazis had removed and exterminated almost all of them, along with Jews of all other professions. At the next Medical Faculty meeting I raised the subject of Dr Lewin's applications. There was a dead silence! Then Professor Veidt, the Dean, attempted to provide a clumsy excuse. He claimed that his qualifications did not cover their requirements. I quoted details of Lewin's academic and medical record and qualifications. I also pointed out that they were in urgent need of his services, and there were no other applicants. There was a long silence. I then told them clearly that they had not yet eradicated the awful crime of anti-semitism from within the university. This crime had impregnated their systems, to their shame and before the whole world. As academics, people of supposedly higher intelligence, this crime was unforgivable. Then I rose, saying "I cannot personally engage anybody for your University. I simply leave it to your conscience, with your duty and responsibility to the students and patients of this, your University of Cologne."

A week later, I discovered that Dr. Lewin had been engaged officially and at his proper grade. At our following Faculty meeting, I was astonished to hear reams of praise for the way Lewin had energetically set about his work. He was already popular with the students and gave interesting, lively and informative lectures. The hospital patients were also extremely grateful to be receiving proper treatment at last. My admonition had penetrated. It took just one month for a complete turnaround in attitudes and everybody was happy. Lewin was grateful and kept in touch with me after I left Germany. He was offered a senior post in one University after another and became Dean and Head of Gynaecology. He had a distinguished career until he eventually died from the effects of the Concentration Camps. His wife informed me of his death. He was a gentle, lovable soul, who finally achieved well deserved fame.

Now I had to turn my attention to the physical and material state of the University. The conditions for study and the personal situations of students left a lot to be desired. Cologne had been heavily bombed by the Americans and the centre was in ruins. However, the Dom, the twin towered cathedral, had only suffered slight damage. Curiously, the offices of Thomas Cook on one side of the cathedral, and the Swiss owned hotel Excelsior on the other, were quite undamaged. As one walked through the broken streets at night, little lights seemed to flicker underfoot; they emanated from cellars that had withstood the bombing and been converted into homes. The Rathaus Council area had been completely destroyed, along with the shopping centre, theatre, cinemas and the electricity and water systems. There were over twenty thousand breaks in the water and cable systems around the University area. Consequently it was a desolate place.

The winter of 1946 was the coldest since the turn of the century. For me, who had not long returned from the heat of the Eastern sun, the bitter cold was excruciating. I wore two sets of everything, but still rattled inside like a pea in a pod. Students wore all the clothing they could find, and sat huddled up in each draughty lecture room. These rooms were without windows and doors, and without heating. Staff meetings were held in an attempt to resolve the problems, but in vain. Even the Mensa kitchens below, though scarcely damaged, were out of use. Previously they had been a great feature of University life. The food was served by nuns and the meals were cheap and wholesome. Now they were inoperative and the students were left to their own devices, to forage for any food available.

I was invited to the Town Council Meetings by Adenauer's sister, to discuss plans for the re-establishment of the town. There was a desperate shortage of skilled staff and workers. Returned servicemen were few on the ground and they were at their wits' end. I suggested a feasible plan to restore the University: I intended to persuade students to dig the trenches themselves and repair water pipes and cables in return for labourers' pay and, more importantly, proper workmen's meals. No official contract was needed, just a 'gentleman's agreement.' This suggestion prompted a laugh, but on discussion, council members could see that this arrangement could bring about a genuine advantage to both students and the university. Though unfortunately they could not supply window glass nor timber. However, I was not easily put off. I had gained my first necessity of solid workmen's meals for the participating students. This arrangement was much more valuable than worthless money.

A general meeting of students was called to discuss my project, which was greeted with enthusiasm. Students particularly liked the idea of receiving solid workmens' meals daily, as food was so scarce. The bargain was kept on both sides, and the young men and women did sterling work. I visited glass makers, timber merchants and companies that had been past benefactors. They were surprised to find a British Officer, and friend of

Adenauer, calling on them on behalf of the University. They became co-operative and, to the surprise of Rektor Kroll and Deans, who had made only feeble attempts to obtain help, the restoration work was carried out within reasonable time. I decided that the academics were not good at the material work of administration, whereas the Army was a strong teacher of 'needs must.' Eventually large numbers of male and female students were cheerfully digging and repairing underground cables, just like ordinary workmen. This engendered a new respect and I won new friends; to the surprise of the British Control Commission, who were struggling to gain cooperation with German Industry. I had bargained a straightforward, completely honest deal, that was solely for the benefit of the University and students. There had been no money or favours on either side! I obviously had nothing to gain personally, except the gratitude of staff and students.

At least the terrible draughts had been eliminated. We even managed to persuade some of the nuns to restart the Mensa ovens, and prepare scratch meals of thin soup and grey, lumpy bread. Some of the students were from farming families and they donated sacks of potatoes and vegetables, and meat which they had previously hoarded. Farmers were prone to do this in time of crisis. Gradually the situation improved, as did the general outlook of students. Their attitudes towards me also changed, from deep suspicion at first, to final acceptance that I was working with them simply as an academic. They had expected officialdom, curt orders and the bullying tactics that had been used by Nazi officials.

At that time I was approached by the local theatre management. Cologne's popular theatre had been heavily bombed and was unusable, but most of the costumes and props had been saved. There was a great demand for theatre and music, since these helped to restore community interest and hope for the future. The management had been unable to find a hall big enough and in reasonable condition for their needs. The University had a Great Hall and Aula with its own floor, stage and seating, which had been preserved in fair condition. With some improvement, these could be made serviceable. They were advised by the cognoscenti to approach me first and get my agreement, having heard of some of my ultra vires activities. I clearly saw the advantages and promised to get permission for the theatre to use these facilities. It took time to persuade the University administration, but students were enthusiastic.

The decision provided an excellent possibility for making the University the centre of the town's cultural life. To have theatre, music, and dramatic arts centred in the University would solve many problems. It was a master stroke of luck for the University. It was also my personal pleasure to be in consultation with the theatre directors, management and bursar. The Foreign Office was delighted. Kroll now sought to assume control, but as usual he was all talk and no action. Therefore, we arranged for a reliable team of delighted students to work with the theatre group. The organisation went well and progressed surprisingly quickly. Different departments were organised, and the necessary restoration work was carried out, assisted by my new building friends and many students. The stage was equipped with lights and backdrops. The auditorium had its seating, which consisted of an odd assortment of chairs and armchairs, that were old and restored and obtained from various nooks and crannies. Everybody joined in enthusiastically. We were all united in a worthy project that offered a revival of cultural life. I had started a comprehensive, fully satisfying, voluntary joint effort.

There was a circular gallery that ran almost around the hall, which was divided off into boxes. This structure suited me admirably, since my office was directly opposite a secluded box, which allowed me full view of all the entertainment. The orchestra was recreated, with old and new talent, and rehearsals began with vigour. Within a few months the first theatre performances commenced, in the autumn of 1947. They were absolutely sold out in advance. Despite the cold, because the heating was not yet fully restored, packed audiences came fully wrapped in an astonishing variety of clothes, beneath their coats and cloaks. The theatre was a phenomenal success from the outset, and the University became the centre of the cultural life of Cologne. Many of the artistes, actors, musicians and singers became famous. They were engaged to sing and perform on the Koelner Rundfunk (radio broadcast station) and thus obtained necessary sustenance and fame. The BBC became aware and interested.

The academic life of the University was now progressing smoothly, and I attended lectures and staff meetings, to check that all was well. The English department had suffered badly and newly qualified lecturers had been engaged. I also helped out as often as possible, to the general satisfaction of students and staff. I sought permission from Foreign Office to begin an exchange programme of professors and lecturers. This was agreed, and in 1947 I began to send carefully selected German professors and young lecturers to British Universities. They could scarcely believe that the academic world outside would be prepared to recognise their existence, let alone meet them personally. But I knew the danger of keeping them too closely confined with their feelings of guilt. The Foreign Office had approved my plan immediately, and contacted a range of Universities. The exchange programme was essential in terms of building better relations, and resuming old academic acquaintances. Oxford in particular, was most helpful, and invited me over for discussions. I had enjoyable meetings with many professors who were interested in my projects, especially those who knew some of Cologne's academic staff from before the War. Most interested were Lord Lindsay of Balliol, and the Professors of Classics, German and History of our leading Universities.

At the beginning of the War the Cologne University Librarian feared for the safety of their precious well-stocked library. The books were carefully packed and sent to a safe haven, deep in forest areas. They now lay between the American and Russian Zone. We held secret discussions about the return of that valuable library, with me making a personal 'recce,' to check exact positions and best routes. With the help of the local

Military Government, who enjoyed this secret operation, Army Trucks were borrowed. The journey was made secretly by night and all the books were safely returned to Cologne University. This was one of my most successful enterprises. My new friend was the Bodlean Librarian, with whom I stayed, after being shown all the secret treasures of the Bodlean, above and below ground. Some were chained to posts and carefully concealed from public gaze, mainly because of their great age and value. It was a fascinating experience. He now made lists of German books that he needed and those he could spare for our needs. We supplied many of our duplicates on his list, including Mein Kampf. A fair and equitable exchange was made and a friendly, enjoyable association continued.

Around this time, I was visited by the Head of Cologne Musikhochschule (Music Academy), whose buildings were threatened with closure by local Military Government. They were claiming them for administrative work. He was almost in tears as he quoted the history of this famous academy. It had been responsible for producing some of the greatest international musical talent, and for training great singers. At his invitation, I visited his beloved academy, and was much impressed by the quality of singers, staff and eager students. The area O.C. knew nothing of this problem, that had been caused by the same junior officers who had been thwarted by me from removing 'clean,' good, pro-British professors like Rumpf and Jachmann from their homes. As usual, he was fully prepared to trust my judgement, and warned those unthinking juniors not to interfere with my operations ever again. When I informed the Professor that all was safe he embraced me in typical artistic fervour, and made me honorary President of the Musikhochschule. My reward was to suffer from expected appearances at all their concerts henceforth. To demonstrate his eternal gratitude he continued to send me notices of annual meetings, major concert events and successes, long after I left Germany.

I attended student meetings, and listened to their woes and grievances. Food and lodging came first. Then books, writing and study materials, some of which I was able to supply with the aid of well-wishers from the Military Government. Colonel Kent was most supportive of my efforts and always prepared to help me. He had served with distinction during the war, and was now doing a good job engendering civilian control. Some of his junior, inexperienced, newly commissioned staff delighted in fomenting trouble, even between their own officers. I learnt a lot about these childish, irresponsible actions from Joan Davis, the officer responsible for the visa section, who later became my wife.

Germans could not leave the British Zone without a visa, and these were only granted after proof that they were on an acceptable mission. My professors had no trouble visiting other Universities, until one History Professor came to see me in indignation. He had been refused a visa by a lady Officer. At the Visa Office I was told by this blond young maiden, with great assurance, that she had refused the visa firstly, because he was a Military Historian, who was engaged in the research of battles and wars, and Intelligence thought he was suspect. Secondly, because his mission was to visit a brewery in the French Zone, of which he was a Director. I assured Miss Davis that his only possible crime was his close friendship with Rektor Kroll, and an assertion from reliable sources, that the pair, who were neighbours, were guilty of wife swapping. I then invited her to dine at the Officers Club. This relationship culminated in our marriage, which took place at the British Consulate, Düsseldorf and was celebrated at the Yacht Club.

Although Cologne was a major University, it had never possessed Students' Halls of Residence, or Residential Colleges, like British Universities. This was normal in the days when students habitually wandered between various universities, to study under eminent Professors. Hence the old term of 'wandering students'. But now lodgings were difficult to find and many were compelled to sleep rough in huts or odd shelters. Something needed to be done, but the Town Council had more than enough problems. From local Intelligence, I learnt of a big Nazi-owned country estate in a suburb of Cologne called Burg Wahn, situated near the railway. The Nazi owner had been killed so we had no trouble in confiscating the estate for a first Students' Residence, which became a great success. It was also the best possible venue for the very first International Vacation Course. I planned this first international course with great detail, and it was an outstanding success. Once the idea had been 'floated' through my Principal in the Foreign Office, the academic world outside showed great enthusiasm and eagerly participated.

It was a momentous beginning for a series of vacation courses. Following on from these, we sent German students to British Universities. Their cautious but friendly reception encouraged British students to begin visiting German Universities. Other German Universities followed suit, and opened up their own Students' Residences, and exchange programmes. Students, who were chosen for the first visits, displayed a new optimistic spirit. Like the junior Lektors, they returned full of fresh ideas. Prevalent fears of being hated subsided. Students wanted to prove themselves trustworthy. My real aim was to develop a good core of students, who would adopt a truly democratic attitude for the future. It was important not to leave a bitter enmity behind. But I must confess that I have never lost my mistrust. The generous financial and other relief that stemmed from America and Britain was being used to good purpose. The Education Minister for the Rhineland was Frau Teusch, who visited me and showed great interest in my Student Hall of Residence project. Seven further Students' Residences were opened for Cologne and Bonn Universities. Bonn was about 20 miles distance away but also my responsibility. It was originally the Prussian University, and had fortunately escaped the tremendous damage that had been inflicted on Cologne.

I had a visit from a party of British MP's, who approved my work and asked me to guide them around the town. They were particularly keen to see the famous Dom and meet Cardinal Frings, who was a courageous anti-Nazi. Though short in stature, he was an imposing and thoroughly independent figure. Several times the Nazis, who hated his outspoken criticism of their brutality, sought to depose and imprison him. At one time a posse was sent to drag him from his Cathedral. He dressed in full panoply, and slowly descended the steps wearing all his orders and red robes, bearing his great Staff of Office. The officer was so intimidated, that he bowed and withdrew with his men, and never returned.

The freezing winter of 1946 caused many civilian deaths. There was a lack of coal and heating fuel, and a new German verb 'Fringsen' was created. Trains passed through Cologne carrying briquettes made from coaldust. Cardinal Frings preached in the Cathedral that the Bible permitted parents of families with little children to 'help themselves' to essentials, that were needed to keep their families alive. He would not condemn, as police had demanded, the citizens who waited at certain places where trains had to slow down, then jumped onto the trucks, and threw piles of briquettes to their grateful families and friends. That operation became known as 'Fringsen,' and I watched it secretly. The whole operation was carefully planned and executed, to give some families the warmth they needed in their homes, and fuel for cooking.

Problems now arose from the volte face of Bevin, who was now Labour Foreign Minister. Our previous remit had centred on eliminating the Nazi element and laying a firm foundation for the future, trying to encourage good, anti-Nazi, democratically minded Germans. This had been a major task, which had required careful preparation. The emergence of Cold War politics, had shifted foreign policy towards a focus on anti-Communism. My Intelligence Section, especially Officer Faitelson who was deputed to guard my safety and keep me informed on German reactions, informed me of the latest instructions. All our work plans and schedules became an absolute fiasco. Intelligence Group had kept me informed on political movements, and taken me to some Communist Party meetings. They were poorly attended and full of revamped old clichés, that were mainly directed at still surviving Nazi members. Communists would ferret them out and pass details to Intelligence, in the hope that they would deal with them. But there were only a few poorly organised Communist cells.

Our British Royal Engineers discovered the German Volkswagen plant within the British Zone. They found the original plans of the real Volkswagen, known by the Germans as the People's Car. Hitler had promised one of these cars to every German worker, with each contributing a percentage of their weekly wages. It was another total deceit by Hitler. The money was punctiliously collected, with all believing that they would become owners of these beetle shaped cars. None were made. Instead they built armoured Jeeps for the Army. Our clever Royal Engineers built the authentic, original

Volkswagen, from the draft plans they discovered. They then received permission from the Foreign Office to manufacture a small quantity. These were offered to a selection of senior officers. For £110, I became the owner of an original Volkswagen. Although we were allotted confiscated German cars, it was my pleasure to drive my own little car.

Unfortunately, six weeks later it was stolen. My Intelligence friends immediately informed the International Police Network, and warned me that it was unlikely to be recovered. Cars were stolen daily, and driven over borders to be sold with no control. However, about three months later, I received a phone call from the International Police to go to Police HQ in Antwerp. On arrival, I recognised my car and heard the story of a policeman, who'd spotted it in a back street garage, kept under surveillance. I was invited to examine the battery that was fixed under the rear seat, and was amazed to find two batteries, one under each seat. One was fixed correctly. The other a dummy had been used for diamond smuggling. Hence the neat little cells inside the mock battery. Only diamond dust was left, they said. They sent me on my way rejoicing.

On my return, my students unveiled a plan to recover some wine. University Library books were not the only things to be concealed in other Zones. A large quantity of quality wine had been carefully stored in what had now become the French Zone. Petrol was scarce and almost unobtainable by ordinary citizens. But here I was with my own private car, fully stocked with petrol. 'Surely I must look reasonably on their most deserving case!' So I arranged visas for them to leave the British Zone with the most trustworthy in charge. Two days later they returned with my car laden with this precious cargo. I was invited to their celebrations, but thought it wise to excuse myself on the grounds that I did not drink. However, I discovered that my Intelligence friends attended, for they had monitored both the operation and me. Always acting, they assured me, as my guardian angels, whilst enjoying the spoils. The student entrepreneurs had sustained a slight accident with my car en route, but one's father owned a garage and overhauled and repainted my car. They returned it in impeccable condition, except for the colour. It was now a beautiful shade of yellow. Consequently, everybody knew where I was at any given moment.

In 1947, I was approached by the Intelligence Unit to investigate an awkward trade union situation in Bielefeld. This was an industrial town famous for cars, bicycles and railway work. A trade union leader named Jahn was so strongly anti-Nazi, that he was forced to flee from Germany with his family, and was given refuge in England. Now he had returned to Bielefeld, and was being prevented from entering his own house, and from returning to his work on the railway. He was also unable to reassume his union leadership. In fact, the Mayor had made it clear that he was unwelcome and should return to England. The family was ostracised and in great difficulty, because there was a strong clique who remained in total power, and had deliberately frozen him out. I drove to Bielefeld and met the local Intelligence Unit, who provided me with the facts. I discovered that Bielefeld, which had been taken over entirely by Nazis in the 1930's, was still totally under Nazi control. The Mayor and Council were all ex-Nazis. Jahn's Union had been smashed by the Nazis and was only just reforming. The union needed his help to fight against the Nazi Mayor and his supporters, who were still in power.

It took just one interview with the Mayor and his cohorts, to have the whole den of thieves removed from power. They were forced to return all the property and possessions they had confiscated. They had been ruthless in their wholesale thieving, and had even stashed away some of their ill-gotten gains outside Germany. With the aid of the British Police unit, who were gladly supported by a great many townspeople, this operation was quickly carried out. Herr Jahn's house and possessions were restored to him, and he immediately began to reform his Union. It was a quick concise operation, which I thoroughly enjoyed. It felt like I had cleaned out a horde of evil rats. I left it to my Intelligence colleagues to clear up the town. Courts and judges were reinstated and I returned to Cologne. With the Jahn family back in their own house, they embraced me and presented me with a big red-covered Book of Bielefeld at my final farewell party. This gift was inscribed with their thanks and it remains a precious memento. Intelligence colleagues were now ordered to cease their worthy anti-nazi efforts. They believed that it was completely the wrong policy, to switch their efforts totally to the elimination of a few Communist cells, which had little validity; except in East Berlin, which was under Russian rule. However, I continued doing my original job and was still supported by the Foreign Office. Every day was important in our efforts to re-educate the students.

Before the end of 1948 came the final blow from Bevin, who issued bureaucratic instructions without seeking our advice. We were told to begin handing over responsibility to the Germans, to run their own affairs. This transition was exactly what we were aiming for, but only when the time was right. We had planned for general hand-over in 1950, after their valueless currency had been changed for a new, valid currency. I believe that Bevin's decision was taken too early and without proper consideration. He was generally disliked throughout our Occupation area, since he never sought any advice from us. Petty dictator Kroll, now revealed his plan to become the life long Rektor of Cologne University. The rules of office were carefully laid down at its foundation in 1388, and these insisted on the annual election of Rektor and Deans. Kroll had visions of greatness, as Commander in Chief, though he'd never worn a military uniform. He had built a group of supporters amongst Deans and senior staff. He had been the last Rektor under the Nazis. Now he was craftily seeking to change the ancient established rules in order to allow him full power to rule continuously. He was so besotted with a power complex that he no longer had any desire to teach. He simply wanted to be the all powerful Führer of the University.

He quickly brought back some of his old supporters, and tried to lay the foundations for his future control of the University. He had convinced them that he alone had the power to deal with the harsh, iron-fisted British officer. He was a petty dictator, who attempted to abrogate full power to himself in perpetuity, by taking full advantage of the present situation in the aftermath of war. I knew that members of the anti-Kroll group considered it dangerous to leave him in power, in his beloved semi-military, dictatorial posture. He began by using wholesale flattery towards the British, with tributes to Britain's great history and democracy. He promised to give his full support to restoring the true values of his University. He tried to convince me that his was the real strength and momentum behind the re-opening. I reminded him that the University was closed and empty, until I tackled all the mountains of repairs. Kroll was generally mocked and caricatured by his staff. But he was a dangerous man though undoubtedly skilful with words. Nevertheless, his habit of repeating set, polished phrases, soon became obvious. He had glibly agreed at our first meeting with all the rules that were laid down. Then he proceeded to go his own cunning way, thinking that we would not be able to discover his clever manoeuvres. It had been unwise for him to underestimate us.

I reported to the Foreign Office that Kroll's major plan was to establish himself as permanent Rektor; the supreme Head of the University in every sense. To this end, he was engineering an amendment to the ancient rules of the University. I declared against this move with a quorum of academic staff, maintaining that official authority was needed for the enactment of any major change. The University was only just recovering its strength after a harsh Nazi dictatorship. Then the urbane mask slipped, to reveal the hard face of the real Kroll. He told me that it was none of my business, and that he knew far better how to handle his University than I, who had never reached senior rank in any University.

This I thoroughly enjoyed. I let him run on and display his first passionate, revealing outburst. Once he'd started, the words poured out. He was THE rightful Rektor, THE man of experience, skill and knowledge. He was accepted by all his colleagues as primus inter pares. He knew best of all how to deal with the authorities, and obtain the help the University needed. The only possible Real Führer! Eventually he stopped for breath and his face crumpled into wrinkles. His harangue actually lasted about twenty minutes, but he was exhausted. I explained quietly that I was in overall control of Cologne and Bonn University, where they were much more reasonable and had no desire to prolong their stint in office. Unlike Kroll, they disliked the administration work and longed to get back to teaching. Was it not time that he too returned to teaching?

I was acting exactly in accord with my instructions, and helping the University recover. He knew he was at my mercy, and then begged me to forgive his outburst, which was due to his hard work day and night. He then gave me another harangue about his heroic behaviour during the Nazi period and since the end of the War. At the end of his apologia, I again reminded him that I was in overall control of the University. He was duty bound to report to me regularly on all his activities on behalf of the University. This included every admission, which it was my duty to oversee and check. I would allow his re-election, contrived improperly this year, on condition that he gave me his guarantee to hold open elections in the coming year. He agreed and we parted. He clearly regretted his outburst and having to humble himself before a young British officer. But he was determined to have his way again.

The news soon leaked out, for the University was an echoing chamber. There was a celebration of this first victory over Kroll, at the home of Professor Jachmann, who taught Classics, with Rumpf and other dedicated anti-Nazis. Jachmann, who literally lived for his books and teaching was a devoted anti-Nazi. The Professor of Law, Nipperdey, was a very quiet man who never wasted words. He was against Kroll and regarded him as superficial. He was highly respected by all students. He showed no favours, never raised his voice and had somehow gained respect from the Nazi overseers who had actually studied under him. He stuck firmly to the Law and sought no other position, but he was regarded by the majority as a good choice for next Chancellor. The Professor of Economics, who was also qualified in law, could have been mistaken for an average Englishman. He always wore tweed suits, brogues and a tweed hat. These clothes had all been bought in pre-war England and carefully hidden. He was grateful to me because he had broken his pipe and I presented him with a new briar, which I had bought before giving up smoking. He presented me with a book of the Nazi Leaders that had clearly been sketched by him at the Nuremburg Trials.

Some senior staff now drew up a quietly determined plan for the next election. They advised me that some of Kroll's old cronies had also become dissatisfied with his dictatorial iron rule, and could now be coaxed to join them in an honest vote next year. These elections were not only to elect a new Rektor, but also to give other Professors the opportunity of becoming Deans of their Faculties. I reported the situation to the Foreign Office, who sent Professor Cohn, Head of University and the Law Department, secretly to stay with me for two nights. This visit enabled me to show him around and reveal what was happening 'on the ground.' I introduced him to the good set of academics, who were prepared to talk to him and give their opinions. He promised to come again and congratulated me on my achievements, and the obvious respect I had gained.

Professor Cohn said that the Foreign Office had been truly impressed by the success of my exchange schemes. They were planning a lecture tour of other Universities, who wanted me to inform them of the present state of German Universities, along with the attitudes of staff and students. I went to Oxford first, where I stayed with my friend, the Bodlean Librarian, then on to Cambridge. I also visited Nottingham where the students explained the history of the Boots foundation, and finally I went to talk to my own

University of Bristol. There I was greeted with enthusiasm by staff and students and the British press gave me splash headlines. Debates with the students took place at the Victoria Rooms, but all did not go quietly. There were many who thought that British officials should not be busy rebuilding Germany, nor should the British have forgiven the Germans so readily. Some asked "why waste taxpayers money on the Nazis and their sheep-like followers, who had nearly cost us our liberty, and the loss of millions of lives in two horrible wars?" I thought that these were good points, well made. I reminded them that I had come at their invitation to talk about our work with the German Universities. They listened as I outlined the basic reasons for eliminating the Nazis, and supporting the ideology of democratic principles. They gradually grew more interested and questions were not as sharply loaded. Eventually we came to an amicable understanding that British participation in the restructuring of German universities was a good investment. We finished with a good evening of merry making, Bristol fashion.

Back in Cologne, I prepared for my next visits to Leyden University in Belgium, and then to Bern and Zurich in Switzerland. I still had no help in my work at Cologne, though I was supposed to have had a junior assistant from the outset. Fortunately Bonn was a smaller and more preserved University. However my Intelligence colleague, Faitelson, looked after Cologne University in my absence. I drove to Leyden where I was warmly welcomed and cross-examined on many details. I found that the good Fathers were extremely well acquainted with much that I was doing. They expressed approval and entertained me well, though they were somewhat aghast to learn that I was not a drinker of good wine, nor yet a Catholic. But when I mentioned my good friend Father Fred Coppleston, the leading Jesuit Philosopher and told them my story of how he came over to me in Cologne at my request, and dealt efficiently with Existentialism, the pseudo French philosophy, which I described as 'hanging in the air without touching the ground.', they were both delighted and amused. German students had fallen for it completely and I could not persuade them otherwise. But he had accomplished in three talks, the complete destruction of the philosophy, by simply holding up a flower and removing each theory, petal by petal, in his quiet, assured manner.

Chapter 10

America and Canada

By 1949, German officials had resumed control of German industry, education and general administrative affairs. America and Britain, had supported them long enough. The British government was busy dealing with its own problems. Internationally, the process of decolonisation had begun and the British Empire was crumbling. The emergence of America and Russia as the new Super Powers, had effectively undermined British foreign policy, and the nuclear arms race had created a climate of fear. The vast programme of welfare reforms that were pushed through by the Atlee government, severely stretched the British domestic economy, as did the American lend-lease programme. Although the implementation of Keynesian economic policies eventually boosted the economy. However, a shortage of labour and materials delayed the reconstruction process, and Britain was forced to embark on large scale immigration programmes in order to rebuild the country's infrastructure. I was to be promoted to a senior position at our HQ at Bad Rothenfelde and opted for a three week visit to America. My two sisters were there, and had invited me to visit them and relatives. They were all longing to see their English warrior cousin. On route to America my British Airways VC10 landed in Shannon, Ireland with acute engine trouble. We were informed that a new aeroplane was going to be flown out, and this would, hopefully, only take a few hours. We waited patiently English fashion, and hours later took off afresh, heading over the Atlantic. We were buffeted by gales and strong winds but eventually landed in Newfoundland with further engine trouble. I had achieved my boyhood dream of following John Cabot to Newfoundland, now deep in snow. We took off the following morning in a snowstorm and landed a day late in New York.

Fortunately, my relatives were there to greet me and drive me to Perth Amboy, where a big family group was assembled. The Stess family owned a candy store called Raritan and I enjoyed sampling their wares, especially American chocolates. There were innumerable questions and answers, as many family members dropped in to inspect this odd English offspring. I was so different from the rest in looks and manners, but was pronounced the genuine article, and enjoyed their full hospitality. My cousin Harry, a famous artist who signed his name in a circle, illustrated Damon Runyan and P G

Wodehouse stories. His work was published extensively in Colliers, Cosmopolitan and American newspapers and journals. His studio was in Greenwich Village, New York, the home of artists and writers. Another cousin, Charlie, a leading solicitor of Perth Amboy, was an enthusiastic sailor. When war broke out with Japan, he had offered his yacht to the nation, and was placed in charge, as Chief Petty Officer, guarding 'Home Waters.' He was a man of many talents and accepted as head of the family.

Charlie offered to sail with me to Washington to see the White House and Pentagon. Washington looked serene and stately with immaculate green lawns. Here were the hallmarks of George Washington's worthy foundation, and the legends of those early years. Now the United States of America were growing ever more prosperous. Yet I could see no trace of the war which had dominated the world since 1939. I had just left the rubble of my home city of Bristol, crushed under Nazi Luftwaffe bombs. But here were no signs of German or Japanese attacks. Everywhere you looked, there was the surge of prosperity, while Britain had paid a heavy, bitter price for her steadfast stand-alone battles against the German and Italian armies. But we bore our battle honours with pride. Britain had played a crucial role in saving Europe and the World from the Nazi terror.

We visited the huge Pentagon Military Headquarters. I had worked with CIA, formerly OSS, at WW1C HQ in India. Therefore, I was made most welcome as a senior officer and escorted around the Pentagon. Charlie was delighted at my warm, cordial reception, especially by the American Intelligence Officers. On our return we were met by other cousins who offered to take me on a visit to Montreal. We travelled along the colourful Route 9 and visited Niagara Falls. The broad highway, north of New York, led through wide expanses of rocky country, great colourful trees and greener, wooded areas, which reminded me of Yorkshire.

The people were plain spoken with attractive northern accents, still bearing traces of British country dialects. We drove through rocky areas to visit Niagara Falls, and managed to get behind those great, cascading, rushing waters. Thus we were able to view the Falls from behind, getting rather damp in the process. It was a truly magnificent sight of the terrific power of water. Next stop before Montreal, was McGill University, which I had to visit. I had promised Professor Amundsen, who'd visited me in Cologne with his students during my vacation course at Burg Wahn. He heard my discussions with students and staff, and remarked on my fluent German. Subsequently he invited me to join him as senior lecturer in the German Faculty of McGill University.

He welcomed me with a Canadian bear hug, and showed us around. McGill was a truly fine University, built of grey granite stone. Its clean lines stood out in a lovely wooded green background. It had its own well-kept grounds and campus and the feeling of a classical British University. I must admit that I was tempted to accept his offer there and then. Though the salary was not that good when translated into pounds sterling, the conditions and prospects were most favourable. Professor within five years, my own good living quarters and a free hand to remodel the German Department. It was not far from Montreal, where I was immediately accepted because of my fluent French. It seemed a most attractive proposition and I promised to keep in touch.

In the meantime, my American cousins drove to the Canadian border, which was guarded by the Mounties in full uniform. They examined our passports. My dark blue British passport, with its Imperial crest and my photograph in uniform within, produced a welcoming salute. They also produced a chair for me to sit and watch their very different treatment of my American cousins. They had to submit to preliminary searches for arms and contraband, first of their persons and then exhaustively of their car. My cousins were quite humiliated at receiving such different treatment. They had considered Canada to be part of America and had expected to be welcomed as fellow citizens. I had to explain the Canadian adherence to the British Crown. One Mounty was French Canadian, and gave me the hotel addresses of relatives in Montreal and Quebec. This is where we lodged and were well received and looked upon as honoured guests. My cousins were mollified and treated me with new respect.

We explored Montreal and Quebec, from the Heights of Abraham, now folklore, to the ancient French style buildings. The dress of many of the inhabitants seemed to step back in time. When I told them I was from Bristol, just like Cabot who had discovered and named Newfoundland, they immediately arranged a small party in my honour. Indeed, we enjoyed many merry nights of celebration before setting off back to New Jersey. I think I could have been really happy living in Canada. The truth was, that I felt so tremendously happy, free and content in those early post-war years, that I had no desire to settle down to normal life. Like a great many other returning warriors, who found it extremely difficult to settle back into pre-war routines, that were dull and colourless in comparison with the war years. Even the post-war years under the Foreign Office, in my enjoyable role as SO1, had meant a satisfying change. The post had enabled me to throw myself into a completely new, challenging job. Trying to change the mind set of the German people after the spurious deceits propounded by Nazi doctrine, was a momentous task. But I believed in converting this mind set into a more democratic way of thinking, and a desire to live at peace with their fellow creatures, of whatever race, colour, faith or way of life. This was just the demanding task I needed to bring me back to semi-civilian life, after celebrating the end of the War.

When my leave was nearly over my new found American family arranged a huge party, with masses of relatives in attendance. The party was held at Billy Rose's Diamond Horseshoe in the fabulous Latin Quarter, the American version of Folies Bergère, with Billy Rose's 'Long-stemmed Roses' entertaining us with gusto. It was a wonderful family gathering and a fantastic night, full of fun and good fellowship. They urged me to return and settle in America. Cousin Sam was a lecturer at Rutgers University, New Jersey. The Dean of his Faculty, hearing of my adventures, expressed a keen desire to meet me. We met over an elaborate lunch, but they appeared more interested about the war, than about my academic background and experience. Then the Dean actually offered me a position. Not in the German Department as I might have expected, but in the Department of English. He claimed that my knowledge of English language and literature was taken for granted. Indeed, they seemed to assume that all English academics were Masters of all Arts. It was a very tempting offer. With the offer however, came an apology. They explained that the pay and conditions were probably worse than in England, and were in a constant battle for higher salaries and improved conditions. I whispered to Sam "Is this a genuine offer?" He just grinned and nodded his head. Back in his car after a pleasant leave he explained that they held British Universities in high regard, and thought that they were all similar to Oxbridge. From what he had told them, they honestly believed that I would not accept a post lower than the level of professor.

I was not tempted to live in America. Instead, I felt an enormous draw back to my roots. Wherever I have been, often in the most enjoyable of situations, like Durban, India, Egypt, Montreal, America and Cairo, I have always enjoyed returning to England. I loved to be safely home again, with that feeling of security and belonging. My early creative childhood years and, 'boy to manhood' feeling of freedom to make my own way, left an indelible mark. It is like a seed born in one, which continues to grow and develop throughout one's life. With birth, comes a multiplicity of complex inherited genetics of indescribable strength. These combine to hold and shape you into an integral part of your country. I believe that the enthralling history of the British Isles, undaunted in strength and courage, different from all other countries and peoples, should be taught from childhood, to all who have the privilege of being born here, or have been allowed to come and settle.

My journey home on the Queen Mary cruise liner, was far more pleasant than my scary outward bound plane flight. The seas were kind, sunrise and sunsets brilliant, as were the many kinds of fish we spotted en route. The atmosphere was enhanced, by learning that the 'Queens' had been used to carry thousands of American and Canadian troops to England during the War, without a single mishap. We arrived at Southampton precisely on time and duly disembarked. Customs Officers proceeded to go through my garments item by item. As the nylon stockings that were hidden about my belongings by my American family descended onto a table, other passengers began to laugh as my face went redder and redder. The fine was but small consequence, compared with the ignominy and shame I felt as those piles of nylon stockings cascaded from all my garments. They were held aloft by the Customs Officer to exaggerate my crime. Of course it was not a criminal offence, as he well knew. The nylons were not confiscated, so I at least had the satisfaction of pleasing my mother and sisters on my return. I resolved from then on, never to attempt to conceal anything from Customs Officials. There is such satisfaction in moving confidently through all customs areas, declaring any item taxable. Strangely though, during all of my frequent journeys, I have never been stopped by Customs Officials, or asked to 'open up' since that embarrassing incident.

Chapter 11

Completion of the Cologne Mission

Back in Cologne water and electricity had now been restored, and the Mensa reopened at the University. The students had settled to their studies, and I held regular meetings with them to discover their views and hopes for the future. At first they were understandably pessimistic, downcast, guilt-laden. I had explained how the world in general had been horrified by Nazi brutality. It was not easy for anyone to understand the massacre of millions of innocent men, women and children, even babies in their mother's arms, who were sent callously to their deaths. Nor the arrogance with which Hitler chose to pursue his overriding ambition to rule the world, and dictate the lives of so many different peoples. These students had witnessed some of the atrocities at first hand. Their duty now was to face the facts squarely and decide on their future role. Germany had lost the respect of all nations. It was up to them to win it back by peaceful means. To seek forgiveness and rehabilitation with all countries and peoples, by cleansing their minds of Nazi poisonous indoctrination.

I explained the British role in terms of education and reconstruction. Firstly, British officials intended to educate the German population about the root causes of Nazism and their current situation. Secondly, they would find and destroy all remnants of Nazism to prevent further brutalisation. Thirdly, they would provide every assistance in rebuilding the infrastructure of the country, in order to prevent the likelihood of future conflict. Thus British representatives would help to reconstitute German administration, state machinery, institutions of education, hospitals, industry and agriculture. Germany needed to recover, repair and return to self-sufficiency. The nation needed to establish itself as a democratic society that could peacefully cooperate with the rest of Europe and the world. British aims in assisting this transition were viewed as an important democratic gesture.

However, I was not there to preach to them. As an ex-soldier I had seen enough of War and was only interested in preserving peace. We all had a duty to prevent future wars by settling disputes, by discussion, debate and arbitration. Wars caused the sacrifice of so many young lives. There needed to be freedom of thought and expression, and joint responsibility in terms of decision making. They needed to work together to assure and preserve democratic freedom. The students held free and open discussions about these issues and all inhibitions were removed. They enjoyed their freedom to debate, and the openness of visiting professors and lecturers. Konrad Adenauer approved of this debating process, even though he was busily engaged in developing his Christian Democratic Union Party, for the forthcoming 1949 elections. He had hinted that his election platform would be based on notions of self-reliance. He thought I should stay at the university for least another year. Certainly the students and staff had requested that I stay a further twelve months. I had my reservations however, but throughout all the student debates about politics and democracy, I managed to conceal my own real doubts, which were based on my own factual experience of German leaders.

The German currency remained useless and the shops were empty. People had recourse to use the Black Market. The Allies arranged a conversion to a new value Mark This would be issued on a secret day, when detailed preparations had been completed. Then public announcements were made universally throughout Germany. Each adult was allowed forty new German Marks, with no exception to this rule. Queues of people, including members of the Military Government, came to receive their new Marks, on positive identification. All went according to plan. The conversion was a great success and conducted in perfect order without fuss. The birth of the new Mark.

All those shops and stores that were hitherto empty, were suddenly filled with food, clothing, and other necessities. There were even luxuries that had apparently dropped like a miracle from heaven. Overnight, all those blank, empty shop windows suddenly revealed hoarded goods in great quantity, now they could be exchanged for the new Marks. The Black Market gradually diminished and eventually disappeared. Shopkeepers became wealthy from their concealed goods. They had long been pleading poverty and had totally deceived their own people. Seemingly, they were resistant to their genuine hardship and need.

About this time a series of visits were arranged for Military Government staff. Firstly they were taken along the Rhine in big Rheindämpfer. They saw castles perched on the hillside and were shown where the beautiful Rhine maidens (mermaids), sat combing their golden locks, and luring sailors to their death with their plaintive Lorelei songs. In the French zone they were introduced to the wine country, well chosen by the French for occupation, with its hoarded stocks of choice wine. Some were almost untouched by the War. Those were enjoyable expeditions that were followed by grimmer, heart-breaking visits to Concentration Camps. These revealed the barbaric slaughter of the innocents by willing followers of Hitler. These sights burned into one's mind with revulsion.

Then they were taken to Essen and the Ruhr. This was the centre of Nazi armament construction, weapons made in the huge works of Krupps, Thyssen and other armaments producers. This was a decided shock for many, as they came face-to-face with the hard reality of German war preparations. The officer in charge pointed to some great piles of twisted metal and said, "Don't be deceived by this great sight of RAF destruction, it is only the top framework. The foundations are still preserved with concealed underground works. Within two years of regaining freedom, they will have rebuilt a huge modern plant, producing everything from cooking utensils to armaments, with their war machines again ready for action." I believed this to be a sound prophesy.

Berlin was a skeleton city in ruins. Remembered State buildings, hotels, restaurants, jewellers, and boutiques in Unter den Linden had been smashed and flattened, just like my home city of Bristol. Beggars were everywhere. The Black Market flourished and people approached us boldly, with offerings that had been dug out of the ruins. Berliners seemed to be crawling out of holes in the ground, or cells that had been dug out of piles of rubble. Some western districts had escaped the intensive mass bombings of the RAF. Bomber Harris had accurately pinpointed military targets and prepared the way for a final Allied onslaught. Harris and Dowding had commanded the fighter aircraft and made an outstanding contribution to the British war effort. In my opinion, their crucial role was never fully recognised in terms of praise and awards. Just as we, the secret, invisible code-breakers, were not recognised nor honoured. We had to work in strict silence to supply these commanders with urgently needed, deciphered information. They needed to know the strength and strike plans of Goering's mighty Luftwaffe at all times.

Dowding could not reveal how he came to know of Luftwaffe plans, targets, timing and the direction of flight-paths. Our decoded messages and signals were passed to him secretly as C.O. Even Churchill was sworn to silence and could not mention us and our work in any of his books or speeches. General Eisenhower informed him, that the prior knowledge gained from our deciphering may have reduced the length of the war by at least two years. It was the best kept secret of the war and never leaked! Hence the current interest in the rebuilt Bletchley Park. It was a unique British enterprise maintained by devoted workers. These included thousands of Wrens who rigorously maintained complete silence. Disproving men's claim that women cannot keep secrets.

Hitler's well-built bunker with its deep, solid construction of underground rooms, offices, radio equipment, sleeping quarters and defences, was a revelation. We gathered solemnly around the spot where his body was burnt, and stared down at the tarpaulin, which covered his remains. We heard the stories of his mistress Eva Braun, who died with him, and the suicide of Goebbels. The latter was that evil Minister of Propaganda, who killed all his family and himself with poison. Berlin was a city of horrors. Though I was keen to see the remains of the Reichstag, that had been twice destroyed. The building stood in a semi-derelict state, naked and bare. It was stripped of its much vaunted, 'solid gold' decorations. The stripping process had revealed that it too, was but a sham. There was just gold paint on a stucco surface façade, a thin covering to the rough brickwork. It was now being rebuilt according to the design of a British architect.

Russian strength was visible everywhere; they were now the real masters in the Eastern Zone. Eisenhower had refused to follow Monty's wise plan, which was to head along the coast with British and Canadian troops, in a direct route to Berlin. Had this plan been followed there would have been no Communist East Germany and no construction of the Berlin Wall. The British and Canadian troops would have arrived in Berlin before the Russians. But Stalin had demanded his right to Berlin and Roosevelt had complied. Eventually, there was a compromise of shared occupation. The sick and near dying Roosevelt had given in to the personal blandishments of Stalin. He had weakly agreed to let him take over all the European States near his borders. These included Hungary, Rumania, Czechoslovakia and Poland, who became enmeshed in the tightly drawn Russian net. Roosevelt was at the mercy of Stalin, who was as guilty as Hitler. He had been responsible for the deaths of millions of his own people, including the majority of his senior officers shortly before the war. These two dictators, Hitler and Stalin, stand out as the two biggest slaughterers of mankind during the last century.

The British Labour Government had decided that it was now time to hand back power and responsibility to the Germans. Immediately our powers of persuasion began to wane. In education we were relegated to a back seat. However, to my great pleasure, the senior academics had summoned up the requisite courage to get together and vote Kroll out of office, and back to teaching. Even before that memorable event, they had changed his appointed Deans of Faculties, and voted in a far better choice. I had succeeded in bringing about the democratic changes I had long wanted. I was delighted that there was now a quorum of truly independent academic thinkers, who were no longer afraid to stand their ground over important issues. They were capable of democratic judgement and independent thought and action. This situation was my best reward, and I considered the de-nazification process a job well done.

My term at Cologne from early 1946 to 1950 was drawing to a close. The University had a firm foundation with forward-looking students, who were running their own associations. They were well able to look after themselves. Those tough, early days of 1946, when students had striven to rebuild their university with hard labour, had fostered real comradeship and congregation. They now had their Students' Union Association, that was inspired by the British. They also printed and published their own newspaper, and helped to organise and run students' residences and vacation courses.

When the news broke that I was to leave Cologne, staff and students wrote letters of protest. But 'orders is orders', and I had a strong feeling that the British future was now under consideration. Certainly Britain could not afford to maintain a costly reconstruction programme continuously in the British Zone of Germany. On the whole we had done a good job, but I really could have done with just one more year, to finish the loose ends and wind it all up properly. Fate was busily deciding otherwise for me.

One of my best memories is my achievement of establishing a new Chair at Cologne University, that of Brewery. The owner of a large brewery in Cologne came to seek my advice and help. He informed me that Cologne was the seat of a number of important Breweries. They were most impressed by my amazingly quick resuscitation of the University, and wished that the Town Council had worked as efficiently. Their great idea, was to found and finance a completely new Chair of Brewing at the University. There was a good laboratory, which they would improve and equip, to do the necessary research into the whole science of brewing. They would be responsible for all financial costs, staff and equipment. It was a wonderful offer, and I promised my full support. When I put their offer to the Bursar and Dean's Assembly, for the first time ever there was no delay. Instead, there was immediate, enthusiastic accord. It would bring fresh finance and more employment to the University. More professors, lecturers, laboratory assistants and free beer. It would enhance the forward looking reputation of the University, as well as providing much needed funds. All were delighted and congratulated me as a successful innovator, who never drank beer.

These jolly beer barons became my new friends. They then hired three of the biggest Rheindämpfer for a celebratory trip down the Rhine with staff and students. It was one of the happiest, carefree days of my time in Cologne. There were so many drinks in my honour that it was enough to make one dizzy. Of course, many of them were, by the end of that highly successful voyage of inauguration of the Cologne Seat of Brewing. It was beyond my wildest dreams that I, a non-alcoholic, should be responsible for the foundation of a new Chair and a Department of Brewing. Maybe I should have married Freda, the daughter of one of the brewers. I could have become Chief Brewer! Or even professor of Brewing, a completely new and unique post. At least I had left a lasting mark in Cologne in the form of a liquid monument.

Chapter 12

Marriage, Birth and the Return Home

Joan was transferred to I.G. Farben in North Cologne as supervisory officer. We were married at the British Consulate, Düsseldorf, by the British Consul himself, who signed our Marriage Certificate. Then we celebrated with a cheerful reception at the Yacht Club, with many friends. For our honeymoon we'd planned a very happy, carefree tour of six countries. First we visited Belgium, where I managed to get lost in the thick forests of the Ardennes. From the delights of Belgium, which was completely free of war restraints, we drove into Holland and watched the twenty four hour recovery work that was taking place under arc lights at Rotterdam. It was truly awesome to see those intrepid Dutchmen beavering away. They were determined to restore completely and remove all traces of Nazi bombs and destruction. We thoroughly enjoyed Holland, and its people, who welcomed us with open arms as liberators and insisted on sharing their meals with us. At this time, the British were the acknowledged leaders of Europe, a country that had freed them from a brutal dictatorship.

The museums and art galleries were still in place. It was like coming back to civilisation after the wilderness. They had hidden most of their great paintings, but the Nazis had stolen many. The work of those master painters was awesome, and I could not bear to leave them. We were also shown the fascinating work of diamond cutting. There were astonishing stories of how the diamond merchants hid themselves and their wares from the Nazis' greedy clutches. Now they had returned to their trade unhindered. We gazed at magnificent displays of blue diamonds that were well beyond our reach. Bulbs too, were carefully hidden during the war, especially the unique black tulip. Our worst moment came when we were surrounded by a great mass of cyclists, who were all pedalling furiously as they raced homewards. We were completely enveloped and brought to a standstill. What a blessing if London were similarly cram-full of cyclists, instead of the masses of poison-spreading cars.

From Holland we drove into France and enjoyed a night in Monte Carlo, without succumbing to the temptation to gamble. We had just enough funds to visit all six countries. We drove up through Switzerland and stayed at a friendly hotel on the Swiss-Italian border. There they spoke their own individual dialects of Swiss Italian and

Swiss German (Switzer Deutsch). Then we drove through the passes to Italy, where we enjoyed most of our month's holiday. Here was all the exuberance of post-war Italy, with holiday makers rushing about in a frantic desire to be seen enjoying themselves. Nobody nowadays, could possibly imagine how quiet and peaceful Viareggio was at that time. We found a lovely villa where, as first post-war English visitors we were made exceedingly welcome. Especially when they learned that we were on our honeymoon, with me still in uniform.

My uniform acted as the best passport in every country we visited, including Switzerland. It assured us of a warm welcome as the heroic liberators. We heard so many grim recitals from everyone, everywhere, of terrible brutalities and murder. People described how their Jewish friends and neighbours were forced into cattle trucks, on their way to extermination. The stories sickened us. It was as though the soul of Europe was slowly reviving after that terrible, Nazi invasion. I had an introduction from Professor Jachmann to visit his friend, the Professor of Classics in Lucca. He was delighted to show us his walled town of Lucca, and explained its origin as a priestly training centre. It had an atmosphere of quiet culture and learning.

We spent two nights in Florence and loved every moment. The beautiful churches and elegant architecture. The superb sculpture, especially Michelangelo's David. We wandered across bridges peering into the little shops, that were full of hand-made leather goods. Then we watched glass blowing and miniature making,. We found them quite irresistible. This graceful city, with its fine architecture and serene atmosphere welcomed us warmly. Our last visits were to Pisa, with its famous leaning tower. Then on to Venice, where we discovered a beautiful old villa at the edge of the lake, with its own gondola. We climbed old, well worn steps to reach the entrance, and then climbed up the wooden, creaking stairs to our lofty pungent-smelling room. It was a truly Victorian setting. We fed the pigeons in the square and generally behaved as tourists, though there were few about. It seemed strange to find the town almost empty, it seemed as though even the pigeons had not returned to their former strength.

We had already made a brief visit to Paris. The city was still recovering from German occupation and it evoked old memories. We had few records of our adventures and decided to make a special visit later, deciding that we would devote a holiday entirely to France in the future, since the country had special childhood memories for me. We also planned to return to Italy, where I dreamed of owning a villa like the one that we were offered in Viareggio. It was a very reasonable price and the previous occupant had been killed by the Nazis. But I could not raise the money on my meagre Army pay. Until then, the acquisition of money had not featured largely in my life. It was a sorry state of affairs however, to consider the chances that I had missed because of a lack of money. But it was a pleasing dream, to own one's own villa in Italy. It would have provided a refuge to escape the pressures of everyday living. A dream that belonged to the 'If only' world.

Back in Cologne, I received my orders to move to Education HQ at Bad Rothenfelde. Joan was devastated to learn, that women had to resign from the Foreign Office after marriage. This was particularly bad news since she had just passed a Civil Service exam, and had been promoted to a permanent, senior administrative position in the Foreign Office. It would have enabled her to travel to different posts around the world. This was her real ambition. Unfortunately, the regulations at that time, permitted only single women in the Civil Service. Marriage meant the end of a career for Joan. With such a narrow system, the Civil Service was thereby constantly removing some of their best talent for no viable reason! Joan never forgave me for robbing her of that coveted permanent position. Had we but known, I think we might have risked not marrying, but at that time it would have been construed as living in sin. Thus we moved to our small house in the village of Bad Rothenfelde, with its one grocery shop.

Our offices were in a big house just outside the village, where I found myself buried in paperwork, detailed reports, analysis and records. It was like living in a backwater after the busy, active life in Cologne, where we'd been surrounded on all sides by people and movement. Of the other officers there, some were permanent Foreign Office staff of various grades. But although the work was important, it seemed soulless to me. It was a general analysis of our closing operation in Education Control in Germany. I missed my busy, active life in Cologne, and certainly could not contemplate a humdrum, confined married life, bound to a desk in Foreign Office.

Joan, perforce, was left much on her own in our small furnished house. The nearest British doctor was two hours drive away at a British Military Hospital near Hanover. Joan was now pregnant and with the baby due in the late Summer of 1949, she was becoming uncomfortable and constantly in need of my help. Eventually the hospital's Welsh doctor thought it wiser for Joan to remain there, since he anticipated an early birth. At this point she was experiencing some pain and nervous anxiety. Fortunately, the male chief nurse was a cheerful cockney with a fund of jokes, and completely at home when dealing with pregnant women.

"Don't worry dear" he said to Joan, who regarded him nervously, "we get all sorts here, in every possible condition from 'earliest' to 'latest', but in the end, its all the same 'orrible result. I don't know why you bother, 'cos its trouble before, during and after." He was a friend to every patient and kept them amused. All the nurses were Welsh, like the efficient little doctor, who spoke with a strong Welsh accent. It made my work easier, knowing Joan was in safe hands, and I made regular journeys to the hospital. Soon she became friendly with Army and RAF wives and especially with the wife of a Lt.General, who'd been through it all twice before. This woman provided Joan with a tower of strength, knowledge and experience. It amazed me how they all seemed to revel in some of her gruesome stories and experiences. Yet when Joan was at home, she was so nervous that I had to keep trying to calm her down. I had yet to learn of her highly strung condition, and other unknown problems.

When my son was born we called him Nigel. The nurses called him the 'blond angel' because of his platinum fair hair. He was quite content whilst fussed over by them. But when we arrived home and put him into his beautifully prepared wicker crib he began to bawl endlessly. Joan did everything according to Dr Spock's book, which she had followed like the bible, but to no avail. We could not face the journey back to hospital, so in desperation I called the local German doctor. He looked at Nigel, then calmly stuck the baby's thumb in his mouth and the crying stopped. "But that is forbidden in Dr Spock's book" said Joan in horror. "Maybe" said the doctor, "but your baby hasn't read it and this is natural to all early babies. He will change later." But Nigel did not change. He continued to yell loudly on every conceivable occasion. After another long journey to the same British Consul's office in Dusseldorf, to register Nigel's birth, we tried to settle with him in our village home. The locals had grown used to us and offered all kinds of advice. Nothing worked until we discovered that the constant rocking of the cradle or pram, or even the motion of my car, gradually sent him off to sleep.

During his last visit with a group of lecturers, Lindsay repeated to me his verbal offer of sharing his big responsibility of opening the first post-war British University. He had accepted the challenge and knew that his retirement as Master of Balliol College was due. He said he was not well, but thought that the change and challenge would be good for him. He asked me whether I would be prepared to give up my work soon and help him establish the Department of German, with the prospect of a future Senior Lecturer position. What a challenge, and what a wonderful opportunity to become one of his foundation team! Without hesitation I agreed a commencement date towards end of 1950 and gave notice to Foreign Office, explaining my reason. We had already been advised of a termination date in 1950, as educational costs were now too heavy for the British government to bear. Therefore, we were all due for release.

We were packing and almost ready to leave, when a telegram arrived announcing Lindsay's death. My future was blown away like a colourful bubble. Obviously Lindsay's successor would pick his own team, so all verbal arrangements were cancelled and my hopes shattered. This was a terrible blow to my dreams of a future in the academic world. I always thought that I was destined for such a career. It was a sad end to a dream. The challenge would have suited me well. I had already been making notes and sketches to prepare me for my re-entry into civilian life. It was with real sorrow therefore, that I said goodbye to my colleagues and work in Germany. I was now returning to England with my family and an unknown and doubtful future.

When I paid my last visit to Cologne, I received a tremendous welcome from the students, and genuine, farewell gifts from staff and students. Kroll had been deposed exactly as I had planned, and the new Rektor was one of my old anti-Nazi colleagues, as were the new Deans. A happy and grateful Dr Lewin had been offered a senior post as Professor and Head of a Gynaecological department in Frankfurt area. All seemed to be progressing well and my work had reached a satisfactory conclusion. The students had arranged to repaint and refurbish my Volkswagen as a farewell gesture, so we had everything in order for our journey home. I had never imagined such a genuine send-off. Staff and students alike, with exception of Kroll, were truly grateful for my endeavours. They had all gathered to wish me well. At least I had the feeling that a tough assignment had been well tackled during the four year period of eventful Service. They were truly grateful for my successful re-opening and re-establishment of Cologne University, since there had been many changes for the better. The same could be said of Bonn university. I had a great feeling of accomplishment.

Nigel slept most of the way home. The British Customs officer took one look at the peaceful child, grinned sympathetically at me and waved us on without bothering to examine the car's contents. The Volkswagen was jam-packed inside, with a pram perched precariously on top. Joan was nervously anticipating that we would have to unpack everything, which would have been wellnigh impossible to put together again. But I was growing used to her habit of anticipating the worst. Her nature worked against my own deep rooted optimism. I had inherited this character trait from my beloved father, who'd always anticipated the best for me.

We arrived home the next day, to stay temporarily with my mother in the family flat in Scampston Mews. It was just as I had originally set it up. We were living in rather cramped conditions, and it took days to settle in and get used to each other. There was the very real and terrible problem of two women sharing one kitchen. Moreover only one of them was a skilled cook. Fortunately they eventually seemed to accept each other. Though my mother regarded Joan as a strange being, who was unused to household management, an unskilled cook and very amateurish with children. Joan certainly learned many of the fundamentals of household management from her new mother-in-law, who was quiet, calm and experienced. But my mother was also worried about Joan's disposition, for she was in a highly nervous state. However, mother taught Joan the essentials of cooking and how to care for Nigel. Fortunately I could not see into the future.

In the meantime I was seeking a post. Wearing my demob suit, which was hardly of the cut, shape or style that I would have chosen personally, I visited an Officer's Bureau that had been set up to help officers find posts. All the good positions had already been snapped up by the first returned warriors. I was a 'Johnny come lately' and they had nothing to offer me. They advised me to sign on for the 'dole,' otherwise known as unemployment relief. Oh what a fall this was! I could see my careful savings disappearing rapidly, while I vainly sought employment.

My grocer friends offered me a management position, even though they did not need a manager. I was toying with the possibility of emigrating to Canada to join McGill University, but Joan was horrified at the thought of living in Canada. An offer arrived for the position of school inspector which I did not fancy. Then I received an offer to become the Head of Education for Libya, from the King of Libya. I was also offered a similar position for Hong Kong. All of these were anathema to Joan, despite my interest, for I would cheerfully have accepted either; she used Nigel as her main weapon. The Foreign Office welcomed me back and my friends celebrated. They recited their own woes with regard to staff reductions. There was nothing available, despite my good record. My friends gave me lunch and told me how they, too, were being reduced in numbers. There was nothing available, despite my qualifications and good record. England was financially broke and the immediate outlook was bleak.

Fairfield Grammar School
1925
Age 11

Fairfield Grammar School
Matriculation 1930
Age 16

Bristol University
1933
Age 19

Camping at Brean Down, near Burnham, Somerset with
Bristol University Students. Pictured on my Raleigh
bicycle, a gift from brother George.

Volunteer ARP Warden
September 1939

Bristol University Officer Training Corps Camp 1934
Third from left.

At the Bletchley Park code-breaking course, Abbottabad, India.

8th Army Code-breaker,
Cairo 1942

8th Army, Alamein.

"Lady of Shalot", Srinagar Kasmir, 1942.
On leave after Alamein prior to joining Wireless Intelligence,
Anand Parbat, Dehli.

Adjutant to Lt. Col. Stevens, O.C.
India Wireless Intelligence Service.
Pictured with R.A.F. Intelligence
Officers.

Srinagar, Kashmir, 1942

O.C. Int. School "C",
Calcutta 1943
Outside the Officer's Mess.

Bomb damaged Cologne 1945/46. The twin spires of the Dom (Cologne Cathedral) remain undamaged.

Cologne students repairing water and electricity supplies in order to resume studies.

Part of war-damaged Cologne University, 1945.

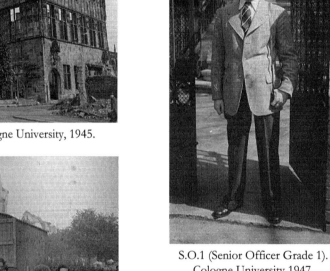

S.O.1 (Senior Officer Grade 1). Cologne University 1947.

Cologne students worked as labourers for 3 meals a day - better value than the worthless German currency.

Partly repaired Cologne University, 1946/7

Burg Wahn: First ever Cologne University Hall of Residence.
(A former Nazi Officer's home)

Official opening of Burg Wahn.

The sign over the entrance at Burg Wahn.

Princess Margaret, with husband Lord Snowdon,
wearing a summer outfit made by Atkinson
Rhodes for Paul Smith shops.

Founder's Plaque
Cundall Manor Preparatory School

Cundall Manor Preparatory School

Presentation of the Conservative Party Long Service Award - 2004
by the Rt. Hon.William Hague MP and Rt. Hon. Michael Ancram QC MP.
photo: Deryc R Sands ©Parliamentary Copyright

Pctured with Dr Green and staff at
Ailesbury Ward, Savernake Hospital, Marlborough -2004.

Chapter 13

Return to Wakefield

All in all, Britain in 1950 was in the doldrums and so was I. Britain had heavy debts and industry was just recovering. The Donners came to London to welcome me back and recounted their troubles. They were unable to obtain men's shirting material in wartime. Herma had implemented the bright idea of making ladies shirt blouses with the spare collar. Quantities of plain and fancy materials, suitable for ladies garments, were available at reasonable cost. Therefore, they made ladies shirts with extra collars, which were an instant success and kept the company afloat. Now they needed me to rebuild men's shirt production and stimulate trade, as I had done originally. They'd come to London to plead with me to return, and bring the company back to life. In return, Donner promised to advance my future role from manager to director. In the meantime, they had engaged a few ex-servicemen, who needed training in sales techniques. The Company needed me back.

Joan was shocked; she had married an academic, who was lecturing and developing a University career, not a commercial salesman. But she knew my pre-war history, including the co-founding at Double-Two. Still she raised problems, she did not like the Donners and did not wish to live in the North, 'the back of beyond,' as though Yorkshire were next to Alaska. I reminded her of my responsibility to maintain the family, and a lecturer's poor remuneration fell far below the standard of living she sought. I also wanted to enjoy this new challenge. I relished the idea of rebuilding the company we had so bravely founded in that difficult, pre-war period. I had been idle too long and was itching for action.

Finally we compromised. I settled her contentedly with baby Nigel in a hotel at Westgate-on-Sea, while I tested the situation in the North. Joan hoped that I would now dislike industry and Yorkshire and return South. But I was bored with enforced idleness. I needed funds for the family upkeep and an outlet for my energy. My hopes and ambitions for a return to academic life had been dashed with the death of Lindsay, and all other suitable posts had been snapped up. Joan would not consider living abroad. I remembered Yorkshire with affection, since I had developed much good relationships there.

My guiding spirit indicated Yorkshire, and I was ready to answer the call. I have always believed in a guiding Spirit, some call this spirit Fate, Kismet or Schicksal, which has moved me in and out of so many odd situations. Double Two urgently needed reorganisation. Once the factory was competently producing perfect DoubleTwo shirts, it was imperative to obtain a continuous flow of orders, to ensure production at full capacity. I concentrated on sales and sallied forth! I found the process of renewing old acquaintances, swapping yarns and persuading them to buy full ranges quite enjoyable. They remembered me from our first opening and were glad to welcome me back They wanted to hear of my adventures and regarded me as part of the original company. My earnings mounted quickly with my sales. In addition, I now had two homes to keep, one in a hotel. This situation urged me to rebuild our depleted finances.

I also turned many ex-service warriors into agents. They received commission on sales, which acted as a spur to develop accounts. They followed my advice, which was to show pride in British Industry, and our company's determination to produce the best garments. I compared the situation with the army, where it was important to have pride in your Regiment. Gradually we became firmly established and confidence grew overall. They became part of a good sales team, after they had adapted themselves to the different pace of civilian life. Mr. Donner sought my advice on problems of style and presentation. I discovered that he was colour blind, and had bought red material thinking it was brown. The factory organisation of packing and despatching needed modernisation and we resumed our original good relations. Sales increased continuously as did my earnings, which the partners claimed were more than the Prime Minister's. I replied that he was not as successful a salesman. The difference being that politicians were selling themselves, whilst we were selling garments of tangible value. Making real profits for all concerned.

Joan had decided that I was positively settled, and joined me with Nigel in a small house in Ruskin Avenue, Wakefield. She disliked the town, especially its residue of grime and dirt, which was a leftover from its coal mining days. However, she did accept my old friend Mrs Forsythe, who was now forewoman and our near neighbour; with her extensive family and humorous little Irish husband. Mrs Forsythe was one of the first hands I had engaged originally, when she was desperate for work. Consequently she was always very competent, loyal and affectionate to me, claiming that she owed me her employment and escape from poverty.

My wife and Nigel received her great affection and support, and her children were instructed to help Joan, who began to feel more at home in Ruskin Avenue. However, she never accepted the Donners and always caused friction. To her, my association with a shirt company betokened a descent into a lower social level, though she was now prepared to accept my rapidly rising earnings from mounting sales. Joan also failed to respond to any friendly gestures, invitations, or parties, despite the many efforts by the

Donners and friends. Wakefield and its 'semi-primitive' condition, after the clean, sea air of the South failed to please her. I offered to send her back to the south, but she refused. Actually she preferred to be left on her own, since she found it difficult to make contact with people. Having made it abundantly clear that she disliked Wakefield and the North, all friendly visits ceased and she became isolated. Subsequently she demanded more attention from me and was jealous of every moment I was away.

However nature itself intervened. In 1951 our daughter Jennifer was born on St.Patricks Day on one snowy morning at Manygates Hospital, Wakefield. Initially she had a mop of dark hair which later turned auburn and then really fair. Unfortunately, Jennifer was born with a narrow trachea and was unable to swallow or breathe properly; she could only be fed with drops from a pen-filler, day and night. The situation was becoming desperate. Dr.Gall said that he could widen her trachea with forceps, but recommended taking Jennifer out of the murky air of Wakefield, which was affecting her breathing.

I drove straight to Harrogate Spa, where there was no heavy industry, only good clean air and the Stray. This was an area of about two hundred acres of unspoilt, green land. It encircled the centre and acted as its lungs. There by good fortune. or my good Spirit's guidance, I found a big Yorkshire stone house For Sale. The house lay in its own grounds and occupied a corner site, surrounded by high stone walls and fronted by a tall hedge. Stone Lodge, Chelmsford Road, was the first house in that area to be constructed out of the old Knaresborough Forest, as the ancient deeds confirmed. It took an hour to settle all details with the owner, who was a widow and anxious to leave. Her son was a solicitor, and on learning of the urgency, arranged for her to join him in Scarborough the next day. Joan accepted the house at first sight, and we moved in that very weekend. We took Jennifer in her pram with Nigel, for our first walk across the Stray. It was a little miracle. From that first day, Jennifer's breathing became easier. Within a few weeks she was completely cured. I shall never cease to be thankful for that quick discovery of Stone Lodge. It was there that our children grew healthy and strong, and went to their first schools.

Nigel's Prep School was owned by a man who ran schools as a business, mainly to extract profit from high charges and low salaries. My son was never happy, nor well taught at that school. Therefore, much of his teaching took place at home. He baulked against Joan's strict discipline, which prevented him from amusing himself. Nigel and mischief were inseparable, despite the dire beatings he received from Joan. He was irrepressible and difficult to control, always bouncing with energy and high spirits and rushing headlong around our surrounding gardens, through trees and bushes. We had a big glass greenhouse at the end of one side of the garden. Nigel came full gallop down the side lawn, and crashed headfirst into the glass-panelled greenhouse. Amazingly, the glass broke cleanly and his head was stuck in the frame. He did not even have a scratch. Joan screamed, then shook him violently to compensate for her fright and anger.

At school, he fell off the wall-ladder and damaged a leg and ankle. He enjoyed sketching on the plaster and never lost his high spirits. He found an outlet by fighting and wrestling with boys at school. Both he and his clothes were in constant need of cleaning and repair. Despite my warnings, Joan beat him often in my absence, but failed to change him into the well-behaved child she desired. I believe young boys especially, have a spirit of mischief which has to find an outlet. Sometimes sport provides the answer. With Nigel it was wrestling, adventuring, teasing his sister and upsetting his mother. He knew just how to annoy her and raise her wrath.

My sales area covered the greater part of the North, from Yorkshire to the borders of Scotland. By careful assessment, I found I could cover this tremendous area by dividing it into four and devoting four days of each week. This left me with a local area for Friday, which enabled me to spend more time with my family. I was also able to help with the weekend shopping. Joan refused to shop on her own, saying that she dared not leave the children, because she feared trouble from Nigel. I bought her a Morris Minor to drive them to school and enjoy Yorkshire's moors and dales, which they loved to explore. In addition I was able to bring home shopping from my journeys, especially when I visited farming areas, with really fresh fruit and vegetables.

However, I became more and more worried about my wife's mental state, and her relationship with Nigel. He was constantly in scrapes at school and at home. He loved fighting and wrestling with other boys, which made his clothes torn and muddy. This situation exasperated Joan, who tried to beat him into obedience. This was obviously the wrong strategy as I explained to her, for it had no effect. He would not conform to Joan's strict regime. He needed quiet coaxing, but that was beyond her nature. Once roused, her temper seemed to be uncontrollable. I insisted that Joan refrain from beating him, but he seemed to provoke her into semi-hysteria. I sought advice from our family doctor, who, to my surprise, already had notes on Joan's mental state from his experience in Wakefield. He called at our home, but she refused to see him.

Subsequently therefore, I decided not to stay away from home for more than two nights in any week. I engaged and trained a sub-agent to deal with the most northerly areas. I would leave home early Monday morning and devote the whole of Monday and Tuesday to the furthermost areas. I worked at speed and gradually moved homewards, usually arriving home by midday on Wednesday, which was early closing day. Thursday and Friday were covered locally, enabling me to be home by early afternoon. Now I was able to devote more time to my family, I took them on expeditions. They loved Yorkshire with its hills and wild, heather-clad dales. We roamed through ancient villages with their hand-built stone walls. It is such a strong, virile County, with a vibrant history epitomised by the ancient towns like medieval York, typified by its soaring Minster. Those were days full of quiet pleasure and family enjoyment. But those pleasant interludes did not last, and I could not neglect my duties.

Return to Wakefield

Unfortunately my wife had more bouts of hysteria and refused to accept daily help and care, demanding my presence continuously. This was truly a dangerous situation, which was getting worse by the day. Dr Gall then made a surprise call on her, accompanied by a specialist colleague. They talked to her alone and afterwards she was unusually quiet. Dr. Gall said that my wife urgently needed treatment in York Retreat, where she might eventually recover and, hopefully, return to normal. Joan had accepted this suggestion. I was left with my two young children, to explain that Mummy had needed to go away and rest for a while. Friends willingly helped and the children did their best to co-operate. They assisted with the housework and enjoyed helping to prepare meals. The atmosphere had changed completely. I had their full co-operation. Jennifer had always behaved well, so very different from her brother. He was always restless because of his exuberant energy.

Dr Gall said that medical staff at the York Retreat would notify me of any improvement. Six months later I brought Joan home, quiet and subdued. There were no further beatings, but Nigel kept his distance, and their relationship never grew warmer. We agreed that it would be safer and better for our children's safety and future well-being, to find them good, reliable boarding schools. Our children accepted this solution, though they were not taken with the thought of leaving home.

Joan's affection for Nigel deepened over the years, once they were separated. But he could never forgive, though I taxed him with wilfully causing her problems. Once Nigel had left home for London to live his own life and eventually qualify as barrister, he did soften a little. Joan then tried to help him as much as possible. But there was always an unbridgeable gap between them. I believe he tried to improve their relationship years later when she began to suffer heart attacks. Happily the mutual trust and bond between Nigel, Jennifer and myself grew stronger over the years. Some measure of acceptance gradually emerged. Joan's love for her children grew as they matured to success in their studies. In later years, she devoted herself more and more to finding ways of helping them alike, in those difficult, costly early years as barristers. While they were seeking Chambers, and understudying experienced colleagues in Court.

My personal sales and commitment to my area had now produced peak performances and my team responded well. I reminded Donner of his promise to me in London, of a return to my original status of co-founder, if I returned to rebuild the company. This I had done in full measure, so he should now restore my proper authority. Donner then told me abruptly that I was by far his best salesman and supervisor and, in his opinion, this was where my best talents lay. I put it to him bluntly that what he really meant was that he was using me only for driving up sales, and did not intend to keep his promises. They, especially Meyer, were adamant. I surprised them both with my resignation on the spot. I told them that I could see no future working with them. They said "You can't resign, we need you." I later discovered that they had calculated that my major earnings

137

would prevent me from leaving to an uncertain future. But they had underestimated me and, before they'd recovered from the shock, I simply left and never returned.

The self-confidence I had developed in my early years had matured with war service. It was high time for me to become master of my own future, which I could no longer fulfil working within their selfish compass. Our company solicitor in Wakefield, who had always held me in high esteem, offered to train me, saying that I would make a good lawyer. This opportunity really interested me, but my family situation made it impossible for me to continue to work by day and study by night. My worthy sales team all phoned to beg me to reconsider, and several threatened to leave if I would not return. I told them that I was just following my own star. I could never harm Double Two, for whose birth I had shared responsibility. But they were better off staying where they were, earning a good living by their own efforts. Some of my oldest and most loyal customers wrote and phoned me. They even visited Donner personally to argue my case and tell him that they wanted me back. They had always regarded me as Mr Double-Two, partner of the firm. Donner was obdurate and did not communicate with me for years.

I decided to learn more about all aspects of the garment industry, in order to decide which branch I would concentrate on. I had offers from some of the best, like Kilspindie of Scotland, who made fine quality knitwear and were exceedingly pleasant in all their dealings. I refused offers from other shirt companies, including Van Heusen, Anchor and Bonsoir. I always admired Van Heusen as a company, as well as their high quality shirts. They and Bonsoir each offered me a fully responsible post as Sales Manager. The post came with a car and expenses, a good salary and a bonus. Though we would have to move to London.

Joan urged me to accept, especially as it meant leaving the North which she detested. But I had all my memories of founding the Wakefield Shirt Company and could not face selling other shirts. I told her that I had an inbuilt loyalty, which I could not betray for any inducement or bigger reward. Although Donner had not kept faith with me, I could never forget my first introduction into the unknown world of industry. I had even invented the name of Double Two, which still exists as the company trade-mark. I had also written all the literature and advertising material. They had been exciting times for an academic, thrown, into the hard, practical world of industry with no experience. It was good training for my war years.

I admired the men's garments that were made by Simons, a high quality Leeds clothing manufacturer. I recommended them to customers who were seeking good clothing for their shops. Simons asked me to call on them since they were curious to meet this stranger who was recommending their garments without seeking commission. I explained that my business was selling shirts, but I believed in looking after my customers in every way possible. My shirt sales increased as a result of building goodwill.

They insisted on making a suit for me and offered me their agency. Now I told them that I was ready to join them. They had shown me all the details of their production and I found their quality tailoring quite fascinating. There was so much detailed work in every garment, and I enjoyed watching the whole process. In fact, I became very successful in selling their garments to many of my old customers. There was a world of difference between the straight forward manufacture of shirts, and the highly complicated garment designing of sports and leisure jackets, trousers, suits and overcoats. There was a whole gamut of complications, into which I threw my lot and my fortune.

Most of all I enjoyed studying the different departments and learning the process of tailoring. There was a separate dining room for directors, and I was installed as a member. One of the three brothers had been in Canada during the war, helping to train RAF pilots. They were fascinated to learn of my war experience, and always referred to me as 'The Colonel', despite my request to be just plain Mister. I was invited to study the many tailoring processes, and grew deeply interested in the high quality materials and ever changing designs and cutting patterns. I was also interested in the sewing skills, whether they were done by hand or machine. As my interest grew, so did my close study of quality tailoring and the challenge for my future.

Years later when I had established a successful tailoring business I had a visit from Donner, who had to admit, grudgingly, that I had created a new and successful company. It was a confession of his own guilt, which at least he had the good grace to acknowledge. He claimed that they all missed me badly and he should not have let me go. We should have had a proper discussion, as had always happened in the past. He blamed Meyer, but I reminded him of our beginning, and erstwhile good relations and trust. He had relied upon me implicitly for everything from our first foundation of the company. I had now proved myself capable of founding and developing my own company, in my own way. To his surprise, I had done this in less time than he had built Double-Two, with my help. Nevertheless, I still held fast to my memory of our early days when, as a refugee from Hitler he had relied upon me completely. He first introduced me to the industrial world. I could never forget our first venture, when we counted every penny. We had achieved a lot along the way. Like building bricks out of straw, during lean, hard, difficult times. Those memories live with me for ever.

Chapter 14

Foundation of Atkinson Rhodes (1958 to 1983) and Retirement

I had followed my spirit guide, and decided to become a clothing manufacturer, founding my own Company. Cloth fascinated me and I visited famous Yorkshire and Scottish mills. They produced fine worsteds and rugged Scottish tweeds. I revived a famous name, Atkinson Rhodes, with myself and wife as partners. I hoped that this would give her a real interest. Suitable premises were available near the bus terminus and Leeds Markets. This was an ideal position for worker access, shopping and communications. At the age of forty four I had the will, energy and self confidence to pit myself against the experience of mature competitors in Leeds. This was the home of the clothing industry. I had succeeded against the odds with my first venture into British industry. Now I was in the senior division. At least I would be well covered. The manager of Lloyds Bank, Harrogate Branch, with whom I was already on good terms, granted me an overdraft. He then invited me to bank functions, and gave me an insight into economic affairs. Any spare time I had, I gave to my lifetime interest, the Conservative Party. Simons recommended Ellis as a production director. His father was manager of a big clothing company and had trained his son to be a practical tailor. He had avoided Army service by pleading that he was needed for the production of Army uniforms. Thus he had accumulated capital which he now wished to invest in a clothing company. He did not impress me as a trustworthy person. However, he had sufficient funds to warrant becoming a junior director, and I needed somebody who was skilled in all the various operations. He was a product of a tailoring family, born and bred into what was known as 'the Leeds jungle,' whose devious habits I was to learn about later. However, he set to work to organise the workers we had engaged. He sorted them into their proper positions, whether cutting, sewing or pressing, and they became the balanced team I required.

I was introduced to a leading designer named Tempest, who had been seasoned in the trade from apprenticeship. He had acquired design skills from the best in the industry. Mr. Tempest was a thoroughly decent man of high standard, and had lost his son in the Navy. He took a great interest in my Army career and worked loyally for me, keeping a close watch on the factory in my absence. I was delighted to find such a trustworthy father figure, on whom I could rely. The whole responsibility of producing first customers, and developing continuous sales, fell entirely upon me. We produced top quality garments, impeccably tailored and punctually delivered. There I relied on the expertise of my production team, who became a most competent, painstaking combination. Tempest impressed all customers with his expertise and pleasant approach, and became my reliable, right hand man.

Tempest had known Ellis for years and did not like or trust him, although he did his best to work amicably with him for my sake. Tempest was not only a top designer, he also took great pains to ensure that the cutters worked exactly to his patterns. He made sure that the sewers, both hand and machine, knew just what he expected on each design, down to the exact seaming. We developed a well-knit team of workers, with whom I enjoyed excellent relations through those first tough years. A period where we struggled to create our first group of satisfied customers, with patient perseverance. My first real problem with Ellis arose from his devoting so much time to his family, who called on him regularly at work. He enjoyed using his office to sort out his domestic problems. Whilst I had to leave my home in Harrogate early and devote myself to work until closing time. I also had to travel extensively to develop the capacity and financial viability, of our company. His mind did not extend beyond his craft since he had left school early. He had no conversational ability with customers, except with regard to the details of make. However he had plenty of cunning, as I was soon to learn.

Naturally, sales were my responsibility. I journeyed forth and produced the first orders, leaving Ellis in charge. Tempest reported that Ellis often turned up late in the mornings. He then disappeared early afternoon for golf, family affairs and socialising with his cronies, leaving Tempest in control. He had an odd concept of a working director's responsibilities, and believed that all problems beyond production should be left to administration and clerical staff. Fortunately, I had also engaged a factory engineer of sterling quality and experience, whose two previous employers, had gone bankrupt like many others in those difficult post-war years. Like Tempest, Ken was thoroughly reliable, an ex-Army mechanic and always present, in all weathers. He kept the heating pumps working and the electric power engines running, so that all operations worked successfully. He knew how to make machines hum with sweet efficiency and was never beaten by any problem. Dependable and trustworthy, he said that he had faith in me as a reliable employer. Ken and I were the first to arrive in the morning, and the last to leave at night. We ensured that all was safely secure. He was very knowledgeable, and would advise me which quality machines to buy at a sale. These sale items were usually obtained as a result of the frequent bankruptcies in our trade. He was indeed a treasure and worked solidly and uncomplainingly for me throughout the years. Such men are always a great asset, but sadly becoming rarer. At exhibitions home and abroad Ken was my right-hand man. He would set up stands with everything in its rightful place, exactly according to my sketches. I simply dressed the models and made final adjustments.

I discovered that Ellis had previously been accustomed to producing lower quality material such as war uniforms, at top speed. He had no knowledge of detailed costs, overheads, wage structures and all the minutiae and capital control of a company. He practised many cunning ploys, such as making suits for friends and pocketing the payment. This had been one of his earlier tricks of the trade, which he still continued.He also supplied all his brothers with their garments at our cost. Further discoveries emerged from loyal staff, and led to a showdown. I could no longer set off on a week's expedition in the full knowledge that all would be well. I began dropping in unexpectedly on an afternoon, to find him missing. When faced with these facts, he promised to behave properly in future and work only for the good of the company. Especially as I now had our first export prospects, which would necessitate my flying abroad. I simply could not face a week away, leaving him in charge, in complete confidence. I was to learn much more about the seamier side of the business world.

Our first years from 1958, showed the expected loss, from expenditure on plant and machinery, and operating costs. But by 1960 we were able to reach a near balance. However, we now needed more capital. I held a Directors' meeting and proposed that we each added further capital in shares. Ellis disagreed and offered only half the amount required. Naturally my share total increased against his, which gave me more security. I put up with the drain on my own capital, for we had to buy quantities of expensive quality, pure wool worsted and tweed and other unavoidable oncosts. He soon returned to his old habits. He supported his brother who was a private tailor, with private orders that were made up free of charge in our plant. Rumours reached me of an Ellis plot to force me out now that we were becoming successful. This was partly revealed when Ellis suddenly exclaimed that he was, "Fed up of it - being constantly watched and supervised." I replied that he only had himself to blame for failing in his duty to me and the firm. He cried, "Well if you're not satisfied, why don't you buy me out?"

I was astonished at such a direct approach, which must have been carefully prepared. He could raise money in his family, since they had all done well out of the war. Whereas he knew that I had sunk everything in the business, and had an overdraft. He had garnished a lot of money one way and another during the war years. Hence his desire to become a boss himself. His plan had been to join me as junior partner, to 'learn the ropes', since he had no knowledge of how to set up and develop a company on a sound foundation. Now that I was succeeding he had developed cunning plans, aided and abetted by his brothers. Information was gleaned from previous employers that revealed his intentions. He wanted to get rid of me and revert to dealing with large companies, who gave the biggest quantity continuous orders, at the lowest make-up prices. Obviously this was a policy that I would never consider. The main advantage for the Ellis brothers, would be a continuous stream of work, without the necessity of seeking individual retail customers. Small profits, producing regular mass orders, with the ever possible danger of losing such price-conscious customers to under-cutting rivals. This was why the Leeds garment trade was known as the 'jungle,' it was full of snares and traps. At least in war, you know your enemy!

Their cunning scheme was a take-over. They knew that I lacked the capital necessary to buy him out. I said that I would consider the proposition, but Ellis demanded an immediate agreement. I knew that at such early stage in our history, the whole business could not be valued by independent auditors at much more than our original investments. I would therefore have to raise his investment plus, at the most,15% increased value. I demanded an audit before final arbitration. They agreed and calculated that, being in debt to my bank, I would not have the resources to match theirs, and would therefore lose the deal. They had underestimated their opponent. They were confident that I had invested all my capital and was now at their mercy.

I had invested in the stock-market during my years with Wakefield, while I studied company reports on those long, solitary evenings in hotels. Thus I had my own private holding of good quality shares. I also enjoyed good relations with my bank manager, who had great influence in those days. In a private meeting I revealed the whole situation, and produced my shares, including those with Lloyds Bank. He was greatly impressed and said, "I always suspected you were a deep cove, playing your cards close to your chest. Why did you not show me these shares when you asked for an overdraft?" I replied, "Because you would have taken them as collateral and I would have lost them. As it is, you thought me worthy of trust and issued the overdraft. Your judgement was right." He smiled, and said, "Oh I knew you were trustworthy from reports I obtained."

I now handed over sufficient shares to warrant his cheque for the full amount required, which actually came almost exactly to the amount I had estimated. I instructed my solicitor to indicate concern to Ellis's solicitor and beg for more time. Then I spoke to Ellis, pleading for more time to try to raise the money, indicating my desperate situation. Of course he refused and I could imagine their celebration, as they enjoyed my desperate struggles! As the ultimate day approached, Ellis found it difficult to hide his exultation. An air of gloom had settled on the workers, who had been put in the picture by Tempest and Ken. They were fully on my side, and loathed the dirty tactics of the Ellis brothers. It suited me well to have Ellis full of the joy of anticipation.

When the day came, I left the factory with Ellis watching triumphantly. My solicitor pocketed my bank cheque for the full amount and off we set, grave-faced. There they were, Ellis with his brother and solicitor, with the documents spread on his desk and a bottle of wine on a side table. "Well" said their solicitor, "We are now at decision time." "I'm afraid so" said my solicitor. He opened his case and produced our document. The

Ellis brothers stood up in eager anticipation. As the bank cheque for the full amount appeared, all three looked at it in utter amazement and disbelief. Ellis reached for it, but I said, "This is the property of your solicitor now," and handed it to him.

Their solicitor took their defeat well. He shook hands with me and opened the bottle to celebrate the deal, even though it had not gone as anticipated. I shall never forget the reaction of the Ellis brothers. Their jaws had dropped at the sight of the cheque. Consternation, disbelief, then dawning realisation that they were completely defeated and excluded from my founded company of Atkinson Rhodes, which they had literally sought to steal from me. Just as Meyer and his brother had planned to do against Donner. My solicitor returned to the factory with me to confirm the good news. All work stopped and there was an immediate celebration, which continued way past closing time. Old Tempest was in tears, and Ken was so emotional that he shook hands holding an oily rag. They all saw me off to continue my celebration at home. Though my wife could scarcely believe that I had won against those Ellis heavyweights. But I had studied war tactics, to learn the enemy's strength and weakness, and turn it to one's advantage.

Thereafter, I was able to travel for days without fear of consequences. As trade expanded I engaged more workers, supervisory staff and a skilled woman sewing manager. We opened another three floors. The top floor contained large quantities of valuable quality cloth, with a hoist to lift and lower. Then there were big rooms with large cutting tables, with rows of hanging garment patterns of suits, jackets, trousers, overcoats and dress-wear. All presided over by Mr. Tempest in his designer's office. The main floors were divided into sewing operations, with a separate group for hand-sewn edges and button-holes. These were high quality experts and it was fascinating to watch their hands moving at dexterous speed and accuracy. We sought to incorporate special, important and novel features to mark us out as different from competitors. Our production rose to fullest capacity to maximum targets and beyond. This was the reward of outstanding quality, which was maintained to everybody's satisfaction.

We survived the first lean years, and gradually grew bigger and more successful. Our name was respected for the high quality on which I always insisted. Having built up a good clientele base in the North and Midlands, I spent more time in London. Here I successfully opened accounts with Jaeger, Austin Reed, 'Cue,' Harrods and Gieves. The 'Village Shops' Group specialised in country tweeds and the famous John Stephen fashion shops. London was now becoming my main centre of activity. John Stephen, 'King of Carnaby Street,' was the fashion designer/ leader of the youth of the 1960s/70s. During this period I met the Beatles, Rolling Stones, Bee Gees and other musicians, writers and artistes Television and radio stars always crowded around and this was most enjoyable, especially as most were wearing JS outfits made by Atkinson Rhodes. I always produced special samples for John and partners, in the different designs they envisaged. I also invited them to Leeds, which they thought of as the 'outlandish, North.' They were actually fascinated by all the intricate operations and especially the rows of various cutting patterns, that were clearly marked 'John Stephens.'

As our fame for quality and service grew, more and more buyers came to us, instead of my having to visit them. Thus Jaeger buyers would visit the factory twice a year to discuss ideas for new designs, materials, styling and fitting. They were the first to experiment with double-knit jersey, and we made considerable quantities of Blazers for them. John Stephen's fifteen fashion shops in Carnaby Street were all under different names, they were also on the King's Road and Old Compton Street. America and Italy were featuring extra slim jackets and wide bottomed trousers, with dark navy overcoats, worn de rigeur. This was a highly successful operation and they relied on my advice, which they accepted without demur. They claimed that I was their only supplier who was capable of interpreting and producing satisfactorily, large quantities of any new design. They certainly kept us on our toes, since we had to cater for sudden style changes. In fact, they set the styling and fashion for the majority of the fashion trade. Everyone copied John Stephens. Burtons 'Top Shops' requested similar lines and Austin Reed called me in to help them start their 'Cue' Department, which was devoted to that same close-fit styling. We made all their orders and opened Cue in fine style, and they continue to be successful.

Browns of South Molton Street, owned a string of successful high fashion and expensive ladies shops. The owners were a charming, efficient couple who came to seek my help in starting a men's department. Their son, a veritable amateur was in charge. He insisted on our making his own concept of designs and styles. These were not a success. I advised him to use our specific designs, which had stood all tests of good fitting. But he insisted and countermanded the advice of his stylist, who preferred our fittings. The stylist promptly resigned and came to see me in Leeds. He said that he admired our garments and wished to sell them, first of all under our name until he was established. Then in cooperation with us, he wanted to run his own enterprise, for which he gave his word, having nothing else to offer.

His name was Paul Smith. His father owned a half shop in Nottingham, where he had learnt about men's clothes. Paul had a natural instinct for quality and style, and admired our garments. He asked whether I would trust and support him, in starting to sell under our and his own name in London. I liked him immensely, and agreed on the spot. I was certain that he would succeed. He started off with samples and then small orders, which expanded rapidly, especially on jackets and trousers. He was always so modest, yet knew exactly what he wanted. The girls all enjoyed his visits. He would arrive in his ancient sports car with stories about his London adventures.

Then, one day he approached me personally, with a quite different story. In the midst of the much coveted Covent Garden, a building was for sale in Floral Street. It had been neglected for years by its previous owner. Paul had the opportunity to buy it before it came on the market, where it would reach a far higher price and would be beyond his reach. "This" said Paul, "was the chance of a lifetime. Exactly what I have been seeking and dreaming about." "Fine" I said, "go ahead and snap it up." "Only one problem" said Paul, ever a man of few words, "MONEY". "Well, tell me - maybe I can advise," It seemed that he was short of the amount required and needed £25,000, today's equivalent of over £300,000, in addition to his own arrangements. The building needed a lot of work, but he was prepared to do much of it himself.

Could I ? Would I help? Of course I would. I recognised his quality and gauged him as enterprising and imaginative. He had the sustained courage and determination to see the project through. I offered to invest in a share in his company but he declined. "I am determined to go it alone." So I wrote him a cheque on the spot for £25,000. This was to be repaid in easy stages, without interest and without contract, solely on his note of hand. I instinctively believed in him, for he was down to earth, resourceful, imaginative and trustworthy. I enjoyed working with him and could foresee a great future, with his talent, skill and capacity for sustained hard work. Like me, he was a 'one-off' individual, and deserved support. Nobody had ever helped me in any way, but I had successfully fought my way through many problems. Had somebody backed me when I had needed just £3000 to match Donner in 1939, I would have been his equal partner. I would have shared the major success of our enterprise. I made my gesture to Paul, even though it strained my resources. I could ill-afford to gamble on his future success, when I was just beginning to see mine emerging.

He phoned me with reports of his manual labour repairs. Then the great opening day dawned. He and his helpers had spent hours and hours preparing the shop, and dressing the windows to perfection; only to have some lout smash the main window and destroy his hard work, stealing his best models. Being Paul, he just gritted his teeth and rebuilt it all, working through the night. The shop was a success from the outset. It was the realisation of all his dreams. It was the foundation of his future, which I had foreseen from the outset. Thus, I helped him found his empire, for which I never sought and never received reward. Even when his turnover turned into millions, boosted by his own extraordinary genius and judgement. My pleasure has been watching his amazing progress, and enjoying our ever continuing friendship. It is my boast that I believed in him and trusted and supported him financially, almost from our first meeting. I have enjoyed his success almost as if he were my own son. In fact, it was I who suggested his knighthood, in order to enhance his growing sales abroad, especially in Japan, America and Europe. He progresses around the world at a rapid pace, with Pauline, opening Paul Smiths fashion shops in every country, including Russia. I only wish that he had accepted my first offer of shares instead of a repayment, since I had believed in his ultimate success at the very outset. In the early years he would drive up to Leeds in his big antique sports car, or phone for my advice on production, and financial matters. There were times when he was rather overwhelmed by his own quick success, though he appeared cool and 'laid back.' He had his own innate sense of choice of materials and designs. He moved firstly by accepting our ranges, and then quickly to his own concept of style and fashion. He studied all our operations down to final pressing, that confirmed the lasting shape, style and fitting. Now, world celebrities shop at Paul Smith enterprises, shops, boutiques and quality tailors. They all enjoy the excellence of his unique instinct for taste, quality, colour and design. He is now Sir Paul, older, wiser but basically the same tall, angular, self-possessed youth who impressed me long ago. He still finds time to keep in touch with his friend, who set him on his way.

Thus I was proudly involved in the true birth and development of the Paul Smith Empire. His speciality from the outset was 'separates.' He loved our Jackets, Blazers and accurate fittings. He would make his own selection of speciality cloth and materials. He thought our trousers, especially the cords, were the best cut, fit and finish in the whole of the trade. All the stars of stage, screen and the music world, and the royals bought regularly from him, and wore Atkinson Rhodes/Paul Smith garments. Eventually he repaid everything as his business prospered, adding his own fine gesture of gratitude in his own inimitable style. As Paul himself wrote of me: "Without his trust and support I could not have progressed to where I am today." Moreover at least I can claim that I taught him the principles of tailoring, building a business and organising the size and construction of his orders, as well as the principles of finance. He created the rest with his own enterprise, good taste and personality, with the aid of his charming, intelligent, designer trained Pauline.

My first Savile Row account was with Rupert Lycett-Green, who was John Betjeman's son-in-law. He'd discovered the maker of Paul's cords, then came to Leeds to meet me and give his first order. He considered ours the best in the trade, so my good relations with cloth makers had paid off handsomely. Those British cloth weavers were the best in the world, at a time when British manufacturing was acknowledged as being supreme. It saddens me to see that it has vastly diminished over the past few generations, along with many other good old customs. Eventually I opened further accounts in Savile Row. There were many who were willing to buy our ready made jackets and trousers, but made to their own design and label. It pleased my workers, satisfied my ego and enhanced our reputation. Thus bringing in more buyers and bigger orders. As my Yorkshire friends said: 'Tis all grist t'mill.' 'A good name's tha best currency.' They taught me well. Their simple philosophy was, that top quality speaks all languages. I therefore became a successful industrialist and a leader in the men's garment industry. It was my great pleasure to prove Donner wrong. He had said that I was a good salesman but lacked the ability to run a company. I had now, unlike him, done it entirely on my own, like the popular song: 'I did it my way.'

My first experience in cloth buying was extraordinary. In early years I needed only small quantities. Therefore, when the elegant representative of a famous Yorkshire Mill called to see me with his elaborate set of cloth patterns, I ordered just one piece. This was sufficient to make about twenty five suits. He said that he would have to confirm such a small order. The following day a Rolls Royce appeared, and out stepped a big man dressed in a tweed suit. It was the Mill owner himself, who proceeded to ask me searching questions. I stated clearly that I could only buy within my requirements, since I had only just started the business. Then he drove me to lunch at the Millowners' Club in Huddersfield. We sat at a massive round oak table, which was covered with an old-fashioned, red plush velvet tablecloth, that had round, plush baubles around the edges. I was introduced by my host as a 'new lad, just starting in the garment trade, fresh out of the Army.' They all welcomed me without question, simply on his say-so.

Lunch began with a Yorkshire pudding, that completely covered each plate. It was delicious and as light as a feather, served with hot gravy. Then a big dish of roast beef and vegetables appeared, also covered with rich gravy. This was followed by roly-poly pudding with custard. A real Yorkshire man-sized meal. My host whispered to me, "Look around you, everyone is a millionaire, though you would never guess. But they will accept any order you give now, no matter how small, with never an argument as long as you pay promptly before your next order. But if you order twenty pieces and fail to pay, the black ball goes in yon pot, and you'll never get another order accepted from any Mill." These were words of advice that I never forgot. Furthermore, I enjoyed the company of those down to earth, bluff Yorkshiremen, who talked straight, did not mince words, and never let me down. They enrolled me as a member of their Federation of British Industries.

I enjoyed their plain-speaking down to earth attitude, and was delighted to learn that they regarded me as 'a lad with plenty of bottom.' This was Yorkshire speak for having the 'guts to succeed.' It was the best real, honest compliment that I had ever received. I came to love Yorkshire, with its sweeping hills and dales and independent villages. Its plain speaking folk were 'not bothered' whether you were wealthy or not; as long as you were acceptable and trustworthy to them and not afraid 'to get hands mucky,' for 'where there's muck there's brass.' I had no idea in 1940, on our first visit to Wakefield, that the major part of my future life would be weathered in doughty Yorkshire. My home city of Bristol saw me through my growing years and education. The War had developed my manhood. Then Yorkshire gave me fame and fortune, along with the love of England's greatest and biggest county.

I remember an old second-hand dealer. He wore an old, baggy tweed suit, and an ancient cap that was always perched on the back of his head. He looked as shabby and poor as the proverbial church mouse, yet he owned a huge, spreading warehouse on the outskirts of Leeds. It was full of the biggest and weirdest assortment of furniture, fittings and machines that he could find, including spare parts of all kinds. He loved buying and selling more than eating. He always looked worn and down at heel, yet his daughter confided in me that he was 'simply rolling in it, had no need to work.' He was a wise old bird with a hidden fund of knowledge. My children thought that he was a magician, and loved roaming around his vast empire. Ken enjoyed bargaining for work benches, machines, chairs, tables and spare parts. Later I bought the first desks, chairs and furniture for Cundall Manor from him. He actually visited the school and fell in love with it. His daughter drove him over at weekends to sit and look at my school's activities. It became one of his favourite spots. Dickens would have loved him as a genuine character. He died wheezing in his old armchair, leaving his caring daughter very wealthy.

Those were happy times in the 1960's and 1970's when our garments were in great demand. We took a Stand each year at the annual International Men's Clothing Exhibitions at Earl's Court or Harrogate. Our new models were always selected for exhibition and we won two Oscars for the best UK garments of each year. Most successful was our lightweight, black dinner jacket suit. The jacket reversed into white and was unique. The garment gained an Oscar unanimously. I was a member of the Federation of British Industry, consisting mainly of weavers and mill owners. There were two other small organisations. At a meeting in the 1960's, it was proposed that we all amalgamated, in order to become more powerful. Thus the Confederation of British Industry was born, and I was a Founder Member. I attended the monthly meetings at Tothill Street, Westminster and was made head of Operations of the CBI Branch in Leeds. I had many a tussle with Trade Union Leaders, who all had place cards, each with OBE writ large, these initials were short for Harold Wilson's Old Boys Enterprise.

British Exports were weak in men's clothing and this prompted a demand for more effort. I had been flying to exhibitions in New York and Europe for some years, and had found it quite easy to open accounts for English clothes, especially for tweeds and blazers. The French and Swiss especially admired our blazers, and I sold them to Saks on 5th Avenue, Bloomingdales and Barneys. British country clothes were popular in every major town, especially in our characteristic tweed and cord designs. The British blazer has retained its popularity all through the years, and we were established as THE top quality supplier. This entailed the storage of large stocks, in order to cope with the continuous demand; with gold, silver, or special club or group crested buttons that were suitable for most occasions.

Some of my happiest and most successful visits were to the American and Canadian Forces PX Stores. I flew by helicopter to Luxembourg, over the long, white lines of First World War cemeteries, with huge flames from mining works lighting up the night sky. I was welcomed as Colonel Harry and they were pleased to see an English clothing maker in person. I flew home with big dollar orders and gifts from PX for my family. The CBI complained that we were failing to expand the export market, and I agreed. The British attitude in those days, certainly in our trade, was anti-export. They claimed that my success was due to my fluency with languages. But I told them that most Europeans spoke English. It was the most popular language. I actually arranged export visits and good contacts for other British firms. Sir Joseph Lockwood of HMV, wrote me a letter of personal thanks for the introductions that I arranged. The export market did gradually improve, and I am glad that I helped them get off the ground. But I received little recognition for all my efforts, most of which had been exerted using my own time and money.

Our house was near Conservative Offices, where I met the agent, who told me that the current MP was due to retire in1959. He suggested that I stand for the Harrogate area. Had he suggested this move before I'd invested all my capital, I would have accepted. He countered with a fresh suggestion. Would I consider standing as a Conservative Councillor for my Ward, East Central, which badly needed strong support? I agreed and did my own canvassing, with the help of our young Conservatives. They were a strong group. I gave them my close support and held a series of talks, which they seemed to enjoy. They were very responsive and eager to help me. They worked in pairs and created a very good impression. But Joan took a dim view of my becoming a Councillor, fearing that she might have to play a prominent public role herself. Whilst I was always a social animal, she did not like meeting people. For her, the world was black or dark grey with no silver lining, even when we were obviously becoming prosperous. Though she was a partner, she adamantly refused ever to visit the factory.

I succeeded in becoming a Conservative Borough Councillor at my first attempt. I eventually became Chairman of committees, especially those dealing with education, property and planning, and was voted Management Leader. I had always been deeply interested in politics. As a life long Tory I enjoyed the regular tussle with the Liberals, especially when they became Liberal-Democrats. People no longer seem to enjoy politics, and open discussion in the same way. Some will not even answer the doorbell, or allow time for an exchange of views. They prefer to have news and information doled out by TV and radio, along with the scaremongering headlines of the national press. Stories that are usually blown up out of proportion for daily scandal doses, and dished out to eager readers looking for more exciting 'bad news.'

The 1970s were characterised by the smug hypocrisy of Ted Heath and the crude dictatorship of some major unions, who were busily corrupting our great industries.

This was especially true of 'Red Robbo,' the scurge of car making and shipbuilding, with its white lines causing endless warfare between union factions. We strongly supported Margaret Thatcher when she faced down Joe Gormley's Union Empire. Yet again, when she brought to an end Scargill's ill-advised, ill-led, unhappy and unprepared coal miners' strike. This strike grieved me sorely. My comrades in the R.E.s at Ripponden in 1940 were all Yorkshire miners, and I would gladly have gone to war with them. During the strike I still felt their troubles, no matter what difference the years had made, and I grieved for them. I contributed secretly to their sustenance. Though I would not support their misguided leader, Arthur Scargill. He was busily fighting his own road to fame, on the backs of misled, honest miners. Quiet and peaceful negotiations, between parties who were really intent on finding a solution, could have agreed a suitable settlement. I would have been glad to have represented the miners. They were the salt of the earth and beavered away in terrible conditions, for our warmth and pleasure. Some of those mines will eventually be needed again.

As the British economy slowed and suffered, I made more frequent sales trips abroad, since I needed to devote more time to selling. Business increased steadily with Paul Smith, who made regular visits to the factory with Pauline. We now made all Paul's suit, jacket and trouser styles, in different materials, from cord and tweeds to linen and cotton. His buying trips were most welcome and refreshing, for me particularly. He was also beginning to develop sales in Europe. He even persuaded the British Embassy in Paris to allow him space for his exhibition. He had a natural gift for choosing expressive materials and designs for the future season. His original Covent Garden shop became more and more popular, not only with stars of radio and television, music, theatre and the art world, but also with Members of Parliament. Lord Snowden and the Royals, who normally had their clothes tailored in Saville Row, now dropped into Floral Street, to try Paul's latest designs. These included original materials, neckwear, colourful shirts and pullovers. He gradually widened his scope and opened more shops. He developed his own export trade, and became an all time favourite in Japan. I have never changed my good opinion of him from the first day of our acquaintance. He stands out amongst all others as a beacon of good British strength and determination. He also has an in-built courtesy, tremendous patience and a constant level of coolness. He has never allowed success to go to his head. If only others would follow his example!

My orders in London grew apace and I became well known as a designer. I had a strong feeling for fashion, new styles. materials and fittings. London was leading the fashion world, and we were on the ball with every changing trend. My team responded enthusiastically, and enjoyed the excitement of every new set of orders. I opened a new London office, as my major business was now centred there. Once a name becomes well known as a major supplier to top fashion houses, the connection seems to flourish by itself. Therefore, we were always busy with repeat orders. I found that Burtons wanted to implement a quality line in clothing, just like John Stephens. Gieves were interested in the styles I was making for Jaeger. Dunhill's famous shop in Jermyn Street began a men's clothing department and gave us their first orders. Those were truly exciting times and they provided a welcome relief from my problems at home.

We were not a Union shop, a fact which I made clear from the outset to all workers. But we never had a strike, because I promised the Garments Makers Union, over interminable cups of tea, that I would never pay less than the full going rate. In fact, I paid slightly over, plus the odd extras for overtime and special occasions. None of my staff ever left, unless of course, they had extenuating personal circumstances that forced them to do so. Workmates would get together and help each other whenever needed. I also found ways of helping those in trouble, although the workers had tremendous self-pride and would not readily ask for help. This was a great asset that I have always admired in British working class citizens. Even from my young days when I was growing up in St. Paul's Bristol. I remember when there was a pawnbroker on nearly every corner and the Pearl Insurance man calling for weekly payments.

Since we were not a Union shop, the Garment Makers' Union insisted that our workers appoint a representative, to speak and act for them on all occasions. Meetings were held in lunch breaks and votes taken after much discussion. "Who have you chosen?" I asked my workers. "You" was the reply. "But I cannot be your Representative. The Union will not accept me!" Oh, but my girls insisted and the Union accepted this situation for the first time in history. A truly historic event! The following year the Union called an all-out strike, because of the failure of some employers to keep to agreed pay conditions. All workers from all factories had to come out. My girls did not want to strike, but were afraid of the Union. "No need to be afraid" I said, "as its a general strike, which affects everybody, you must join in." "We'll only go if you will lead us as our Representative." Consequently, for the first time in Leeds, and probably in British history, people witnessed a boss leading his workers out of their factory, to join the strike. The Union representatives were 'gob-smacked,' and rushed over to shake my hand. They were laughing fit to burst. I have never lived it down, and it is the absolute truth. Indeed, I have dined out on this story many times. I was 'sent to Coventry,' by some owners, who refused to speak to me. They called me a renegade.

My workers were always very important to me. Some of them had been working in the garment industry all their lives. A lot of them had left school aged 13 or younger. I respected them all, and treated them accordingly. In return I received their ungrudging support. They were so enamoured with our trade, that they actually enjoyed coming to work. The factory was always clean and warm, and the workers had great expertise that had been gained from a lifetime of sewing. They enjoyed working in the relaxed atmosphere surrounded by all their mates. Instructions were given quietly and cheerfully. Ken ensured that the machines were always in good running order. Spare machines were always on standby, and the rooms were cleaned and polished every evening. I was determined to provide the best working conditions and atmosphere. Thus I earned the trust of my workers. They knew that I was always ready to listen to their problems, and advise and help whenever possible. Walls and ceilings were painted regularly and the workers chose the colour scheme. They had lunch in our canteen and shopped in their lunch hour in Leeds famous, enclosed market opposite. The bus station was at the lower end of the markets, so they wasted no time in hurrying home.

Their jokes and quips flew from bench to bench. They made their own clothes at home during what little time they had to spare. There was a constant flow of gossip and stories from my contented workers. At Christmas the girls decorated the whole factory with coloured tapes, ornaments, lanterns. They had their own committee, and I donated funds to the Christmas Party. Then we all sat down to Christmas dinner, which was cooked in our own ovens. Although the baking and making of all kinds of goodies had been done at home. No outsiders were allowed on the first day, except for old, retired hands. Tempest, Ken, management staff and committee members and myself, served dinner in the beautifully decorated canteen. It was a really homely affair, with singing, dancing and lots of old songs. The happiest day of the year and worth every effort, to see them all so content.

When I bought a small van to carry our exhibition props at home and abroad, I handed it to Ken saying, "This is in place of the Rolls Royce I never promised you." He loved that van and took his family on regular outings, much to their delight. When I took stands in exhibitions, it was Ken who loaded and drove the van, and built the stand with his young assistant. Everything was all ready for me to dress with the prepared model garments. He was the person I missed most when I eventually retired. When old Tempest had finally retired he continued to drop in often, to keep an eye on the cutters and sewers. He also liked to have a cup of tea and a chat. He could not bear to be away from the action. He was like an old warhorse and kept a fatherly eye on me.

Smoking was strictly forbidden in our factory. There was one perilous occasion when Ken had just finished his rounds, and I thought I could smell burning. We retraced our steps and, sure enough, somebody had tossed a cigarette end into a waste bin. Gradually it had set light to the waste. It was just beginning to flame as we spotted it. We could have both been on our way home, only to be called out later with the awful news that the factory was in flames. After that incident we were doubly cautious. We gave our workers the grim news, that they were nearly out of a job. There was no surreptitious smoking thereafter. In the difficult post-war years, there were quite a number of factory fires. Although some of these were started deliberately, by firms who were facing bankruptcy and seeking to use the insurance money for a fresh start.

Our suit trade was now growing strongly. The garment trade is so driven by immediate changes of fashion, that suddenly suits were in demand for seasons. This demand was abruptly followed by a demand for sports jackets, tweeds, flannels, cotton and linen, and for different style trousers. Sometimes a sudden switch came in the middle of a season. A demand for lightweight suits for instance, whilst we were producing orders for heavy Ulsters. Fortunately, we had increased the number of workers and were able to establish a special team. This team were responsible for coping with sudden changes in fashion trends. American orders in particular, often came at widely differing seasons. My only real problem lay in finding a good, reliable, accountant, not only to balance the books , but also to deal with the Inland Revenue. All records were kept in accurate order by my administration staff. They consisted of two middle aged ladies who'd had years of book-keeping experience. They kept precise records under my firm instructions and guidance. From the very beginning I was determined that everything would be accurately and correctly recorded. I had heard astonishing stories of the 'tricks of the trade,' and some were almost beyond belief. Keeping two sets of books was a well-known ploy. In all, I employed three sets of professional accountants in Leeds, one of whom was too sharp in his tax dealings. The second was very stupid and made too many mistakes. Finally and unwittingly I employed an alcoholic. He was once brilliant but had gradually grown slovenly. He was always late and had an indecipherable scrawl.

To our amazement my wife eventually offered to keep the accounts at home. In essence she took over the bookkeeping responsibility. My clerical staff prepared all the accounts for Joan, who kept them in complete order. It was truly amazing, as she'd had no training in this field. With both children away Joan became more stable. Keeping precise, accurate accounts, was a pleasure for her and a daily duty she enjoyed. My staff were amazed at how quickly Joan assimilated all the details of costs, expenditure and income. Within a year she was balancing the accounts completely and accurately. From then on, the Inspector of Taxes had no complaints. They even wrote a few words of praise for her neat, precise statements. Actually, Joan had long been keeping detailed records of our personal accounts, and investments.

Joan also learnt about the Stock Market, after years of vilifying me for 'gambling hard-earned money, which should better be saved for the children.' When she saw the factual gains that could be derived from solid companies like banks, she began to take more interest. I bought her some shares as her first investment. It was astonishing how quickly she learnt about the peculiarities of the Stock Market, and she began to follow my favourites. This process helped to offset her claustrophobia, as she rarely left the house except for shopping expeditions with me. With no real friends or outside interests, the Stock Market opened up a new and fairly exciting world for her.

Atkinson Rhodes flourished and my export business increased. I made regular flying visits to America and took part in International Clothing Exhibitions in New York. On one such visit I had a suite in a 5th Avenue hotel with my samples neatly arranged in one room. When I awoke next morning I found that the room was empty. All my beautifully tailored samples had vanished. The hotel police said it was an 'insider job' as the thieves had opened the door using a key. I attended the Exhibition with photographs and pattern bunches and my own extra garments. I still gained orders, especially from established customers like Saks, Barneys and Bloomingdales Stores. The latter had once offered to buy my whole range and season's total production. This was an attractive offer, but it would have deprived us of regular customers. These customers had been carefully and painstakingly developed over the years, so regretfully I turned down the offer.

However an American garment manufacturer at an International Show, introduced himself as Phillips from St. Louis, Missouri. He also had a proposition. His company would sell Atkinson Rhodes Jackets, Blazers and Pants (trousers) through their sales team around America, if I would sell their garments through my sales team in Britain. I could not tell him that my sales team was principally me, but I declined politely. I stated that American prices were so much higher than the British, that the process of making and selling their products in Britain would be impossible. Nevertheless, he invited me to visit their 'Plant' in St. Louis, so I flew over and was well entertained. They were considerably bigger than my company, but their garments not as well tailored and finished. This they acknowledged, and wanted to consider a deal whereby we would tailor their garments in England. They admired our English design and styling, which competed within a lower pay structure than their own. I envisaged them swallowing us whole. We would simply become a Phillips Branch. The deal was so heavily weighted on their side, we would have become a vassal unit.

Again it was an offer I had to refuse, with regret. But they were still not finished. They gave me orders for our Yorkshire and Scottish Tweed Jackets, Blazers and Pants at keenest prices for quality. These were duly made and delivered as per contract. Their sales team added them to their ranges as 'English Make.' They sold so well that we quickly received repeat orders. Then their salesmen refused to sell our products, since their popularity had prompted a reduction in the sales of their own garments. By mutual consent therefore, we finally parted company. Within a year I learnt that they had suffered a setback from internal dissension, and had finally sold out to another manufacturer. My instincts had been correct, but it was a pleasant episode.

When I returned to England, my staff were busily packing a large quantity of our stock garments into long wooden boxes. They were delighted to tell me about a magnificent order they had accomplished in my absence. A Nigerian company had placed a wonderful order, which would have cleared out nearly all the stock we held against repeat orders. They had written a letter, which claimed that they knew of our high reputation and had an immediate demand for our products. They required express shipment and had enclosed their cheque from a well known Nigerian bank for £20,000. They trusted us to send full quantities of a size-range laid down. But they demanded immediate despatch within seven days, otherwise the order failed. I found activity at fever pitch. Everybody had joined in to ensure the great triumph for the 'Boss,' with this fantastic super order, which was to be despatched before my return. They were taken aback when I stopped the packing. I said, "Just wait until I check." "Oh, we have checked, the bank is well-known as being one of the very best in Nigeria.""Yes I know, but have you checked the credentials of this company? Why, without any experience of us, do they give an open order trusting us to send top quality garments in the quantities requested? Doesn't it sound too good to be true? Would you give a complete stranger such an open order, for so much money, without properly checking?"

Crestfallen, they acknowledged that they had been so taken by this magnificent order, they had not made any checks on the company. They had also been motivated by the seven day time limit so as not to lose a moment in putting together such a marvellous, all embracing order. I phoned the Nigerian Embassy who verified the bank as being one of the very best, but could not vouch for the customer. They sent a cable to the bank's H.Q. in Nigeria for verification. They gave us the answer 'name unknown, no such customer,' and issued us with a warning about the clever tactics of such crooks. My staff were desolate and promised never to consider sending such huge quantities again, without first checking with me. A loss of £20,000 at that time, plus oncosts, including packaging, flight charges, and all the wages and incipient costs, could have caused major problems. We'd had a truly lucky escape.

We now had further problems, stemming from Prime Minister Ted Heath's three day week. Beaten and humbled by Joe Gormley during his battle against Union power, Heath was now facing economic chaos. His reaction was completely negative, and he forced his three day week on British Industry. Many good companies went under from loss of production, and an inability to fulfil orders. Britain reeled from this stupid, negative act. British industry protested, but to no avail. However, I was not prepared to let Atkinson Rhodes die a death because of Heath's cuts. We had a full order book, a reward for all our years of development. My workers were panic-stricken. They had families to support and could not afford to lose their jobs. Unemployment was high, and there were no other jobs available. I reminded them that we had come through problems before, and that this was no time to lose heart. We would seek a way around the problem, as we had always done. Tempest, Ken, managers, forewomen and supervisors were all invited to suggest solutions or alternative plans.

Suddenly a solution came to me, like the breaking of a cipher. Instead of working the habitual full days we could split forces to part-time working. If half the workforce worked one week mornings and then part-time afternoons, and reversed the following week for remainder, all would theoretically switch to part time working. Then if we switched halfway through the week, and added an extra hour split between am and pm., we could actually cover the same amount of work time equivalent to a full week. I explained my scheme in detail to Tempest and Ken, then to the Head Cutter, design team, supervisors, forewomen, workers and down to the packers. All agreed that it was a workable solution as long as everybody complied firmly with the rules, and did not discuss the changes outside. They were just to say they had been put on part time. Ken altered the clock-in machines and all was set. It worked magnificently and the workers even took shorter lunch breaks. All orders were made and delivered on time. Consequently, we received more orders and repeat orders, as other firms were failing to deliver. Since they had not found their way around this new regulation. Other companies gradually broke the regulation, cursed Heath and crept back to work. We simply found a way around the problem and succeeded. My workers thought I was a miracle worker. I was amused to learn that at the Wakefield Shirt Company, they'd simply obeyed Heath's orders, worked only three days and suffered great difficulties.

Heath continued to annoy us with his next move, which was to trick us into Europe. I remember all the meetings and discussions we held in Harrogate and Leeds. I actually led discussions, that were attended by big gatherings of our active Young Conservatives. The lies, if not actually put out as such, certainly had the truth twisted. According to Heath there were "250 million prospective buyers in Europe just waiting to give us orders." He persuasively stated, "Think of the trade awaiting us from Common Market fellow traders. What have we got to lose?" Only our Sovereignty, freedom in Law, movement, trade, general democratic freedom, that was won over centuries, with hard battles! There was no mention of the truly negative side. Heath and Rippon continued to lie, denying that there would be any loss of sovereignty or legal rights. They knew all the time that they were betraying Britain into an unelected, unknown consortium, that would be at the mercy of unelected plotters. We needed a Churchill, but no champion arose. Instead, subsequent leaders fell for the same plot, to their shame. Only Thatcher seemed to become aware of all the deceits. By then it was too late.

However my greatest adventure into industry was now reaching the high target I had secretly set from the beginning, to my own amazement. Despite all the initial problems everything eventually worked out successfully. I enjoyed every challenge and fresh struggle to reach each objective. At a time when Companies were avoiding export markets, I was enjoying successful flights to Europe and Scandinavia, especially the wonderful receptions in Denmark and Norway. There were productive trips to Paris, Lille, Basle, Bern and Zurich. We actually won the International Gold Award for top garment exports. But at the same time our trade was growing ever stronger at home, especially in London.

I ceased attending major CBI conferences, which had become a mere talking shop in London. They scarcely ever expressed real, concrete facts or views, and I confined myself to real activity at local conferences; and factual meetings in CBI Leeds office. There we held direct dealings with Trade Union leaders and Government officials, to tackle problems that affected Yorkshire and the Northern areas. We were able to make genuine progress, which enabled us to put sensible proposals to CBI HQ. I also chaired the CBI Northern Education Committee. I suggested that school leavers entering British Industry should receive further education and training. I remained an active member of the CBI until my retirement. But while our Yorkshire Branch held a farewell lunch in my honour, no word came from Tothill Street.

Since I was approaching my 70th year, I decided it was time to prepare for my first real rest from responsibilities. My children were now safely ensconced in their career as barristers. Nigel joined friends, including Pat Scotland (now Baroness Scotland), in setting up new Chambers at No.1, Gray's Inn. Jennifer fell in love with and married fellow barrister James Munby, who is now my respected son-in-law. It has been a wonderfully happy, successful marriage from the outset. While I was considering retirement, I had tentative approaches from people who were interested in making an offer to take over Atkinson Rhodes. One actually came to me personally with his accountant. He had been a sales manager in his father's company of knitting wools. He had become bored with dealing with small orders and sought to deal in bigger ranges of clothing, like mine. He seemed genuine and his accountant supported him, so eventually the deal was confirmed. I reluctantly parted with my very special foundation.

Farewell parties and retirement celebrations, now brought to an end my highly successful career as company founder and director, over some 25 years of devoted hard work. I had reached and passed my original dream target. However, I could not envisage myself settling down at 70, to enjoy a quiet retirement. I certainly anticipated a well earned rest, but then fresh activity either in politics or some other new enterprise. Yet when I explained this to my wife, she simply would not believe me. I made the usual plans for a major family leisure trip around the world. Unfortunately this was never to be. My wife's heart problems grew steadily worse and she needed regular treatment. As she would not accept any carer or nursing establishment I took over her nursing care. I also devised regular day trips over the beautiful areas of Yorkshire, with daily walks in the Valley Gardens. Joan seemed to enjoy these above all else.

Strangely, she now seemed quite fond of Yorkshire, especially Harrogate and no longer wished to return South. With her children gone, but rarely visiting, she was trying to come to terms with her past relations with Nigel. He had finally proven his ability and innate intelligence, by becoming a barrister. He had passed all his exams successfully and acknowledged our financial help and support over the years. The joy and privilege of attending the registering ceremonies of both Jennifer and Nigel in the Inner and Middle Temple, as fully qualified barristers, remained her undimmed, bright memory. Her remaining years were happily spent helping her children and grandchildren. Indeed, Thomas and Charlotte, the children of Jennifer and James, gave her the greatest pleasure of all.

Chapter 15

Family Life

Our family life was not quite the connubial pleasure I had always envisaged. During my four years War Service in the East I'd had literally no social life, and had rarely seen a white woman. Thus I was totally unprepared for the close company of English female staff working in Germany. I was captivated by the attractive blonde visa officer, Joan Davis. We became good companions after my first two years of resurrecting the Universities of Cologne and Bonn. Her Danish family was only mentioned after we became engaged. Joan's Danish grandfather Cuiksen founded the Victoria Carpet Company in Kidderminster, where Joan was born out of wedlock, in October 1917. Such conduct was then regarded as beyond the pale, and the children suffered as a result. Joan's mother was hastily married off to Davis, a teacher, but was so unhappy that she died soon after. Joan always suspected suicide, which preyed on her mind. Neither the Danish family, nor her grandfather would recognise her, but she was given a good education in Switzerland. Her unhappy childhood naturally affected her attitude to people.

Such stories emerged at odd moments, like during my memorable sales visits to Denmark. The Danes were so friendly, hospitable and completely pro-British. They told me how their Royal Family had defied the Nazis, and refused to obey their command that all Jews wear the Star of David on an armband. The King wore one himself, and his people followed, much to the Nazis' confusion. Both Danes and Norwegians smuggled many Jews to neutral Sweden at night, in blacked-out boats. The Danes had a more cavalier way of life. They preferred adventure and were more inclined to gamble than the Norwegians. But they were also temperamentally subject to mood swings. They could suddenly switch from merriment to depression and had a higher suicide rate.

I began to understand the mixture in Joan, for she was subject to depression. When we learnt that she was pregnant, I said that we must get married immediately. Joan was reluctant for she was studying for a permanent position in Foreign Office, but I insisted that we owed it to the child. How different the modern outlook! Our marriage took place in the British Consulate, Düsseldorf, but, en route, Joan had a presentiment that I would live to regret it. I laughed away her fears, but later recalled her foreboding. Even now, I wonder how different my life and that of my children might have been....for Joan never revealed the real truth about herself until much later. We had a wonderful honeymoon, but our return was spoilt by the news that Joan had passed her exam and had been appointed to a permanent position in Foreign Office. Spoilt, because of the F.O's ridiculously strict rule, which prevented the employment of married women. Joan had to resign and never forgave me. A permanent position in the Foreign Office had been her dream, since she had always lacked security as a child. The dream had been snatched away and I certainly had to suffer the consequences!

My father had died while I was in India. Somehow I could not bear to think of him dying. I still see him plainly, as that firm, sturdy figure of my youth. He never showed great emotion, but would give me a warm hug, especially when I came home with my degrees, the realisation of his dreams. But that abiding, quiet love was always there. I had reached all my targets in life successfully, but could not match his serenity. Such people, sometimes work ceaselessly and devotedly all their lives, often for little reward. They are the strong core of communities, holding them together and sacrificing themselves without hesitation for family and country. Unnoticed, they receive no awards or commendations and are usually just taken for granted. My parents belonged to this group of people and they'd laboured that I might succeed. Like the unknown soldier, they deserve the highest honour. But I know of no monument in gratitude of family sacrifice.

I was now unemployed, with a wife and child and we were sharing cramped quarters with my mother and one remaining sister. What a sorry state after ten years' devoted service. Then came the urgent recall to Wakefield. When I found myself back in Yorkshire I felt remarkably at home, and ready to renew my previous mastery of that branch of British industry. Since I was now a family man with extra responsibility and urgently needed to earn enough money to raise and educate my children. Prep Schools in Harrogate at that time were of poor quality. Clifton House School was owned by its Headmaster. Indeed, he owned a chain of preparatory schools. He was concerned primarily with profit, therefore he underpaid his staff and spent little as possible on buildings and equipment. The welfare and the education of the boys came last. After several non-productive interviews, I realised that Nigel would never make good progress there. But he needed to be separated from his mother. Eventually, we decided on Oundle, which seemed to offer a good all-round training, with art and workshop facilities to suit Nigel's special interest. Unfortunately, the master in charge of the first year entrants at Berrystead House, was a sadist. He would beat boys soundly for every misdemeanour, and the slightest breaking of his stringent rules. Whilst playing classical music loudly he would whack the little sufferer with one of his collection of canes. Berrystead House gathered an ill reputation, but the master continued his beatings, despite protests.

Several boys ran away and were punished when caught. Nigel revealed that, when one of his friends was caught after twice running away, he was so severely beaten that Matron had to keep him in sick bay for over a week. Nigel then told me everything, and, after corroboration, I complained to the Headmaster, Knight. He refused to believe that a member of his staff was responsible for any wrongdoing, until one had to be sent to an asylum. Knight himself left soon afterwards and improvements followed. We transferred Nigel to Bootham, which was a Quaker school for boys, set in the lovely city of York. It was a quiet, well-run school that did not resort to corporal punishment to maintain discipline. It seemed ideal and Nigel soon settled in. We were also able to visit him more often. Above all, he enjoyed my personal calls. When I was driving with him through Yorkshire we had good, frank discussions, and he frequently sought my advice. He was truly artistic and could draw and paint well. He also loved music. I discovered that his happiest moments at Oundle were those spent in the art studio and laboratory. With hindsight, he might have been best suited to study at Art College, but Joan would have considered this highly unsuitable.

Gateways School lay half way to Leeds on Lord Harewood's estate. It was a good girls' school and Jennifer settled there contentedly, after the poor quality Harrogate school. I drove her there in the morning in her neat green uniform, and she returned home by bus. Joan now helped Jennifer with her homework. A good student, she mastered her subjects well, especially languages. Latin was not taught at Gateways, so Joan and I taught Jennifer at home. Joan became so proficient, that she developed a love for Latin and Jennifer responded, and made good progress. When Jennifer herself expressed a desire to attend boarding school, we took her on a tour of possibles. Her final choice was Cheltenham Ladies College. The Headmistress, Miss Treadgold, was a large matronly figure who appealed to Jennifer immediately, as did the college. When offered the possibility of a scholarship, Jennifer accepted the challenge. One cold winter's day we drove through icy roads and snow banked hedges to a warm, friendly Irish hotel, close to the college. Scholarship exams lasted three days and the results were astounding. Jennifer came top and was awarded a scholarship. Fortunately Jennifer enjoyed both her studies and games at Cheltenham, and finished her schooling by achieving top grade A levels.

We made regular visits to both children during term time. Jennifer especially enjoyed the fine performances of Shakespeare plays at Stratford. With her love of horses she also enjoyed polo matches at Cirencester. After her A levels, Jennifer decided on Law as her career and chose London University. Once she was happy living in London, I visited her often on my regular business appointments. When I opened my London office in the West End, Jennifer found it a useful way to earn money, by working part time for me. In the meantime Nigel had disappeared into London. He had joined a group of young rebels, who ran stalls in a big underground market in Kensington. They sold their own kind of modern music and lived a hand-to-mouth existence. They enjoyed each day in their own company with no thought for tomorrow. Music was all important and they were rebels against the system. When his whereabouts were eventually revealed to me, I helped him find more suitable accommodation. Then I discussed his future and discovered that he still preferred Law and, like his sister, longed to become a barrister. When I explained that this meant a two year course, with fairly tough exams, he said he was prepared to get back into serious study, if I would help. Of course I was happy to help him now he had decided on his career direction.

After the children left home, Joan found our house too big and the grounds too extensive. Our gardener, dear old Rayner, was a lovable First World War veteran. "He was lazy and incompetent, and our housekeeper was careless with her work." Both had to go, especially as Joan could no longer climb the stairs. We moved to a bungalow that was large enough for Joan to have her own quarters. It also had a surrounding fence to keep out the neighbours. Situated in a quiet, tree lined, residential area, protected on all sides, Joan's agoraphobia grew worse and she refused to go out alone. I therefore did most of the shopping. I also drove her to the Valley Gardens, which was her favourite walking area, or around the Harrogate Cricket Ground, which was conveniently situated at the rear of our bungalow. Gardening became her hobby and she seemed to grow stronger and more active. Secure within her own domain she devoted herself to our children's welfare.

When, eventually, she offered to take over the company accounts, explaining that she had received some early training in basic book-keeping, I was worried about whether she would have the patience to keep the books regularly. But she insisted, and as we were having so much trouble from professional accountants, I agreed to a trial period. The result was amazing. Within three months the books were in order, and she had corrected errors made by staff and accountants alike. Benefits accrued to all, especially my wife. It also meant that Joan was able to maintain our various schemes for our children's future upkeep and training costs. We needed to support them through to the Bar until qualified and thereafter; until they were at last working in Chambers and earning their own living as barristers.

Many people fail, or have to leave the Bar because they are unable to raise the heavy financial costs necessary to see them through. Some have to find part employment elsewhere, or become solicitors or work for Insurers. Nigel the rebel had to live for years in rented damp, basement flats, usually at the mercy of unpleasant, sharp landlords. Now a hardworking barrister, he needed a place of his own. We encouraged him to look for suitable offers from estate agents around Notting Hill, ever our favourite neighbourhood. Eventually he chanced upon a small row of renovated ancient cottages, in an unbelievably quiet place. They were tucked away from the traffic on the outskirts of Notting Hill, within easy reach of four Underground stations. He negotiated the price down to a reasonable sum and we offered to supply two thirds. The deal was closed and we drove to London to help him move in. Now he possessed his own little house in a lovely quiet spot, almost unique in Notting Hill. He even softened towards Joan. Meanwhile Jennifer was now through her Bar exams, after graduating well from London University. Following her graduation, she gained acceptance at top quality chambers as their first woman member. The chambers were headed by Lord Alexander.

Nigel eventually passed his Bar exams to everybody's delight. His success transformed him! He invited us both to the Inordination Ceremony at Middle Temple, of which he was now a member. He dined with fellow barristers, Q.C's and judges. We were intrigued by this ancient custom of dining at long, polished tables in an ancient hall. It was a real joy to see Nigel called to the Reception Table, to be proposed for membership by a leading Judge, and then sign the official roster. I loved every moment, especially the really happy look on Nigel's face. I had never seen him look so completely contented. He had at last achieved his goal, and was a fully fledged barrister. Though there remained the struggle to gain acceptance at chambers, and win his spurs in legal cases. It was truly a moment of delight for the whole family.

Joan's agoraphobia grew worse and she would not leave the house unaccompanied. I had to bring food home with me from Leeds market, until the big supermarkets opened, with their big car parks. These enabled us to shop in comfort, with me pushing the trolley, and Joan filling it with groceries. Joan always hated my political activities and complained about the time I devoted to being a Councillor. The role required me to take part in canvassing and other activities. In fact, she hated anything that took me away from home. Every moment of my time seemed to be taken up from early morning to late night. I could only manage to enjoy a visit to my Prep school at weekends with my children, who truly loved Cundall Manor and Major Collins on his big horse. With a phone call odd evenings, to make sure the boys were well looked after. I had to forego much of my political enjoyment and duties to my great regret, for I truly loved the excitement of political battles and election contests. I filled much of my time during those long periods when I was confined to the house, with Joan's bouts of illness, by writing books. Though I really longed to be active again and needed the thrill of politics. I found politics to be such an antidote to the concentration of industry. However, I did manage to push through a project for our first, much needed small Conference Hall. It was built at the back of our Victorian Theatre in six months, at total cost of some £20,000, an unrepeatable bargain.

Now I was a lone voice, unable to be present at meetings to prevent the next perpetration. My wife and children were walking home when they heard loud crashes. They were in tears as they watched the demolition of our elegant town railway station, with its turreted plate glass roof portico. It was held up by slender pillars in a Victorian beautifully and tastefully constructed design that were always handsomely decorated with flowers. This was a wanton destruction of one of Harrogate's finest features. We were most upset by such despoliation of our lovely town, which was being torn apart by money driven development. In its place, developers erected the ugliest possible modern cement and glass construction, which acted as a wind-tunnel, blowing open all the doors and regularly breaking their glass. The most elegant railway station front was replaced by an ugly monstrosity. In addition, a faceless high tower concrete block was built, which now houses tax offices.

I was now more or less confined to home, with my wife suffering heart attacks and needing constant care. I only received such bad news about the buildings of Harrogate second hand, or through the local newspapers. I became rather depressed at the depreciating state of Harrogate politics, especially as the last good agent had now left. There was no proper guidance, and I longed to be more active. Any suggestion of my wife taking a spell in a nursing home with full care and facilities was out of the question. Joan would react with hysteria at the mere mention of nursing homes. It was during these years that the big construction of Harrogate's major Conference Centre, was planned and argued over. The project started and then stopped because of the failure of the primary builders. I had to sit and watch as the costs mounted into millions, until it was finally completed. Eventually it stood there, all bright and shining. It became the pride of our town and is now universally famous as a grand British Conference Centre, but yet too small for major assemblies.

Reluctantly, Joan accepted my role as Councillor, Chairman, Governor of Schools and other roles which I thoroughly enjoyed. The local offices became an escape centre, where I would willingly devote myself to all manner of duties. Joan was content most of the time, although she was still troubled by sudden by bouts of hysteria. However, the advent of television was a boon, for she now occupied herself with reading, radio, television and knitting. The latter was a hobby at which she excelled and she made garments for the whole family. I realised at last, that Joan was totally bound up in herself. Some women do not take well to motherhood and Joan had only really cared for her children when they were fully independent, away from home and successful. She did not care for people, especially women, and certainly had never wanted children, nor had any patience with them. Essentially, she wanted no part in other peoples' lives and could not understand why I was so interested in helping others. Thus she was always intensely jealous of any time I devoted to people and children. After two serious heart attacks, she simply pottered about the house and gardens, or watched television, leaving everything to me, but refusing to employ help.

My compensations were work, devotion to our children, supporting the Conservative cause and social and charitable activity. Beyond this was my continuous pleasure in the development of my school, Cundall Manor. Seeking a Headmaster I could trust, who would follow faithfully my original concept and be devoted to the education and welfare of the children. It is difficult for many people who claim to have expertise in the field of education, to grasp fully the importance of each child's physical and mental development. Teachers stand in loco parentis. It is one's primary duty to bring out the best in each child without undue pressure. They should enjoy participation in lessons and games. Only a slight touch of discipline ever needed and consideration for fellow class-mates. Teachers need better grounding in all aspects of children's growth and development, to engender the whole person.

Jennifer made good progress at the Bar specialising in Family Law, and was beginning to enjoy life and her many successes. But, most important was when she met fellow barrister James Munby and they fell in love at their first meeting. They wasted no time in getting engaged, and James dutifully asked for my permission to wed. Joan was most fearful at this news, fearing the worst as usual, perhaps James was 'some ne'er- do-well who'd cast a spell over her daughter.' He might take advantage of her and leave her, like a screen villain. This was hardly a fair picture of quiet, rather shy James. Joan had no idea of how her daughter's struggles through education and the Bar, had brought out her own tough strength. Jennifer told me that once she met James she knew instinctively that he was her choice for life, and he responded equally. It was a love match that has lasted amazingly well. They have a strong family life and my daughter continues to provide me with an enormous source of pleasure and pride.

They decided to get married in the famous London Registry Office without any special ceremony. Then they planned a really big reception at the Inns of Court, in best legal fashion. We arrived at the Registry to meet James' mother, who was a widow, who came alone and, like me, was not a whit apprehensive. We found James already there, sitting quietly waiting. It was an enjoyable marriage ceremony, well conducted. We then attended the magnificent reception. The legal profession really did them proud. The Hall was sumptuously decorated and absolutely full of members of the Bar. James' uncle, who was a Don at Oxford, welcomed us. All the close knit Munby family were there, brother Julian and sisters and relatives. Jennifer and James were surrounded by all their colleagues, whilst we were being congratulated on all sides. We were so proud of our daughter, who looked absolutely lovely and completely happy with James, and Nigel, busily introducing us to Judges and Seniors.

It was a fine beginning to a very happy and successful marriage, which has lasted in perfect harmony. They have two lovely children who are both now graduates of Oxford and Bristol. They gave Joan unadulterated delight towards the end of her life. I am a fond and delighted grandfather. Their father, Sir James, is now a High Court Judge and my daughter is now Lady Munby. Thomas is a barrister following his parents. Whilst Charlotte prefers a life and career in the country, since she has a tremendous love of horses. This characteristic she shares with her mother. They are my joy and pleasure. My son Nigel is now contentedly occupied with his best loved career, as a sculptor and artist, in his ancient cottage in Notting Hill. After over twenty five years at the Criminal Bar, he was glad to retire to enjoy his true vocation as an artist.

The family home within the ancient Frith Copse, which is commemorated by a stone marking it as 891, the HQ of King Alfred, at Manningford Bruce, Wiltshire, is only ten miles from where I now live in Marlborough. Family gatherings are always a pleasure. They are informal and full of fun, with everyone 'doing their own thing,' in their own time and space. It remains my great pleasure to help all my beloved family make their way through the twists and turns that we all encounter, on our journey through life. I hope that I may live long enough to become our joint families' great grandfather, with my grandchildren happily married. As the only grandparent left on both sides of our growing family, I am now the senior figure of the clan.

Chapter 16

Cundall Manor Prep-School

I was so frustrated by the poor quality of Prep schools in the Harrogate area in the 1950's that I decided to demonstrate how a school should be conducted for the benefit, care and education of children. Not the proprietors, nor the staff, who were often impeded in carrying out that primary responsibility. My friend Robert Birley, was Headmaster of Eton College, and I had worked with him on German re-education. He agreed with my concept of a Prep School, as providing preparation not just for further education, but also for coping with life's future problems. Parents should share that responsibility with the school by keeping in close touch with their children at all stages. This way they could learn about their problems, which may so often be blown out of context. Not to mollycoddle their children, but to maintain a watchful eye when they stumble.

When I was introduced to Major Arthur Collins, ex-Guards, we found instant accord. As Second World War warriors, we swopped adventure stories. He heard about my plans to start a new Prep school as a non-profit making enterprise, and offered his own family estate at Cundall. It was originally a hunting lodge and had been unused since the War. During my visits in Knaresborough, he and his wife told me how his father, Colonel Collins, had developed Cundall Manor and its lovely little chapel. They were truly delighted to envisage their estate becoming Cundall Manor School, and promised all possible help. I was happy to have found such an ideal place, and grateful for their support and friendship.

Sir Arthur, as he became, was ever a man of his word. He restored the Manor, which was ready for residence in 1959. The heating and plumbing was in order, and the big Aga cooker worked well. I inherited his old staff and set all in order, ready for the reception of the little future leaders. They were so urgently needed for our country's guidance. Unfortunately, as with the best laid plans, mine soon began to go awry. Hearing about the problems my prospective Headmaster took fright and withdrew, saying he was interested only in teaching. I therefore tackled the myriad of preparations for my enterprise, on my own. Although I was helped with suggestions and helpful lists from scholastic friends, I never envisaged having to calculate the number of beds, wardrobes, lockers, bedlinen, classroom desks, chairs, tables, Headmaster's study and staff rooms. Domestic staff were most helpful, and provided me with lists of cutlery, china, glassware and all their needs. Outside sports equipment was required, the ground needed to be levelled for pitches. There seemed to be no end to the innumerable tasks, and I thought that I had surmounted all possible problems in founding two new industrial companies!

I engaged an acting Headmaster, Forbes, who was a travelling coach for boys struggling with entrance exams. He was delighted to be given a trial for such a responsible position as Headmaster. He was the best of the mediocre applicants. Maybe I raised him beyond his experience, but I thought I could keep good watch overall, and I laid down meticulous instructions. I gave him my trust and he accepted, without question, all my carefully drawn plans and teaching methods. The welfare of the boys had to come first and foremost. He promised to consult me before making any changes, and discuss with me in advance any proposed alterations or amendments to the curriculum. I would not leave him in charge without this guaranteed assurance.

As I had to devote a major part of my time to the development of my own companies, I had to trust him to run my school exactly as I stipulated. His wife claimed to be trained and experienced as both Matron and Housekeeper. Maybe I was too trusting, but I thought their gratitude was genuine. He'd been promoted from the position of being an individual coach with slender earnings, to a salaried Headmaster, with accommodation and the help of Cundall's own domestic staff. I had a large new building constructed to my specifications for the Assembly Hall. It was fitted as a gym and also used for indoor games. In fact, I ensured that the school was properly equipped, down to the last piece of cutlery. This was a truly giant task. We engaged further teaching staff, and drew up a complete programme. It was amazing how quickly the news spread about this new Boarding Prep School for Boys. We opened with a first complement of ten boarders, without any form of advertising. The first example of Cundall magic.

All went well from the beginning, and I kept a close watch and supervision on everything, until I felt that Headmaster and staff were working well together. The boys were happy, well-fed and content. The best proof of this was the increasing number of applications. As every pupil was treated individually, we were soon in great demand. I felt the pleasure and thrill of a dream coming true. I devoted every weekend to the pleasure of Cundall. It was so very different from the hard slog of manufacturing. I also built two modern bungalows for possible married staff.

Whilst going carefully through the curriculum with Forbes, I became aware that he was still using many of his old cramming methods of teaching. These methods were generally used to push backward pupils through entrance exams. I objected strongly to such pressured teaching, which produces only provisional, superficial results, without proper depth. Forbes promised to change to normal, careful graduation, but could not get cramming out of his system. I reminded him of his agreement to follow my instructions, and warned him that my school was not founded to be a crammer of superficial, repetitive layers, without thorough, patient grounding. I'd had my own personal experience of this superficial cramming with Greek and German for University entrance.

Gradually I began to hear of further trouble at Cundall, concerning Forbes and his wife. They had gathered a close clique of teaching staff around them, who sought to dominate others. Some of my staff left in disgust, one actually warned me that parents were being fed innuendoes, denigrating me for no valid reason. Parents meeting them regularly as Headmaster and Matron, had no reason to doubt their statements. Thus he was able to pursue his secret plans, aided by his wife, who was furious at my refusal to allow her unqualified, drug-taking son to teach and guide our pupils. I learnt that young Nick Forbes was being watched by the police because of his drug activity, and had to reprimand Forbes for allowing his son to mingle with our pupils. He had broken his promise to send him away.

Forbes had never risen to any position above travelling tutor. He'd agreed all my terms and conditions, as did his wife. When finally chosen, their gratitude was overflowing, for they had little money and no permanent residence. They were overjoyed at the prospect of good quarters in the main building, with 'all found,' in addition to a salary. Yet Elspeth lacked the experience she claimed she'd had as Matron cum Housekeeper, as my domestic staff soon discovered. Apparently, they began to have visions of greatness, and the respect that was shown naturally by grateful, trusting parents, deluded them into feeling that my school should rightfully be theirs. They insinuated that they were in complete control and that I should now leave, having fulfilled my function in providing the necessary funds, buildings and equipment. They even pretended that they were part founders and rightful co-owners. Such fictional stories were recounted in private discussions with parents. Some parents were persuaded into alliance with the Forbes, who were secretly contriving to force me to hand over Cundall to them, without compensation, and just disappear. They underestimated me. I was trained in a war against much more ruthless foes.

Obviously, with all my other responsibilities I could not be there daily. I had laid down the exact rules and regulations that needed to be followed implicitly, which they had guaranteed to follow. Visiting regularly at weekends, all appeared to be developing according to plan in the first year. Parents enjoyed visiting Cundall with its fine Manor building and extensive, landscaped grounds. All the boys thrived. There was no bullying, just quiet help and understanding, which was given within a family atmosphere. The boys appeared to settle in well, and enjoy school life and games with other schools. Our blue and yellow colours and distinctive blue blazers, cap and Yorkshire rose crest became well known in the area. All woollen pullovers and knitwear were made by my

Scots friends Kilspindie. I had designed all the uniform and crest, and Cundall soon became a respected school.

The first definite signs of trouble came when Forbes' son Nicholas was caught with drugs by the police. The Court accepted Forbes' guarantee for his son, so I was outraged to find that he was being used as an assistant master. A position for which he was in no way qualified. I forbade his presence in my school, and the Forbes resented my decision. Then I checked other staff that had been engaged by Forbes without my knowledge. I found a further two unqualified teachers who had to go. Gradually I was beset with problems, all of which emanated from Forbes and his son Nicholas, who was still, apparently, taking drugs. I was anxious of the possibility that he might try to peddle drugs to the boys. To protect the boys from this danger I ordered his immediate removal.

My instincts warned me of further trouble, although nothing untoward appeared on the surface. A local vicar's wife, who was employed by me from the outset, as school secretary, hinted of problems, but all the boys appeared happy, well-fed and contented. I did raise again with Forbes that he was still using too many cramming methods. He claimed that this was only for basic learning, to develop retentive powers. But basic learning cannot be pursued by cramming methods. Education must be ever expanding, once its habitual firm foundation is established. I disagreed strongly with Forbes methods, which lay deep in his system. I also learnt that Forbes had not engaged any married staff to occupy my new modern bungalows, as Mrs Forbes objected to wives. Again this was a point of disagreement and indicated that he was influenced too much by his wife. There were disturbing stories. Some parents had been led to believe that Forbes had shares or certain 'rights' in my school. He told them that he was not only Headmaster, but had equal say in everything. I could not believe such wild rumours, for I was unquestionably the sole owner. But I was too involved at that time, with the development and progress of my company and my children's welfare, to investigate in detail. I thought that such stories were rumours that were being blown out of proportion.

However, through my loyal secretary and Mrs Gregson, who was a new teacher I had appointed for the pre-prep department, I began to receive more disturbing news. Apparently the Forbes were holding secret meetings with groups of parents during which he accused me of blocking and impeding his work on behalf of their children. He was asking them for their support. There lay great danger in this situation, since I was not personally well known to many of the parents. They only saw Forbes regularly. Naturally, they regarded him as the man in charge of all teaching methods and child welfare. Finally, to my astonishment and concern, I received a letter from a solicitor parent. This letter advised me, on behalf of the parents he represented, that I must now personally leave the school. It requested that I hand it over lock, stock and barrel to

Forbes with full rights of possession. If I refused to hand over my school, they had already taken lien on a large building only two or three miles away, with a view to purchase. They would transfer their children there and expected all the teaching and domestic staff to move with them. They threatened to leave me with an empty Cundall Manor, without staff or pupils, facing bankruptcy.

There was no suggestion or offer to purchase my school from me. Just plain, illegal, criminal robbery, led by a solicitor, and parents who were under the Forbes' spell. One could almost admire the cunning trickery and hypnotic salesmanship of Forbes, in so easily persuading intelligent parents to follow him obediently and blindly. I related the whole bare faced plot to Arthur Collins, who was not surprised. He had met Forbes several times. He had found him to be difficult, rude and domineering. He'd assumed an attitude of ownership and stated that Collins and his horse were not welcome around 'his' school. Arthur Collins offered to help me in any action I cared to bring. As a senior member of a well known group of London solicitors, who acted for the Queen, he was well respected. In fact he later became Sir Arthur Collins CVO. I now had to take legal action that had been forced upon me by the conniving Forbes.

My solicitor sought witnesses who were prepared to state true facts in Court. Two reliable witnesses were our head cook and the school coach driver. Both were prepared to swear that Forbes had tried to persuade them to leave me, and accompany him to new premises, by promising to give them increased wages. Both remained loyal to me. The school secretary was also completely loyal to me from the beginning. She was willing and keen to expose their lies and cunning ruse, as was Mrs Gregson. We engaged leading Counsel, John Wood Q.C. and Harry Woolf, who later became Lord Chief Justice. They went over every fine detail repeatedly, until they were satisfied on every aspect. A special hearing was arranged with a High Court Judge, and I was privileged to attend. It was a remarkable, fascinating verbal battle between two experts. Every point made by Wood was argued against by the Judge, as devil's advocate, who refused to accept any point until he was fully satisfied. The final witness was, naturally, the vicar's wife, my school secretary. It seemed like hours before the Judge leaned forward, smiled and said, 'Your injunction is granted, and, in my opinion, well merited.'

Now it was all over, I held a legal injunction, which clearly stated the names of the main perpetrators; who'd been led by the Forbes and the solicitor. They would now suffer in terms of their reputation and future. They were refused permission to move or start up any kind of school, anywhere in the county of Yorkshire. They had to meet all costs and apologise for their unlawful behaviour, or face the consequences. Their solicitor, fearing that he would be struck off, came personally to apologise and beg forgiveness. This I granted, but only after exposing to him every detail of his unprofessional conduct. He admitted his guilt in listening to one side only and not allowing the owner to state his case. He offered compensation, which I refused. I told him that he would have to live with his guilty conscience and support my school henceforth. His son was allowed to remain as an innocent sufferer of his father's lapse of judgement. From then on he became a fervent supporter, and was delighted with his son's progress.

The Forbes had to pay their costs and leave Cundall immediately. Forbes sought an interview with me, and laid the blame entirely on his wife, as though he were innocent. Naturally I refused to listen to any more lies. They left with his wife swearing in really foul language in front of all the staff, who had happily assembled to speed her off. All was now peaceful and serene. The staff were happy and delighted at my victory, as was their old employer Sir Arthur Collins, who congratulated me. Many teachers had refused to join the Forbes clique and remained with the school. Thus we were able to continue with everyone's co-operation. Most parents stayed loyal. But the leaders named in the injunction had to leave and move far away, beyond Yorkshire. They intended to start up a new school with Forbes, in a distant County at entirely their own expense. They had to fund this costly expense along with all their other costs.

Our numbers quickly increased with the junior prep department and later the admission of girls. My only real problem was replacing the Headmaster. It was surprising the untruths that could be revealed from a careful examination of the many applications. One's apparently first class record was completely false, with no valid qualifications. But eventually a genuinely qualified Headmaster was found and all was well. My school was born of an inspiration to establish a level of teaching excellence for children, who are so often, regrettably, at the mercy of misguided adults. Often these adults were concerned principally with themselves, as were the Forbes. Cundall could not fail now, as Arthur Collins and I had known from our first meeting. It bears our hallmark of genuine sterling quality, that is appreciated by every boy and girl at Cundall. Our school had acquired its own ethos. The healthy combination of a caring Headmaster and staff, and supportive governors. Above all, there were happy parents who now participated in school activities. Together they represented the outstanding Cundall family, of which I am truly proud.

To ensure its future security, I decided to turn my school into a Charitable Trust. This Trust was to be supervised by a well chosen Board of Governors, under the guidance of Sir Arthur Collins. The fame of my school has since spread far and wide. Headmasters have come and gone, but the school has grown and extended over a greater area. There are now more sports and athletic facilities and the latest technological equipment. Technology which I could never have imagined during the 1940's and the war years. When we were inventing the world's first computers in our code breaking struggles. I remain proud of the success of my original, single-handed venture into education, which, despite a difficult and costly start, overcame all problems. It grew into the haven for children that I had first visualised. A school where parents play an essential part, cooperating with the Headmaster.

Unfortunately the misconduct encountered en route, was not confined to business and industry, where it is sometimes provoked Misconduct reaches into all other walks of life, including the arts, education, sport, religion and, of course, politics, my lifetime interest. Our great country should always be able to depend on the wisdom and honesty of those elected to honourable Government. But all citizens have a duty to watch and judge who they elect. Good does not automatically succeed, as it should. However much we progress, there appears always to be a negative side. It behoves us to be ever wary of those in whom we place our trust.

Cundall, my lovely personal dream come true, has successfully weathered its storms and problems. James Napier brought many improvements, and kept in contact with me until he finally retired. Every year our school expands. In 1985 three new classrooms were added to the 'New Block,' followed by the new headmaster's house, which is now the Senior School. Then came our new covered swimming pool, with changing rooms, plus a further twelve acres of playing fields. The Orchard, became the new pre-prep building in 1996. This was the year that Sir Arthur made his tremendous gesture of 'gifting' his estate of Cundall Manor and grounds to our Charitable Trust.

Best of all, financial difficulties that were unknown to me, were actually resolved by the parents. They took necessary measures, which resulted in the appointment of the present worthy, highly qualified Headmaster, Peter Phillips. Along with his capable wife Sarah and family, his firm, quiet guidance has brought parents even closer together. Cundall has put down stronger roots, and is accepted as a leading school. Our pupils are gladly welcomed by all the best schools and readily win scholarships. Parents willingly entrust their precious offspring to us, including our neighbouring farmers. The latter supported me in the early days, and have continued to watch the school thrive.

Peter finds the right staff to fit Cundall's quality requirements, and we attract future leaders. They come to us for grounding, before taking off to establish their careers. These include Cambridge graduate Stephen Fry, who was inspired by Cundall to develop into a famous writer, actor and comedian. He has an outstanding wit. Nick Hawkins also attended Cundall and became Conservative MP , similarly Jonathan Hill. Some of our loyal teachers mature after many enjoyable years at Cundall, like my old friend Peter Robson, who outlasted two headmasters. He taught geography and history, and looked after welfare. He also painted shields for hall and staircase and was always helpful. Now he is a successful publisher in Scarborough, but he is still drawn by affection to Cundall.

Meanwhile Cundall continues its natural growth and expansion, supported by our well established fame and success. Our happy parents, created 'Friends of Cundall,' which promotes new enterprise. This process delights me, for I have always sought parents' close involvement in the school. This is a sure sign of genuine success in our endeavours on behalf of the children, who are the very heart and substance of a good school. They are our real hope for the future of our beloved country. To make sure Britain stays in sure, safe hands. Of all my activities, after a long and eventful life, this would be my best and lasting memorial. I would be truly honoured to have my ashes scattered over my inspired creation of Cundall Manor School.

I have been invited back to Cundall, now as the aged Founder, watching its measured progress and continued success. Cundall is my happiest venture, tucked away as it is, in a beautiful, quiet corner near York. I avidly read its weekly reports that breathe stories of some three hundred happy, contented little people. They are growing up surrounded by good teaching and modern equipment, full sports facilities, keen Governors and happy parents; who form their own supporting committees and join in all activities. Peter and Sarah are the acknowledged best Headmaster team ever, and the creators of the happiest, loyal Cundall family. This family consists of pupils, parents, staff, governors and a range of supporters all over England. Should you doubt me, I challenge you to visit and see for yourself.

Chapter 17

The Death of Joan

I finally retired, rather unwillingly, in 1987 aged 73, having attained all my industrial targets. Had I then been able to enjoy an active political career, helping both my Party and Harrogate Borough, I would have been content. I planned a long holiday for us both, for recuperation and change of scenery. Instead, I had to continue to cope with the diverse problems of my wife, now becoming more difficult to handle alone, but refusing any outside carer. Joan preferred visits to our family in Kennington, where she delighted in playing with toddler Thomas and baby Charlotte. Then to their lovely old 18th Century thatched roof dwelling, Frith Copse, set in their wide-spread woods near Manningford Bruce, Wiltshire. Nigel would join the family gatherings in London, rarely spoke to his mother, but softened a little as he settled, with her help, into his chosen career of barrister. Joan accepted the long car journeys without demur, while still grumbling at our local shopping trips.

Then Joan suffered a major heart attack, needing urgent hospital treatment. Joan could no longer climb stairs, so I found a big bungalow with space for her to walk about freely, in a quiet area, surrounded by big gardens, protected by trees, fences and hedges, from close neighbours, and backing onto fields leading to Harrogate Cricket Club grounds. There we took our quiet, daily exercise, returning to knitting and TV before retiring, leaving me to seek refuge in my close study of events, writing copious notes preparing my next book following "German Universities after the Surrender", with David Phillips, at Oxford University. "Secret Communications," my Code-breaking secrets, and my earlier bibilical studies.

The extra strain contributed to my own collapse, losing my balance, falling unexpectedly, whilst walking. Examined by three consultants, one an eminent neurologist, none could trace the cause. Joan was terrified, fearing my end, leaving her alone and helpless. Finally the neurologist's young Registrar discovered failure of my thyroid gland, threatening death. His thyroxine treatment restored me to my previous good health, to my wife's relief.

I now concentrated on my long-planned book on cryptology, from the first alphabet, followed by simple codes and ciphers. Our well-stocked local library found books I needed, and Bletchley provided helpful material from surviving records. A further heart attack came suddenly, requiring extended hospital care. Just as Joan arrived home, came another from leg vessels. Then in August 1996, just before her 79th birthday, came a massive stroke. We rushed her to hospital, and for three days and nights I sat by her side while she fought hard, but finally succumbed, holding my hand in a tight grip.

Our family came to assist me at the funeral service, and persuaded me to join them in Wiltshire. Jennifer found me a suitable dwelling in Marlborough. So I began sad farewells to Harrogate, our home for nearly fifty years. In June 1997, the Mayor and Council of Harrogate gave a farewell Reception for me, with a big gathering of members of both Parties and worthies of the Borough. The local Press produced a special feature in my honour. I made the rounds of all my friends, acquaintances and the Council. I truly loved that beautiful, well-planned, orderly Spa town, constructed by the wise old city fathers. With ancient Knaresborough close at hand, surrounded by rugged Yorkshire dales, biggest and best of all the Counties, which EU powers sought, in vain, to change into a soulless Region. Long live Yorkshire, where I prospered by hard, honest labour, with good Yorkshire folk, advising me not to do "owt fer nowt, but if tha does owt fer nowt, do it fer thysen."

It will always hold strong memories for me, the growth of my children, the successful foundation of my own company, the co-founding of CBI, the foundation of Cundall Manor Prep School, my entry into Harrogate political life as Borough Councillor, and all my other interests and many good friends. Also sad and bitter memories of my wife's problems, and subsequent unhappy years. Then came an urgent request to call at Wakefield "Double-Two". On arrival, I was welcomed by Mr. Donner, my co-Founder in 1939, with son Ricky, now Managing Director, and staff, all lined up to greet me with a huge Banner: "Hail to the Founder." I was given a gala reception, shown the extensive buildings (shades of our two original rooms), and waved on my way with a collection of their latest products - which I wear with pride. That, I reflected, as I drove South to Wiltshire, was the place where my career in industry really began, before joining the Army, in the ranks, for those ten memorable War years on three continents, which affected my life ever after.

Chapter 18

Retirement

On July 1st,1997 I arrived at my new home in Castle Court. It is situated in River Park Marlborough, within a fairly modern retirement complex discovered by Jennifer. The spacious gardens, extensive lawns, colourful flower beds with roses at my door, trim bushes and trees, welcomed me back to the softer West Country of my birth. The river Kennet flows through our gardens and we are visited constantly by ducks waddling in single file, and rigidly disdainful swans. The town centre is fairly close-by, with the Conservative Party offices in the High Street and Marlborough College almost next door. I am a regular Tutor at the College's International Summer School.

Frith Copse, the family estate, was once the meeting place of King Alfred and his brother King Aethelred 1st in 871. The Swanborough Tump, a stone monument at the corner of our woods commemorates this hallowed spot, less than 10 miles from Marlborough. It is the comfortable home of the Munby family, Sir James (now a High Court Judge), Lady Jennifer and their children Thomas and Charlotte, with Grandpa Harry nearby. Jennifer, retired from her career as a barrister in family law, now devotes herself to her family, gardening and grooming her beloved horses which she rides in competitions and hunting.

Farmer Reid challenged Jennifer to reorganise the whole stable complex and run it properly. There is something intriguing about the captivation of men and women by horses, and their pleasure at risking life and limb in competitive riding events and hunting. Both horses and riders need to be physically and mentally fit, and highly motivated for such strenuous exercise, part of the English scene and ancient custom. An American cousin, Lisa, runs a small farm in British Columbia Canada, breeding Dorset sheep and horses. Charlotte, my granddaughter also shares her family love of horses, riding, competing and the thrill of hunting. My role seems to be that of benevolent supporter, helping to meet the endless costs of their demanding hobby. The stables were left an absolute shambles by the previous incumbent, and Jennifer was fully occupied with restoring the string of horses that were left in a really bad condition. They desperately needed proper feeding and care. I undertook to renovate all the buildings, stalls, tack rooms, food stores, entailing months of hard work. Eventually it was all accomplished and in fine fettle by the end of 1997. Furthermore, the renovated buildings were much admired by all equestrian friends.

I was glad of such physical hard work because it helped to blot out the terrible 1997 defeat of John Major's ill-led, troublesome regime, and quarrelsome Cabinet. I watched from home helpless and unable to prevent Harrogate's slide from an erstwhile fully Conservative Council and succession of Conservative MPs, to a Liberal-Democrat majority and MP. I remembered the semi-bankrupt débâcle of the Wilson Government, which was followed by the even worse regime of Callaghan. Then enjoyed the triumph of Margaret Thatcher, who recovered as much as possible from Heath's handover to the European Union. Heath never forgave her, a woman, for beating him in the election. In my opinion, Heath's betrayal of taking Britain into the Common Market of Europe, has dragged our country ever deeper into the EU's costly, disastrous embrace. The Treaty of Rome changed the pretence of a single Common Market. Britain is now faced with the prospect of a EU Constitution that will herald a Superstate. Thus Britain potentially stands to lose her precious, hard won sovereignty and freedom, with Germany triumphant at last in her centuries-old battle to dominate Europe.

I had regained some of my old strength whilst working on the physical renovation of the stables. Therefore, after a pleasurable first family Christmas at Frith Close I returned in 1998, to my old love of politics. Feeling refreshed and eager to work I was welcomed at Conservative Party Headquarters, Smith Square, Westminster. After years of being semi-house bound, and the disastrous collapse of Conservative fortunes, I felt positively rusty. At this point, however, my energy levels had returned and I was looking for positive outlets. I became a life President of Marlborough Rugby Club and supported the Pavilion Dressing Room, which was constructed near the Common and completed in 1999. I was also invited to a volunteers' celebration at the local Savernake Hospital. Originally founded as a cottage hospital by Lord Ailesbury in 1866, it had grown into a trim, compact hospital, which served a very wide area. I was installed as a life time member of the Friends of Savernake, and have served as a volunteer at the hospital ever since. My regular visits, and the speech therapy assistance I give to stroke victims, are a bright spot in my week. I am recognised everywhere, by staff and patients alike, simply as Harry. I have grown to love this friendly, competent hospital with its pleasant atmosphere, which is so suitable for rehabilitation. I fought a long running battle along with other supporters to save Savernake, when the National Health Service Trust sought to destroy a large part of it and change its substance. I then supported plans for a new, modern hospital. But we still have to raise about £10 million for the cost. I was a member of the inauguration committee Sacsa, whose remit was to start the action and funds for the project.

As a member of the Stroke Association, I was introduced to the Dysphasics' Branch, which is based at Wroughton on the outskirts of Swindon. Patients are brought by coach and car from the outlying areas weekly to the Ellendune Hall. Much patient work is required to enable them to begin to formulate intelligible sounds. First efforts are so often just gibberish. Regular exercises and experiments however, often bear fruit and we are delighted with any success. My own love of language and philological sound formation found a practical use at last. The cheerfulness of these patients is remarkable. They are always delighted to see us and they enjoy our efforts. Indeed, they often make us laugh at their responses, as they gradually gain strength and confidence.

The Conservative offices are in High Street, Marlborough, but the constituency is named after Devizes, which is the biggest town in the area. There I met Agent Ian Ramsey, an ex-Squadron Leader, who welcomed me whilst simultaneously trying to assess my possible value. I was duly enrolled into the Devizes Conservative Constituency Association (DCCA) and cordial relations were soon established. I was introduced to the Chairman, Tony Duck and the President Lord Prentice. My next meeting was with Michael Ancram QC, our genial MP. This meeting marked the beginning of an enduring, firm friendship, and Michael invited me to meet the new Party Leader William Hague. There was a worried atmosphere at Central Office, largely prompted by a lack of funds and support. During Major's last election campaign a lot of money had been misspent and our Party was now flat broke. Staff had to be cut back severely and many advisers and Agents were dismissed. The situation facing William Hague, as newly elected Party Leader was truly depressing. I promised to help as soon as my Harrogate property was sold. Their gratitude was genuine and profound, and William invited me to help with Fund-raising. It seemed that the old fundraisers had departed, as had so many other erstwhile supporters. New brooms had swept too clean, needlessly removing some old talent, including Agents, who are always the bedrock of good constituencies. Michael explained the sad plight of his own constituency and I promised to help restore DCCA to full strength. Like all my other promises, I kept this one in full, since both my Party and new constituency were in sorry state. It has been a real pleasure to work with Michael, who I esteem highly. He is not only one of the best and most honest and reliable MPs I have met, but he is also one who genuinely loves his fellow human beings, and serves them gladly. His charming wife Jane shares his views and works equally, continuously, for Party and constituents. I returned to Marlborough intent on strengthening the Party and Association as much as possible.

The chaotic, rundown state of the offices above the Conservative Club was almost akin to the Augean stables Jennifer had discovered. I alarmed the part-time secretary by ruthlessly tearing up masses of ancient files, decrepit furniture and furnishings. There were tables without legs and broken table tops, collapsing chairs, overflowing plywood cupboards and fixtures visibly cracking. It was a major onslaught and clearout that filled me with great satisfaction. I fully refurbished the offices with good furniture and equipment. They were then given a coat of paint and up-to-date pictures of our MP and present Leader, and new IT equipment. The offices were now fully operational except for secretarial problems. The part-time secretary answered continuous phone calls, and had no time for filing. Moreover, she adamantly refused to work overtime, even at elections. Thus a backlog of work piled up. Ian Ramsey had to cope with a small adjoining room that was cluttered up with old files, like the ghosts of yesteryear. Ceaseless phone calls, and strings of overnight answer-phone messages, compounded the problem. Striving to create order out of Michael's overfull diary and keep abreast of all DCCA activities, Ian sat in the centre of his widespread web. He had no privacy and was at everybody's beck and call. He was also hampered by a lack of space and elbow room. He acted as secretary in the afternoons, phone clerk and general dogsbody. He often worked late in order to concentrate in peace. He needed to consider important operations, plan and devise acceptable solutions to all manner of problems. It was a great relief for him therefore, to find a willing ear; he was also appreciative of my helpful advice, gleaned from my many years of political experience. From then on, we worked closely and amicably together, plotting and planning the future success of DCCA.

After discussions with Michael and Ian, I promised to restore order and put a firm foundation under DCCA. Fortunately, the offices and main operations are situated in Marlborough, and I now had the freedom and wherewithal to devote my mind and energy to this mammoth task. Over the past nine years it has become a tremendous success. The previously impoverished DCCA, now has a new, strong, financial foundation. This has been complemented by an election winning team that has gained total control of both District and County Councils, a feat never before achieved in the history of the Association. The DCCA is now a top-rank constituency, just as I promised it would be. Together we made this area the most successful constituency, as a composite, co-operating community, rightfully named by William Hague as 'The Wiltshire Winners.' There remained a smaller adjoining office, which I also cleared, giving the agent a workmanlike, snug office with computer and sound equipment. He had a good desk and filing cabinet, but lacked privacy. Ian had one special gripe in the shape of an ancient photocopier, which he relied on for all his multiplicity of leaflets, letters, instructions, pamphlets and documents of all kinds. These often amounted to hundreds of copies that were designed for general dissemination. Unfortunately, it struggled to produce even 50 copies before it habitually broke down. Management, who were ever short of funds, turned a deaf ear to his urgent pleas for a new machine. Finally they offered to buy another old, used machine. Ian indignantly replied "So now I will have two old machines breaking down, instead of one." Local printing was very costly, but management was obdurate. Therefore I invested in the latest Xerox photocopier, which quickly recovered its cost in productivity. All became proud of this modern machine, which could expand to A3 size and produce maps, documents, leaflets and posters, at a fraction of previous costs. I have produced enlarged sectional maps for every local Town, District and County election, which we have since fought. This was a mammoth task, helping our volunteers, (including me), to deliver large quantities of leaflets by hand, and canvassing within a close area, saving time and legwork.

DCCA was so impoverished that it lacked members and subscriptions, and could not really afford even a part-time Agent. They regretfully underpaid Ian, who was one of the best and most resourceful Conservative Agents I have ever met. They expected him to work overtime on about half-pay, without time off, but failed to give him any certainty of tenure. His presence was demanded at all Council, Management and Executive Meetings, including those that were held at week-ends. He was expected to set out desks and chairs, take the Minutes, serve day and night, and be continuously at their beck and call, as general maid-of-all work and as part-time secretary. Hence his necessity of working nights to gain peace and quiet. He received no extra pay for overtime or any bonus. He told me that it was only his loyalty to his MP that kept him there. His situation had to be remedied, and I was now free to indulge my abiding interest in politics. Michael and I became good friends and met regularly for joint discussions on the best way forward for our ailing Party. He now benefited from the support of a reliable, loyal team of Ian Ramsey and myself. We worked hard to reshape the future of DCCA, despite the lack of co-operation from Central Office. Funds often seemed to pour in and out of HQ without reaching the weakest constituences, where they were most needed. I have been determined to remedy this lack of DCCA funding.

It is extremely difficult to find and weld together a really strong team of volunteers. Many seek to become 'officers' with high sounding titles, then somehow forget to carry out their duties and responsibilities 'on the ground,' where talk becomes action. It must be brought home to every physically able and competent member of our Party, be they officers, executives, councillors, committee members or volunteers, that they owe a definite duty to our Party to fight every election, whether General, County, District, Town or Parish. This is our only real hope of returning the Conservative Party to Government. We have achieved much in DCCA, by winning elections throughout our constituency, and now control both District and County Councils. We have also returned our MP with increased majorities with the aid of willing volunteers and the goodwill of our constituents. Michael inspires all, helping those in need with his frequent surgeries, spreading goodwill with his cheerful smile and willing co-operation. Yet within exists a truly serious politician, concerned for Britain and our people, a worthy leader.

Chapter 19

Devizes Conservative Constituency Association Recovery Year

The year of 1999 began quietly in the completely refurbished DCCA offices. With our agent Ian Ramsey, my plan was to conduct a thorough review of previous election campaigns, in order to improve the future organisation. We planned meticulously, paying close attention to each area with its own personal and local problems. By proving our support in these areas, it was possible to win votes and gain control of Parish and County Councils. Once constituents were convinced that we intended to continue to work for them, our prospects at General Elections would automatically improve. I maintain that elections are won from the ground up rather than from the top down, as Central Office believes. Therefore, they continuously waste supporters' contributions in huge planning operations, doomed to fail because of a lack of understanding of electors' needs. Naturally, voters are concerned primarily with their own personal and local affairs, national politics often coming a poor second. Thus many of them need to be convinced that politics really does affect their daily lives and their children's future.

Management were yet again unable to fund new equipment, which was urgently needed for the future development of DCCA. I bore the cost alone. Now we sought to revive the flagging membership spirit. We also needed to ensure that the right leadership was in place, to build the strong structure needed for the May 1999 Town and District Elections. In 1998 there was a fairly hopeless outlook; since the complete collapse in 1997 had left a state of general pessimism. To establish 1999 as recovery year, we had to win sufficient council seats. This process was always viewed as the first stage in the ultimate later battle for General and County Council Elections. The latter were expected in 2001. Many members seem to avoid 'hands on' election tasks, such as delivering leaflets or canvassing. They viewed these chores as somewhat demeaning. Despite the fact that they play an essential role in persuading people to come out and vote for our Party. We relied upon a truly supportive minority, who were always willing to undertake any kind of work for the Party. It was like a world of make believe until we won our spurs with first election victories.

Our Trump Card was our worthy MP Michael Ancram Q.C. He was popular everywhere, visited every Branch and appeared at a wide variety of functions. He held surgeries for all those in need of his help or advice. His natural approach and cheery smile and greeting, earned the trust and affection of his constituents. His promotion to Chairman of our Party was universally acclaimed by the media. I threw a grand celebration party. Michael, not to be outdone, presented me with a bottle of House of Commons whisky with his signature 'To Harry to commemorate 70 years membership of the Party.'

The Association was, as yet, ill-prepared to undertake a single by-election. A good deal of hard work was imperative, especially to improve our standing on the Kennet District Council. We only held 9 seats out of a total of 40, Labour 10, Lib-Dems 8, and the remaining 13 were Independents (see chart below). We were easily outvoted. We also lacked suitable candidates and there was no immediate rush of volunteers. But gradually, with coaxing, names began to emerge from each Branch, of people who were prepared to be groomed and instructed.

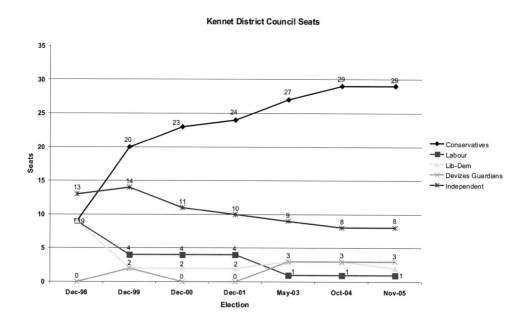

Kennet District Council Seats

I now made my promised contribution to our Party. I handed my cheque personally to Leader William Hague and Michael Ancram at Central Office, surrounded by enthusiastic staff. Michael was absolutely delighted, and has never forgotten what he called my 'magnificent gesture.' I only hope that it was put to greater effect, as William Hague promised. It certainly stopped the erosion of staff at that time, in a depressed and decimated Central Office. I had now become a 'Grandee' of our Party, an intangible title. The only genuine titles I have really enjoyed, were properly earned through army promotions. I am in favour of 'Honours', properly earned by meritorious service to our 'Monarch and Country', on the battlefield. But we old warriors seem to have a different view of service from the modern adulation of those who strut their image on stage or screen.

In Marlborough we were working long hours, planning and organising in detail. We moved potential leaders into their proper positions, including the future DCCA Chairman. When the basic structure was finally complete, I worked personally on every by-election, delivering and canvassing with our volunteers. I wanted to prove that I was not just an elderly benefactor, but essentially, an experienced organiser and active director of operations. As our positive victories mounted, the full extent of my personal activities and sustained enthusiasm became apparent.

Ian Ramsey was still hemmed in that poky backroom, but our new, enhanced image merited a private office. This was necessary both for our MP to hold his surgeries, and for our agent to operate with privacy. Our secret goal was total mastery of Kennet District Council, and Wiltshire County Council. I signed a long term agreement for a major office, which became the agent's Centre of Operations. The office was refurbished completely with good quality desk, tables, chairs, new carpets and fittings. I also redesigned the decorations in Conservative blue and cream, hung just two pictures of Winston Churchill (1942) and Margaret Thatcher, and was content. Michael, Jane and Ian were most enthusiastic. Jackie Dicks, ever resourceful, added a bowl of beautiful flowers.

We now completed our campaign strategy, based on three basic phases for the May Election. I designed and printed maps of each and every area of town and district, with dwelling occupier guides. Then I proofed and polished the first of Ian's inspired leaflets, based on information supplied, both of each Candidate personally, his area and the demands and criticisms of the people living there. Leaflets for each candidate were printed and delivered by hand of our loyal supporters, who turn out in all weathers and carry the real campaign burden. Personal canvassing however, is always the best vote generator! Many members seem scared to approach voters face to face, for quiet persuasion. Personally I enjoy canvassing. Meeting voters and discussing local affairs is always of prime importance. Politics needs only to be gently introduced to establish concord, for after all, politics influences our daily lives. The best canvasser is the best listener and sympathiser.

At the end of Polling Day, Ian and I waited anxiously in our office for the first phoned results. It was a long but hugely satisfactory night for Conservatives: an outstanding gain of 11 new District seats, including our first in Melksham. We now held 20 seats against total Opposition 20 (including 11 Independents). As some Independents agreed to group with us, we now assumed control of Kennet District Council. Town Council Candidates also won 11 seats. This was a far better result than ever previously achieved. I threw a celebration party at the Club, enjoyed by everybody, in victorious mood. Thus 1999 became the best year for DCCA, since the collapse of John Major's weak government. Our recovery year was now well on its way, with Michael, Jane, Ian and myself fully satisfied.

My real tribute came from Michael, who expressed his appreciation of all my work and contributions to the rebuilding of his constituency, in writing. Letters of thanks were also received from William Hague and our Chairman. However, there was much more to be done in 1999. Jerry Willmott was duly elected Chairman at the AGM in June. Since then, he has proven to be the best Chairman of DCCA and Leader of Kennet District Council. He has also been a successful District and County Councillor, and has an abiding love for the Fire Service. He is a thoroughly nice man, firm, yet agreeable, with a good sense of humour. What finally matters, is not the offices, titles or appointments, but the actual number of individual votes cast. I seemed to be almost alone in grasping this salient fact. Politics is often regarded as something apart, not to be discussed, except in small doses. Yet politics governs the life and conduct of our country, and is my daily concern. Many of our present politicians lack the cut and thrust of the old days, when Country, Party and People came first and foremost; and politicians were not busily moving us into unknown, unelected, foreign entities.

Under European Union instructions, our Country has now been divided into huge, shapeless and characterless Regions that effectively destroy our traditional Counties. Our Region covers most of the West Country, through to the Scilly Isles. This is a huge, unwieldy mass, with groups assembling at Exeter for the selection of our MEP Candidates. We actually gained four seats, including farmer Neil Parish, who has become our most hard-working, genuine Conservative MEP. But our MEPs are allowed to speak for only 90 seconds, barely time to make a point, so their impact remains minimal.

Central Office continues to pour out millions to no viable effect. Money would be better spent providing worthy Agents to rebuild deteriorating constituencies to win elections, our prime task to bring us back to government. DCCA Management seemed incapable, from 1997, of producing sufficient funds to cover the costs of their Association, underpaid Agent and office manager. Like Mr Micawber, continuously seeking help to clear their ever-mounting debts, with some contingency or wealthy donor. But as a fully active member, I insisted on full value for all expenditure. The Reserve I helped build, began to diminish, as expenditure exceeded income.

A Party fund-raising scheme I proposed, 'The Golden Circle' vanished into limbo. It was condemned by the dead hand of a briefly employed 'marketing expert' at Central

Office, who lacked political experience. I had even designed new badges in gold, based on my fresh concept of our Olympic torch with clasped hands around the base, indicating joint faith and loyalty. I presented a sample to Michael and Jane, who wore hers with approval. However, I had one most important further task in 1999, concerning the future of our Agent. Ian now refused to continue any longer in the unacceptable conditions under which he was forced to operate by DCCA. Twice before, management had ignored his threats to resign, but now we had reached impasse. Management refused any improvement stating that they lacked funds, so we would have to let him go, an almost suicidal decision. They failed to assess how grave their situation would be without him. He was the kingpin that locked all members together in winning elections, our raison d'etre. His departure would spell the end of DCCA as a viable constituency, and undermine my efforts on their behalf. They lacked a clear valuation of his contribution, and the respect and duty they owed him as responsible employers. He was entitled to a full Agent's salary, pension, working conditions, holidays and a proper contract of employment. They were failing, not only in their duty to him, but also in their responsibility to all contributing members of DCCA, their MP and above all, to our Party, and any hope we might have of winning local or General Elections. After discussion with our Chairman, I made a substantial offer to the DCCA, to ringfence Ian, give him a minimum three year contract, (with extension of further years if he wished to continue), with annual increments, specific details of hours, days and work periods, with clearly defined holidays. Plus, entitlement to a full time secretary, with overtime agreed when necessary, especially during elections. Jerry wrote accepting all points and Ian was satisfied with the contract. Ian Philpott, ex Bank and Building Society, became our Office Manager and soon settled in as part of our team.

Bigger battles lay ahead in 2000, which I named 'Action Year', and firm preparation necessary. In November 1999 came the first intimation of our future contests: 'Melksham Without', a County Council seat became vacant and Liberal-Democrats, who until now had ruled Melksham, had called the by-election for January 2000. Here was a cracking first action entry to 2000. Our Candidate's family name was well known in Melksham. Ian and I made our first full recce of Melksham in November, including the country areas, selecting Bowerhill for major concentration. I drew our maps and plans accordingly; deciding which areas should be tackled in greater strength, and grouping our team members, in order to cover the whole area in absolute detail. Women members said it was futile to expect help before Christmas, since everybody was busy preparing for the festivities. While CC HQ gloomily forecast 'a loser'. Undeterred, we continued planning.

We prepared our comprehensive house-to-house delivery of our first leaflets. These were carefully prepared by Ian, with a clear photograph of our smiling candidate, his personal history and a short introductory message. First hand delivery operations were fixed for 18th December, meeting at the Conservative Club, Melksham. Invited contingents arrived from Wiltshire, Gloucestershire, Dorset, Hampshire and even London. They were welcomed with hot drinks, leaflets, sectional map, blue rosettes and soon were off - eager for action. In the meantime, Michael Ancram arrived and went walkabout in the snow with the candidate. He greeted townsfolk with a cheery smile and a handshake. By lunch time, all groups had reported back, their mission accomplished with military precision.

Now came distribution of that all-important, attractive, double-sided colour leaflet, accompanied by a short, clear history, messages and colour photos of the candidate with our popular MP and County Council promises to Melksham. On the inside pages, positive clear points of Council's pledges were neatly laid out in blue and white. These pledges were clearly and precisely expressed without bombast, and dealt with matters of principal interest to all constituents, especially local concerns and problems. I led our own band of volunteers and delivered and canvassed with great zest and enthusiasm, even leafleting the house of the Lib-Dem leader. Polling Day: the result, much to CCO delighted surprise and the anguish of Lib-Dems, we had established our First WIN in the U.K. on 13th January 2,000. A magnificent gain of a County Council seat! This gave us full Conservative control of the whole Wiltshire County Council for the first time ever! Michael, Ian and I were absolutely delighted at this magnificent result, which proved that all our careful planning and organisation had been completely worthwhile. Central Office's gloomy forecast was now transformed into messages of congratulations on a miracle victory.

We adopted the same detailed planning procedure in February at Urchfont. Ian and I drove there on first recce to meet Colin and Jane, whose Stone family had been the bakers of Urchfont for over 200 years. I enjoyed leading a personally conducted, wonderfully pleasant election campaign with them. We were greeted cheerfully everywhere and won in a canter. One extraordinary story: On Polling Day I took over as Teller from a pleasant, smiling fellow, wearing a blue rosette. He introduced himself as a Labour member, but a great friend of Colin whom he admired. He'd offered to help Colin win the election and had accepted the role of Teller. He waved goodbye with a grin. I suggested to Colin that he should be his first convert. A lady in a smart car stopped us outside the Post office, leaned out and said "If your want me to vote for you, Colin, you had better post these letters for me!", which of course he did, saying "She is a Liberal". With friends like these, how could he lose? A happy, popular GAIN, for a good Candidate whose family had always been staunch Tories.

A Liberal Democrat resigned from their stronghold of the Avebury area, reigned over by Ludovic Kennedy. Ian and I made an exhaustive recce over a widespread area from Beckhampton corner, through Avebury and the Bassets to Broad Hinton. We decided that the latter was worthy of a major effort, since it was the biggest and most heavily populated area. I made enlarged workable map sections, for piecemeal daily coverage of the whole extensive area. The major problem was getting together a team of helpers. Some were tired of efforts in Melksham and Urchfont, and found excuses to avoid the really bad weather. Some failed to turn up at the appointed date, place and time. The giant task therefore, fell to me, with our new candidate Chris Phillips, a recently retired publican. I planned a joint daily operation with him. He was a complete beginner who could not go out alone. As this was a most important seat to win, long held as the solid, top Liberal Democrat safe haven, I decided to devote myself completely to the task.

We worked solidly through every day, in pouring rain, stopping for lunch at a local pub. We canvassed daily and received a good reception, especially when we were soaking wet. We presented ourselves as 'two drowned, crazy Conservatives', and received a welcoming grin in response to our damp smile. "You must be crazy to come out in this weather. Nobody else has been round." Our reply would be: "Ah, but we are <u>real</u> Conservatives, who brave the weather just to meet you." The replies were often unprintable, but always good humoured. We heard their local and personal problems. They were especially glad to be meeting the real candidate himself on their doorstep. Nobody had ever bothered about the outlying country districts before, so I decided to cover every one. We made our presence felt and coaxed some useful votes.

We survived heavy rain showers one week, hail stones and gales the second week and deep snow the third week. It became a standing joke in our office, as to what condition I would arrive in daily with my completed Canvass sheets. Finally, to everybody's surprise we won, beating Lib-Dems on their home-ground with a straight fight, giving us complete mastery of Kennet District Council, with an overall majority for the first time in history. Michael was delighted and I received many congratulations, recognising my well-nigh solo achievement. It was tremendously hard, grinding, daily work, over more than three weeks, but the victory made it worthwhile.

We also helped Swindon win Council seats, though dominated by Labour. They had only a small team of helpers and badly needed our willing assistance. Swindon is a major town of Wiltshire, and has grown piecemeal over the years to become one of the wealthiest industrial towns in Britain. Unfortunately, most of the directors live elsewhere and give their allegiance to other areas, so Conservatives are rather thin on the ground. Labour continues to dominate Swindon with two M.P.s. However, with our help, more Council seats are being won by Conservatives. Our team helped with canvassing at elections and I made major financial contributions to Swindon to retain their Agent. I am convinced there will be a future Conservative gain, especially when given the full attention and support of a team like ours.

In June, a Marlborough Town Councillor resigned. I persuaded Marian Hannaford to stand, explaining the procedure, and canvassing with her daily. The whole area was covered in our usual detailed, planned procedure, with maps and street guides for each helper, and all went according to plan. We won handsomely, establishing Marian as new Town Councillor, and I enjoyed developing her career into District and, finally, Wiltshire County Councillor, serving with enthusiasm, and developing confidence, in her peoples' interest, working assiduously. July brought the resignation of Lib-Dem County Councillor of Bedwyn/Pewsey area. Unfortunately, my friend Peter Shaw (ex-Major SOE.), Chairman of Pewsey, was in hospital recovering from a severe operation. With our good candidate David Fitzwilliam Lay, we followed our winning campaign tactics vigorously. Nobody else volunteered, so I took over personally and covered the whole of Pewsey/Bedwyn area in detail with my hard-working small team. In addition, I went out on my own during the day to ensure complete coverage. Result: terrific Win, consolidating our majority in Wiltshire County Council. August was a quieter holiday month. We were able to take time to review the year's events and plan the future.

By March 2000, our successful recovery necessitated greater printing output. We needed a multiple printer that was able to pour out large quantities at great speed. We also needed to reduce the high external printing costs. Negative reaction from management was predictable, since they feared they might be asked to pay for expensive high-grade equipment. Ian's pleas were met with total silence. We inspected power machines and selected the latest multiple printer by Panasonic, which was able to print two copies per second. Ian suggested I offer DCCA to pay part if they contributed the remainder. But still no response from Management. I simply had to get this invaluable machine, without which we could not have survived the onslaught of 2000. In addition to election material, there were quantity leaflets required by each Branch, as well as masses of other printing including Directories, Campaign guides, 'In Touch' magazine, instruction leaflets, major meetings, conference papers. As we grew in power, and membership, so increased our printing needs, with major office activity.

On the 19th of October I invited a table of guests at the William Hague dinner. This was the most successful event of the year. It was arranged primarily by the Marlborough Branch led by Jackie Dicks, with help from the Conservative Women's Association and our team. Firstly, there was a reception for William at Devizes by the Women's Committee, followed by a sumptuous dinner that was held at Marlborough College. I took my daughter Jennifer to dine and meet my friend William Hague, who made me blush with his lavish praise. Jennifer said she had not realised her father was so highly esteemed by the Leadership. William did not elaborate.

Finally, to finish off the year 2000, we had yet another difficult situation in Melksham. A Lib-Dem resigned from Melksham Black Forest District. We contested it with Andy Milton who had stood previously, but lost to Lib-Dems. With little support from DCCA or West Wiltshire, I took out a small, fragmented team and delivered leaflets and canvassed. I was helped by my trusty friend Basil Davie and we ensured complete coverage of the whole area, despite the lack of cooperation. On Polling Day none of the promised help turned up. Ian and I sat alone staring down the long, empty room. Andy Milton arrived late, and only went out to canvass for a time, when persuaded to do so by me. Eventually Ian and I took turns to go out and canvass one area after another, punctuated by our personal comments on lack of support! We were alone in the Town Hall for the Count, with Andy for Conservatives, whilst the room appeared to be totally packed with Lib-Dems, all laughing confidently. Plus some Labour Councillors in support. We felt very much alone as the Count took place. Andy won as District Councillor, by 47 votes. What a tragic scene for Lib-Dems. Some were actually in tears, since they had anticipated repeated success. Andy was quite overwhelmed, having witnessed a well organised and properly fought campaign, he was completely converted. Ian and I drove home in the small hours, content with our success and all our hard work. This event signalled the end of a long and tiring year. An important year, which established the DCCA for the first time in history, as the complete master by an outstanding majority, of both Kennet District and Wiltshire County Councils.

Chapter 20

The 2001 General and County Council Election

By winning our first County Council by-election in Melksham, handsomely against all the odds, we established a reputation which grew throughout the year. We became known as the Wiltshire Winners. I urgently advised Party HQ yet again, to focus on finding, training and funding good Agents. I suggested that we invited back those who had retired, albeit on temporary basis. But to no avail. They refused to consider my suggestion of researching every constituency in detail, to discover how to develop future success by appropriate planning. Operations like ours, would produce similar results, with Party funds directed to areas needing support.

We even found time to help others. I spent long weekends assisting the Rugby/ Kenilworth Association, with financial help as well as advice. St Ives was in a fragmented state with no agent, and characterised by warring factions and a lack of funds. I took a small team to help Portillo in Kensington. We had a good reception and were even invited to lunch with a group of supporters, whilst canvassing a block of flats. Problems abounded everywhere. With our Marlborough Branch and Women's Committee (a stronghold of DCCA under its active President Lady Jane Ancram), we organised a grand Reception and Dinner in honour of our Leader William Hague. We successfully raised fifteen thousand pounds for the two Swindon constituencies, that were perpetually lacking funds. We also 'adopted' the North Swindon Candidate and canvassed on his behalf.

Ian and I now concentrated on County Council and General Elections. They were expected in May and we planned the whole operation, as Michael's team, to ensure return of Michael Ancram with a bigger majority for another full term, and gain more Council seats. The agent's Operational Guide gave detailed, explicit coverage and was to be read, digested and followed in sequence by every Candidate. Then Ian composed a full set of carefully devised leaflets for every Candidate, giving voters a clear résumé of the personal history and real intentions if elected. Plus a joint photo of Michael with the Candidate, a winning aid. Every leaflet, printed document and written instruction was drafted and proofed, until we were satisfied that each was absolutely correct. Each candidate's message came through clearly, in plain English. In the absence of both

Chairman and Deputy, perforce, Ian and I became Campaign and Operations Directors, ensuring full activity 'on the ground'. What a successful team we were! With the Ancram battlebus in daily coverage, young Ian Philpott competently managing office operations and volunteers who rallied to us. A hard working, happy and harmonious team, that produced excellent winning results and overcame all problems.

Now we needed more office space. Consequently, I made a further agreement with the Club to rent the whole of the first floor. The ever supportive David Blanchard contributed the necessary new kitchen, and the worthy Giles Currie hosted a fine dinner event at Aldbourne to raise funds. We took overall responsibility for the whole Campaign and, with our small band of helpers, we won handsomely. A great celebration was held to thank everybody for their willing cooperation that returned Michael with an increased majority of over 2000. We were amazed at the sorry failures elsewhere, which indicated a repeat of the John Major catastrophe of 1997.

Our President Reg Prentice was now very ill. He told me that he was grateful for all I had done for DCCA. He stated that my quiet contribution in planning and organising, in addition to my major financial support, had not been made clear to the Management Committee. Thus members lacked understanding until the truth was revealed. In July 2000 he wrote a letter, stating his pleasure in proposing me as Vice President, in recognition of all that I had done for the Party and DCCA. It was unanimously accepted by all the officers. By now he looked ill and drawn. When I last called on him with Kay Davie, he expressed the wish that I would carry on looking after DCCA as President. I assured him that I would look after DCCA, but preferred to work behind the scenes. He died soon afterwards and we mourned the loss of a great President.

The sudden outbreak of foot and mouth disease, and the exceedingly inept handling of the crisis by Blair and his incompetent ministers, caused havoc. Instead of isolation or immediate vaccination, which would have stopped the spread, they wasted time and good animals, in a quite unnecessary mass slaughter. They failed to call in the Army immediately, for their capable control. They caused a degree of mayhem that brought grief, terrible loss and bankruptcy to many farmers. They then relied upon their habitual 'spin' tactics to get them out of trouble, having eliminated our export trade.

Blair postponed the anticipated May Election to June. This unexpected move dissipated election interest and enthusiasm, and accounted, to some extent, for the low turnout. We had some four weeks to make fresh preparations. Our Campaign Team punctually delivered the first leaflets, which we had fully prepared. Central Office, without notice, decided to drop our famous Olympic Torch. We simply refused. Instead I proposed a new design, with the aid of my artist son. This depicted both hands clasped around the torch in a sign of joint loyalty and friendship. It was never accepted, like so many of my good, constructive ideas. Candidates were grateful for carefully prepared maps and street groupings. Our great asset was Jane Ancram. With Michael working in Parliament as Chairman, Jane took command of the Battlebus. Day after day she covered every area throughout the constituency with cheerful energy. In retrospect, I can see that our total DCCA victory of the 2001 General and County Council Elections, was absolutely outstanding in present apolitical England. If only all had fought like us! Our Party gained only one new seat.

Following the election came the shock of Ian Ramsey's written resignation, prompted by the longstanding lack of cooperation and support of Management. DCCA was always short of funds, even with my help. They could not afford to pay Ian his proper salary and expenses. Yet they could not operate successfully without an Agent. I suggested that Ian should work three days a week for DCCA, and maintain the same salary. He would then be free to engage in other work to increase his income. My suggestion was acceptable to Ian and duly adopted. Next came William Hague's resignation, immediately after the election. Then began the leadership contest that brought into the open all the factions that had been secretly operating against William. All of them plotting and planning their chosen replacement. The leading faction supported Michael Portillo. Whereas others supported Iain Duncan Smith or David Davis. It was quite a mixed political bag, and the contest revealed the extent to which disloyalty had thrived behind the scenes, whilst William was out front battling away against Blair. However, my opinion is that he is still young and may yet become a strong Prime Minister. He will hopefully mature in different positions of responsibility, but next time he needs to lead a loyal Cabinet. One that is fully cooperative and operates as a united team.

At the first open contest for Leadership, where all members were allowed to make the final choice, Michael gave his support to Iain Duncan Smith, who eventually won. I wrote and gave him my support, suggesting that he take Michael as his Deputy, for his wisdom and experience. To my astonishment, Iain not only chose Michael as his Deputy, but also awarded him the post of Shadow Foreign Secretary, a role to which Michael was well suited. We duly celebrated at our regular meetings. I liked Iain Duncan Smith, a genuine eurosceptic, with good, firm ideas of leadership. Unfortunately his voice let him down. I offered my help in voice training and public speaking, but to no avail. He was not allowed enough time to establish his leadership. Visible cracks appeared in Labour Government policy, and were associated with growing leaks and rumours. Once things began to go wrong, the lack of substance was clearly revealed. Main concerns such as education, health, transport, communications and finance came under scrutiny. The ill conduct of certain individual Ministers, was worse than all the insults of 'sleaze', which Labour in Opposition had hurled at the Conservative Government. As with many good actors, for that, in my opinion is Blair's forte, there is no real substance beneath the surface. How long will the long-suffering public give him rein.

Now came the great tragic world blow from the fanatic Islamic terrorists led by the wealthy Osama bin Laden, who left Saudi Arabia to find support in Afghanistan with the similarly fanatical Taliban regime. There he built up his al Q'aeda terrorist force world-wide, planning the destruction of America, Britain and Israel. He trained his followers ruthlessly in the extreme fanatical belief of self-sacrifice, culminating in the evil airplane attack on the World Trade Centre on September 11th. Thus did 2001 end in the bloody massacre of thousands of innocent people, unlike historical combats between armed forces in previous wars. Despite the fact that such taking of life against the ethics and true teaching of their faith. Israel is their main target, but we are equally under threat, and need to to strengthen our own defences, rapidly being reduced by the Labour Government.

Sadly, 2001 closes on a grim note with universal terrorism menacing countries throughout the world. In addition the increasing encroachment of the EU, seeking to draw us further into this complicated, bureaucratic, uninspiring melange of European States, to become faceless units of a single Superstate. I remain totally opposed to their encroachment on our liberty, and will continue to fight to maintain our currency, our liberty under our own laws, and refuse to to submit to the EU version of the Napoleonic code. Nor yet submit to Germany's aggressive desire to become Master of Europe, if not of the world, as sought continuously since Charlemagne became crowned as Holy Roman Emperor in 800 AD.

The United Kingdom Independence Party was principally formed from dissatisfied members of the Conservative and other Parties. They are totally opposed to British membership of the European Union, and are regarded by our Party as an enemy. Understandably, since they foolishly began attacking Conservative Candidates at elections, including those who were genuine eurosceptics. Instead, they needed to use their growing strength to attack Liberal-Democrats and Labour, who are in favour of permanent assimilation of Britain into the European Union, and often combine forces in elections simply to defeat Conservatives. Obviously the UKIP should be supporting Conservative candidates, many of whom share their views. Joint co-operation in elections, would be to the advantage of both, and lead to a quicker defeat of Blair and the European Union. I have promoted this alliance from the outset, but have met stubborn resistance on both sides. If only these people had been out canvassing with me, talking to people on their doorstep, hearing real opinions and not theory, they would react differently. If they had served in the war, they might well have learnt the value of the ancient truth: 'Your enemy's enemy, must be my friend.'

The majority of Conservatives are now openly eurosceptic. Indeed, a growing number of them have followed me and become wholly anti-European Union. They have considered our options in resuming traditional, co-operative relations with the Commonwealth. Unfortunately, since Margaret Thatcher's great anti-Europen Union speech at Bruges, during which she said, 'No No No' to the European Union, all succeeding Leaders, with the exception of William Hague and Iain Duncan Smith, have been in favour of British membership. Even discussion of Europe has been forbidden. Significantly, this topic has been banned ever since the Maastricht Treaty was signed by Thatcher's unworthy successor John Major. To my mind, one of our worst ever Conservative Prime Ministers. The man who decided, in his own small mind, to eliminate our age-old Honours system, whilst at the same time himself being guilty of sleazy misconduct. A scandal complemented his signing the infamous Maastricht Treaty. Meanwhile, this present Labour Government hands out honours to all and sundry, like toffee apples to obedient followers, and dispenses knighthoods and peerages to favoured supporters. I believe that we need to elect a positive, patriotic Conservative Government and bring about the right climate for change.

Chapter 21

2002 - 2003: The Calm Before the Storm

The New Year opened quietly as we recuperated from our successful labours in 2001. But this was the calm before the storm. Problems were already looming. The Party was desperately short of funds, since millions were spent in vain on the Election campaign. Constituencies were busily seeking new ploys to raise funds. Major donors vanished after this second crushing defeat. The heart seems to have gone out of our Party at present. However, going against the downward trend of our Party, I promoted the recovery and stability of our own constituency, and Michael's position is stronger than ever. Naturally this situation pleases me especially, since I devoted myself to the resuscitation of both the Party and DCCA. I established a firm foundation on which to build our future. But sadly, our successive Party leaders still do not grasp the basic reasons for our maintained success. Nor do they accept my advice on how this may become the model for our Party's return to Government. Therefore, I must continue to strengthen DCCA as clear leaders in re-establishment.

Apart from my political activities, I was invited to join the voluntary readers of the Talking Newspaper, reading aloud for the Blind, with items of the latest news and views. These are recorded on disks and delivered Post-free, to all our blind and near-sighted members. It renders a quiet, thoughtful service by an anonymous group of caring citizens. One of the good qualities I love about this ancient town of Marlborough, is its quiet, unassuming nature. To our surprise we mow learn that we rank as the most charitable town in England. The Malburians are most caring and open-handed, without themselves making any claim to wealth.

The Lottery Fund supported the necessary enlargement and improvements of our Jubilee Centre for daily care of elderly and frail people, mostly living alone. Many I also meet as patients at Savernake Hospital, where I work as a volunteer. Savernake was considered for closure by the NHS, as too small. After a prolonged battle, we not only saved it, but also gained a agreement for enlargement, envisaged to become a medical village in this situation. I suggest a Convalescent Home to cater for rehabilitation before resuming life (usually alone) at home. No such place exists in Wiltshire as yet. My suggestion has borne fruit with an extra wing built at Great Western Hospital at

Swindon for rehabilitation. It would ideally have been better placed in the healthy surrounds of Savernake Forest. We also plan to build low cost houses and flats for medical staff to buy or rent, in our remaining acres, to contribute to costs of the new building.

Bletchley Park staff keep in touch, inviting me to take part in Conferences and Meetings. My books are in increasing demand in the Bletchley Park bookshop, especially 'Secret Communications' now in its second reprint. I have had the pleasure of escorting the coachloads of keen Wiltshire folk to Bletchley, now rebuilt with working models, bringing back memories of exciting war years, especially in the Egyptian desert, India and Germany. These memories remain vivid with invitations to lectures and talks to many clubs and associations, military and civilian. Those very active War years made the biggest impact on my life, and I strive to ensure that we never again suffer even the threat of recurrence.

Gordon Brown's Budget on 17th April was a total volte face. Having promised no Income Tax increases, he has now steeply increased National Insurance contributions for every worker and every company. A terrible blow for industry and all the hospitals they claim to be helping. This will mean cutting back more jobs, with more Nursing Homes closing, unable to meet this Government's ever increasing charges. The artificial glamour, carefully created around Brown, as a capable, intelligent, prudent Chancellor, is fast disappearing as he dissipates the vast inheritance from the Thatcher era, with huge expenditure and waste, with failing results. Taxation grows weightier and more invidious as Britain's debts increase continuously under his mismanagement and misapplied policies. It is estimated that about one third of Britain's employed is now working, in one way or another, for this Labour Government. Part of their continuing plan for centralised control, instigated by the EU.

They have drastically reduced British armed forces armour and equipment, while simultaneously spreading them across every battle hotspot around the world. Famous Regiments, disbanded or amalgamated, have lost their individual images of fame and glory, of past battles and history. All the traditional elements of a Regiment's pride. Subsequently, the armed forces were over-stretched and lacked the support of vital modern equipment, including airplanes and ships. Even the supply of soldiers' basic armour and boots was curtailed. The Territorial Forces were weakened to such degree that they were unable to respond to urgent calls for duty overseas. Historically, Britain had always been able to count on strong defences and well trained fighting forces. But the drastic reduction in these clearly exposes the country to increasing danger. Blair rushed incontinently to support President Bush in his fight against world terrorists. In so doing, he made extravagant promises of British armed support in Iraq, despite the fact that the illegal invasion of Iraq was a huge error. Britain was already stretched to the limit with only slender reserves. Thus it was difficult for British troops to carry out a major role in the East, especially in Iraq and Afghanistan.

Vast millions of oil money were expended, not only on all forms of modern arms and destructive equipment, but also on constructing nuclear bombs, chemical and biological weapons, sufficient to spread disease throughout every enemy country. For the future peace and growth of our suffering world, we must first eliminate the root cause of fanaticism. Strong, continuous action by NATO and a balanced, determined United Nations, would ensure that nations accepted full responsibility for their actions. Each country should be enabled to live at peace with its neighbour, rendering aid individually, as well as through world organisations. Vast oil wealth should be distributed fairly. There needs to be an incentive to seek practical, feasible solutions to the world problems of poverty, starvation and disease. Oil is expendable and other sources of energy must be found.

It is the expressed aim of Western Statesmen to eliminate world poverty, hunger and disease, and to ensure continuous world peace. Not least between religious faiths, yet some still support many fanatical terrorists, in the name of religion. All faiths must learn to live together, share their main beliefs and devote themselves to the welfare of all people. Then they need to combine and speak in a resoundingly strong voice to State and World leaders, and demand that they implement effective measures for world peace. It must be their mission to ensure peace and harmony throughout the world; otherwise they have no right to claim that they are holy representatives of a benign, protective spirit.

How to bring this situation about however, poses an eternal question. How do we find such righteous, political leaders, when those who are currently in power jealously guard their man-made edifices and neglect their duties? The world leaders we need must be greater than these. They need to look beyond the needs and fulfilment of their own people to the world beyond. We need good, strong, messianic leaders. Those plutocrats who are now seeking World Government, might well succeed if they pursued worthy positive missions, instead of the negative, demonic form they now present to the people. Many small movements aim at ending world poverty and starvation, but it needs world leaders to make a real impact. Or perhaps the voice of the people, who, once roused and united, can enforce action to be taken now, beyond idle discussion and wishful dreams. Gandhi made his great gesture on behalf of the poor and downtrodden of India. During my three years in India, my affection for the country and her people grew steadily. I believe that India will be a worthy future world leader. The signs are already there. Despite the millions who remain in dire poverty, there are genuine calls for really honest leaders. Those who do not seek their own enrichment but who are interested in improving the lives of the lowest orders; the people who are still called 'untouchables', and live in enforced slavery.

In 2003, we began preparations for forthcoming District Council Elections, working with each Branch, to find, train and guide suitable candidates to contest every seat. Boundary changes demanded new sets of maps and street guidance for every area. I designed detailed sectional maps of each District. These were divided into individual coverage for every candidate and team of helpers. From my own past experience as Councillor, I knew the wearying frustration of having to seek out unknown roads, alleys and outlying farms, without guidance. Now each delivery lay within a small compass, without strain. Our meticulous, detailed planning produced willing volunteers who were ready to play their part in our victorious efforts. Without the help of our volunteers, everything would grind to a halt. The hidden strength of the Conservative Party lies in its loyal members, who are ever active, even in bad times. My fervent wish is to lead them all triumphantly out of the stifling, unelected, clutches of the European Union, and back to our nation's independent, sovereign freedom. We could then co-operate better with Europe, from the outside, as wise Churchill originally advised.

I have witnessed so many political reverses that were later followed by rebounds, that I await with confidence a future upturn in Conservative Party fortunes. It is my mission to help put that missing spirit back into our Party, and simultaneously regain Britain's erstwhile independence. For Britain to stand tall amongst free, fully co-operating nations, for the benefit of all. Above all, for Britain, for whom we willingly fought against well-nigh impossible odds. I'll warrant that these sentiments will be echoed throughout Britain, once our people become fully aware of just how much, and how sinisterly they have been betrayed. Needless to say, we won those District Council Elections, with an increase from our previous 24, to our best ever 27, with overall majority of 11, leaving Labour just 1 seat, and Lib-Dems 2 seats, in sad disarray. From 9 seats in 1999, we have trebled by 2003, a proud Wiltshire record. We now look forward to the challenge of the next General and County Elections in 2005, from DCCA position of strength as Masters of District and Wiltshire County Council, and Michael our worthy MP, to be returned with an ever increasing majority. It is the duty of our Party to provide the funds to finance the team of skilled Agents so necessary to win future elections, as well proven at DCCA.

In my endeavours to strengthen our constituency, I have walked the streets, alleys and byways of almost every town and village, delivering, canvassing, attending meetings, and above all, winning elections. With our enterprising agent Ian Ramsey, I have carried out a reconnaissance of every District from Melksham to Netheravon, Ludgershall and Tidworth. I have enjoyed meeting Wiltshire folk on the best of terms. But somehow, they no longer find politics interesting. They do not trust politicians, except for those like Michael, who keep their promises and work hard for all in their constituency. It becomes increasingly difficult to persuade the majority to come out and vote. We need new approaches and fresh appeals to rouse interest. Let us hope that our new Leader will be able to find that hidden formula to inspire new hope in a Conservative future. Service to our Country is the only true way forward.

In the meantime, the European Union's hidden, secret masters strengthen attempts to remove from all member states their individual sovereignty and freedom, to turn us into faceless, character-less units of their planned Superstate. The preparatory move is to turn the whole of Europe into Regions, removing our traditional boundaries and replacing with new roughly-hewn Regions, planned in advance. England would disappear, becoming faceless blocks, in place of our clearly defined Counties. Thus our rough-hewn Region now encompasses all counties, swallowing up Wiltshire, Gloucestershire, Somerset, Dorset, right through the South to include the Scilly Isles, with Exeter named as capital centre. Amusingly, Gibraltar now added in August, to be welcomed by our leading MEP Neil Parish.

Wiltshire is a quiet, conservative green County, retaining much of its ancient history. Changes, many begun by our computer inventions at Bletchley, are important for improving our life-style. But, basically, the character of the people remains firm and constant through the ages, generally trusting their elected leaders, slow to provoke, tolerant of others. They become fully roused when their country is threatened, as enemies have found to their cost. It is my belief that such arousal has now begun, as they awaken to their planned betrayal.

Chapter 22

2004 to the General Election of 2005

The year 2003 ended with the dismissal of Party Leader Iain Duncan Smith. This event was plotted by a cabal of MPs, with the requisite number of names to force him to resign. Michael Howard was then elected by the unanimous agreement of MP's. A trained speaker, barrister and successful Home Secretary, especially on reducing crime, Howard maintained iron discipline. He outlined his principles and guidance for our Party to follow. Facing a General Election in about eighteen months, there was no time to lose. But I could not envisage Howard as a leader likely to inspire enthusiastic support. He lacked warmth, and the expression of total sincerity that is necessary to attract mass confidence and support.

In 2004 we geared up for a desperate struggle, in an attempt to win back sufficient seats to beat Labour. But Howard was insensitive to Party members' opinions. He was also too rigid on discipline and inflicted suspensions on leading members who dared to oppose his iron rules. He forbade any mention of the EU, suspending an Association for daring to approve of statements made by UKIP about exit from EU. I wondered why? Did he seek to keep his long, close association with the EU secret and unmentionable? Had he forgotten that the Conservative Party is a broad church, allowing members to speak their minds without fear or favour? Leaders are required to listen carefully before making arbitrary, rash decisions. He overplayed the stern disciplinarian role and failed to attract solidarity like Thatcher, who was truly our best leader since Churchill. Howard failed to get support from the Party and the country at large. We needed a more open, sympathetic leader to inspire faith in our people.

In the meantime, February approached with my 90th Birthday. I planned a small party for family and friends, but learnt that celebrations had been taken over by the connivance of Michael, Jane, Agent and members. I was truly staggered to find over a hundred assorted friends, who thoroughly enjoyed each other's company, and even paused at odd times to notice me. It was a truly convivial, happy event, with a ninety year-old belle of the ball. Outstanding for me, was a huge poster-size Greetings card that bore a giant Yorkshire rose, emblem of my beloved school, Cundall Manor. The children had used multi-colour pieces to construct this wonderful tribute to their ancient Founder. Michael made a lovely speech about a fellow I could not recognise. Invitations followed to special lunches and dinners. The Jubilee Centre held their own birthday celebration for me, with hand painted festoons, that were decorated with greetings from individual members. The Stroke Association at Wroughton, where I worked on speech therapy for dysphasics, held a special tea-party, and the chef at Savernake Hospital baked a special birthday cake. My cup and interior were both full. My many American relatives all sent elaborate greetings and cards, and my ninety years scored 100%. It was an unrepeatable occasion, never to be forgotten.

The new hospital at Savernake was near completion and based on a circular plan differing from the original design. As one of the original members of the planning committee and voluntary worker in the wards, I was invited to the foundation stone ceremony. There was always such a pleasant, caring and relaxed atmosphere at Savernake. Every task was done efficiently and punctually, without undue haste. We volunteers were accepted informally at all times, unless I happened to push a trolley over a freshly washed floor; when I incurred the wrath of the indomitable, industrious cleaners, who insisted on calling me 'young Harry'. Jubilee Centre, which is part of the old Priory, improves continuously. There is a constant demand for membership from the disabled elderly. Not surprisingly, since members are given special care with a well cooked lunch, with fresh vegetables and meat or fish daily, and specially arranged outings in a coach adapted for wheelchairs. With the support of so many sources, our committee is kept continuously busy. Volunteers came daily to assist Carole, the ever-active manager. Without these cheerful, willing volunteers, who undertook all the tasks and burdens thrust upon them by the NHS and other hospitals, care homes, charity work, many of our needy institutions would freeze. I could devote a whole chapter to our wonderful, anonymous, British army of volunteers. They are unhonoured and unsung, yet they merit recognition and awards, with badges of distinction.

Now I am Chairman of Castle Court Residents' Association, and join regular sessions of reading for the Blind and arranging meetings of the Marlborough Group for non-partisan political discussions. I never suffer a dull moment and enjoy continuous activity. My abiding major interest is politics, on which our country's future depends. The dangers increase almost daily under our present disastrous Blair/Brown-led Government. They slavishly obey the ever demanding European Union, to our continuously mounting cost in billions of pounds and ever decreasing political power. Intelligence reports, e-mails, journals, military and other sources of information come my way daily, illustrating the state of the world, and our country in particular. It is a pleasure to be invited to address clubs, associations and other groups on the history of two World Wars. Especially on the process of Intelligence gathering in its various forms, whether spies, agents, double-agents or code-breaking. More Wiltshire groups persuade me to take coach loads to Bletchley Park. It is often a relief to break away from the heat of politics and enjoy the company of one's fellow human beings, on everyday matters. Though Bletchley could hardly be regarded as normal. I am a social animal, and happiest in company of people of all kinds, young or old, fit or disabled. I like to hear their interests or woes and exchange reminiscences. There are many lonely people, not necessarily old, living alone with no friends. They often find mental relief by expressing their thoughts aloud to a listening ear, because sometimes their lives have become complicated and they find it difficult to cope.

As 2005 loomed ominously, I knew that our Party was ill-prepared, despite all my repeated warnings. I had insisted on the absolute necessity and provision of experienced Agents, for every constituency with a conceivable hope of victory. Conservative Central Office and Party HQ were fettered in their own superior belief, that they alone possessed the know-how and mental acumen to solve the eternal problem of winning elections. Despite their continuous losses, they refused to listen. As the longest serving member for 76 years, and Councillor from 1958, I have supported and served our Party diligently. I have given sound advice that has been based on long experience, especially on the use of commonsense to solve many problems. But our present crop of 'leaders' seem intent on creating more complications, rather than providing simple solutions.

Unfortunately, the results of the 2005 General Election proved my point. Our DCCA constituency again returned our outstanding MP, the ever popular Michael Ancram, with an increased majority. But we were forced to watch so many worthy candidates, along with too many ill-chosen unworthies, go down in ignominy. The proper measures were not implemented in time to convince the voters. Leader after Leader is rightly or wrongly blamed and dismissed. The whole process has become a second-rate beauty parade. Strong candidates have often been eliminated by ill-chosen committees, who have lacked the ability to probe for hidden talents, or sense potential leaders. It has become patently obvious that the choice of Parliamentary Candidates has been placed in the wrong hands. Hence many good candidates have been neglected in favour of the second-rate. At least we won back some seats, as voters' confidence gradually returned to diminish Labour's lead. Labour still had an overall majority however, and it seemed increasingly difficult to force Blair out of his disastrous ministrations.

We, in Wiltshire, followed our winning sequence. All the carefully selected candidates for County Council seats were interviewed and instructed on every point. They were fully briefed and armed with detailed maps, house and voter guides, and local information. This enabled each team of volunteers to cover the area completely and methodically, in the shortest possible time. Each operation went smoothly and trouble free. Michael was working at Conservative Central Office, but found the time to return to canvass, meeting old members and new. His indefatigable Jane happily toured everywhere in the Battlebus, which was an ancient local farm vehicle, and cheerfully greeted all and sundry. We achieved our best ever result: we won 11 out of the 13 County Council seats, with only two Swindon seats retained by Labour, and Lib Dems were knocked completely out of the contest. I actually shed my blood for our victory, since I fell down steep stone steps, whilst checking my canvassing notes. I gained head wounds and bruises, and broke my nose for the third time. Once again the Wiltshire Winners triumphed, returning our gallant MP, Michael Ancram QC, with an ever increasing majority, marking every election since he first stood for us in the 1990s, a proud record. But this overall election defeat brought to an end the efforts of yet another failed Conservative Leader. Michael Howard, again with the wrong tactics, failed to convince the public and also lost the faith of our own Party membership.

Labour won again by a landslide, with 355 seats. Our own suffering Party could only finish with 197 seats, and Liberal Democrats 62. Small comfort that Labour had lost 47, whilst we recovered 35, reducing the Labour majority to 67, their smallest share of the national vote. Wiltshire victors were dumbfounded, but I was not surprised. I had persistently warned our leaders and their Ministers, that they would suffer defeat if they refused to change their repeated and misguided 'Top-Down' instructions. During every election, millions are poured into piles of expensively printed, pages-long instructions, mostly written by inexperienced theorists, on how to win elections. The good money of our supporters would be better spent hiring skilled Agents. We have proven literally, by recording ever greater successes, that elections are won from 'Ground-Up' tactics, by 'hands-on' operators, based on local knowledge and experience. It is the 'Groundlings' who bring out the voters, by personal persuasion and dependable service. Better value is also acheived from persuading media support.

A good, experienced Agent, with a reliable team of enthusiastic volunteers, is capable of raising funds and bringing back old members, whilst also attracting new. We have developed good methods in DCCA. Similar, concentrated efforts around our country would bring equally healthy, positive results. But first and foremost, adequate funds must be set aside by Party HQ for the employment of experienced, trustworthy and well trained Agents for target seats. A training school should be set up, with funds to make their future attractive. Every constituency needs careful research in depth to assess its needs for future viability, with the possible help of a successful, neighbouring constituency, if necessary. This is the responsibility of Central Office and represents a major step towards winning elections. First, there needs to be thorough, detailed research conducted by experienced Agents in every constituency. This research would reveal the strength and weakness of each area. Then there needs to be an assessment of the necessary steps to build the weakest up to full strength, and set accurate sensible targets for each constituency, with the co-operation of their leaders. To be followed by an assessment of the needs of each, whether full time Agent or two smaller areas sharing one Agent, or perhaps sufficing with one part-time Agent. This process would build a strong political framework sensibly, from the ground up. Necessary funds need to be devoted to this sensible, solid reorganisation. To date, the current members' contributions are systematically wasted on unnecessary volumes of literature, that is largely unread, but no doubt keeps the Central Office staff happily employed.

I have been urging reorganisation for years, and behold something new has recently erupted from CCO, in the shape of a gigantic solution, obviously evolved from inexperienced clever theorists. This is a new solution that seeks to transform ALL constituencies within each County into one conglomeration. They would all be huddled together in one central office and presided over by one, or possibly two Agents, directing all traffic. They will drain strength, especially financial, from the most successful Associations in order to build up the weaker members. This represents an improperly considered, crash solution. One that has been prepared in a hurry and without a careful analysis of the negative results, such as differences between areas, members, staff and Agents. I fear that there will be a number of unsolvable problems causing frustration. Agents and staff will be overworked, and there will be considerable dissatisfaction when successful constituencies are drained of their talent and resources. Ultimately, there will be a loss of all vigour and sustained output. It all needs careful analysis by experienced experts, in order to implement a workable scheme. Agents should be free to move around their constituency continuously, and study the situation in each Branch. This way they can find solutions to problems, instead of confining them all into the walls of one office to check the traffic flow.

Announcing his resignation, Michael Howard gave new candidates time to prepare by the October Conference, where each would be able to state his or her case, before the usual packed audience. The beauty parade took place in the crowded Conference Hall, with a vast television audience. The front-runner David Davis made a factual speech, as did the others. Then David Cameron, young, attractive and well educated, stepped onto the stage. His speech was clear, concise and different. He spoke about a new, modern face for Conservatives, which captivated his audience. He brought new meaning and a 'modern' message, to which they responded with thunderous applause. Here was their new leader, young and fresh, giving them new hope of improved Conservative fortunes. Cameron won the Party's final vote by a wide margin.

Now we have a new David come to judgement. He will need to emblazon on his shield: 'Let boldness be my friend', and demonstrate, like Thatcher, that he has real courage to deal with major issues. Such as her momentous decision to allow council house tenants to buy their own houses at factual prices. Or her bold decision to defend the Falklands from Argentinian invasion. The people rose to support a brave, courageous British leader, not a modern British adherent of the European Union, as he now appears. Hers was the very stuff of politics and the British spirit of independence. With Germany, our erstwhile enemy, now dominating the European Union, we are in urgent need of a courageous and gifted leader to restore Britain to virile independence. Is that Cameron's role?

Britain is now desperately in need of just such a bold and strong leader. One who can combine the strength and determination of Churchill, the perceptive courage of Thatcher and the wiles and skills of Disraeli. For this is what is needed to bring forth the fortitude and bravery of our nation. Do you have the inner strength and capacity of that young David whose courageous act slew the giant Opposition? For this is what it will take to free us from the clutches of those hidden forces that dominate the EU. Remember that the British Empire ruled the world in the Victorian era, not so long ago, having come to greatness under the first Queen Elizabeth. Throughout our history Britain has stood firm against all attempts at world domination. From the early Britons, whom I admire for their stubborn tenacity and for being the founders of my city of Bricgstowe, to brave Alfred and his brother Aethelred, to withstanding the determined invasion attempts of Napoleon and latterly the Germans, whose last attempted invasion was thwarted by British forces in 1940 and 1941.

Now we face this unelected combination from Europe, who, I believe, are striving by stealth to take us over, lock, stock and barrel. Their intention is now being made clear. The whole of Europe, including all Britain, has already been divided into a sequence of regional blocs, literally doing away with England, which on paper no longer exists, and bonding us with France. Instead of erstwhile sovereign nations, all will become units of a planned Superstate, which their recent Constitution attempted to promulgate without Referendum. This was signed in advance by the heads of all nations within EU, including Tony Blair, who signed away our rights, as usual, without permission of people or Parliament. Once passed, Britain automatically loses freedom, sovereignty, legal rights, and the concept of the nation state. Britain will become just another faceless unit in their Superstate, which will be apparently ruled by a Communist style dictatorship. However, these rulers have underestimated the people of France and Holland, who pronounced a defiant NO in their Referendums. None of these heads of the European Union have ever had to submit themselves for election. We may logically ask then, who assumed the power to appoint them and give them sway over us and our sovereign state? Why have all our own statesmen through the years, since Macmillan and Heath, accepted and been party to Britain's betrayal, as each part of each Treaty has signed away our rights?

At its peak, the British Empire covered one quarter of the earth's habitable territory, and the Royal Navy controlled the seas. It was the largest and most successful overseas Empire in history, and encompassed four hundred million people. India contained two hundred and ninety four million people, Africa forty three million, Asia six million, Australasia over five million and the British Isles itself over forty one million. Global trade was directed from London, which was the capital of the financial and business world. If Britain is still a sovereign nation then, according to our Constitution, largely unwritten but sovereign nonetheless, no foreign law has any legitimacy on British soil. All attempts to enforce foreign law would place perpetrators subject to the Treason Felony Act of 1848. Hence the current Government's attempt to destroy it. But our unimpeachable sovereignty cannot be transferred. Sovereignty implies self-government and the autonomy of the nation. No foreign power may exert any rights over the free British people. But this emerging, unelected European Superstate presumes our Parliament to be an administrative pawn in their game. Despite the fact that they are unable to stop their own internal, wholesale cheating and robbery of millions. A whole series of qualified accountants have continuously and steadfastly refused to balance or pass their plundered accounts, one after another, and each has been summarily dismissed.

To submit now, to an unelected, spurious consortium, which seeks to deprive us of our hard-won independence and turn us into a vassal state, without even a Referendum to voice our opinion, would be to go against everything we have fought for, so bravely and tenaciously throughout our history. British people have always defended their sovereign rights to freedom and independence under British law. But the European Union seeks to deprive us of our proper, inherited rights, for which millions of people have fought and sacrificed their lives. I pray that the good people of Britain will awake from their long sleep of apathy, in time to grasp this imminent danger. Together as always, the British people can overcome these hidden enemies, and cast off the nets of this invidious European Union. In so doing, Britain will be able to stand free again, with the support of our great Commonwealth, America, other Allies and many close friends.

Index